I0799909

POSTCARD HISTORY SERIES

Heritage of the Endless Mountains

PENNSYLVANIA

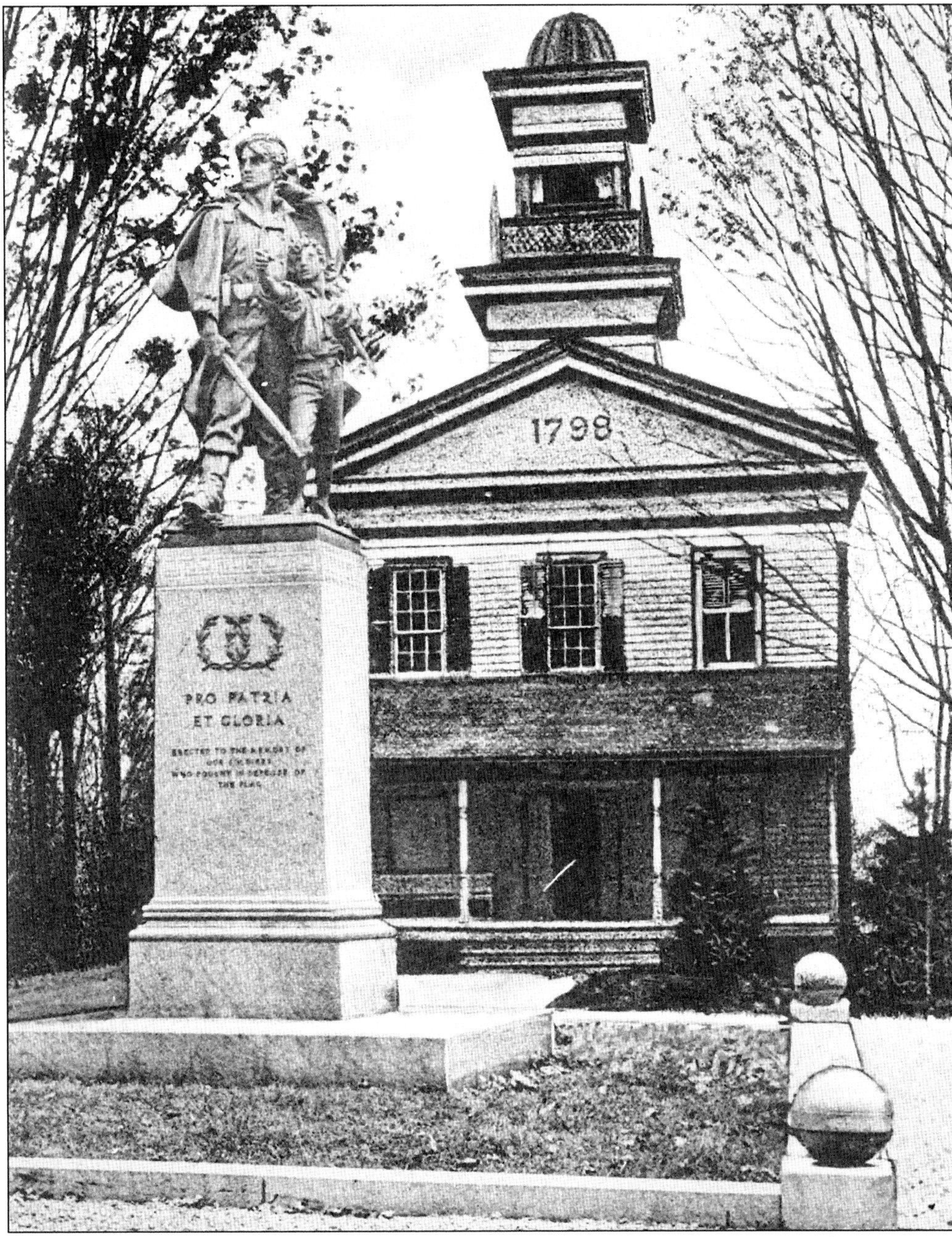

SOLDIERS MONUMENT AND OLD ACADEMY, ATHENS. This monument, erected in 1902 to celebrate the soldiers of all wars, is called "The Protection of the Flag" and is a rare depiction of this theme. Descendants of the pioneer Snell family commissioned George Brewster to create the sculpture, which was cast at the Gorham Foundry in Rhode Island. The famous New York architectural firm of McKim, Mead & White designed the monument. Behind the sculpture stands the Old Academy. By the time of this card the building was vacant, except for occasional civic functions. It was razed in 1924. Pupils' desks and timbers from this building are on display in the Tioga Point Museum, across the street. (Postcard courtesy of the Tioga Point Museum.)

Postcard History Series

Heritage of the Endless Mountains
Pennsylvania

Bonnie Stacy

Arcadia
Publishing

ISBN 978-0-7385-0142-0

Published by Arcadia Publishing
Charleston, South Carolina

Printed in the United States of America

Library of Congress Catalog Card Number: 9961282

For all general information contact Arcadia Publishing at:
Telephone 843-853-2070
Fax 843-853-0044
E-mail sales@arcadiapublishing.com
For customer service and orders:
Toll-Free 1-888-313-2665

Visit us on the Internet at www.arcadiapublishing.com

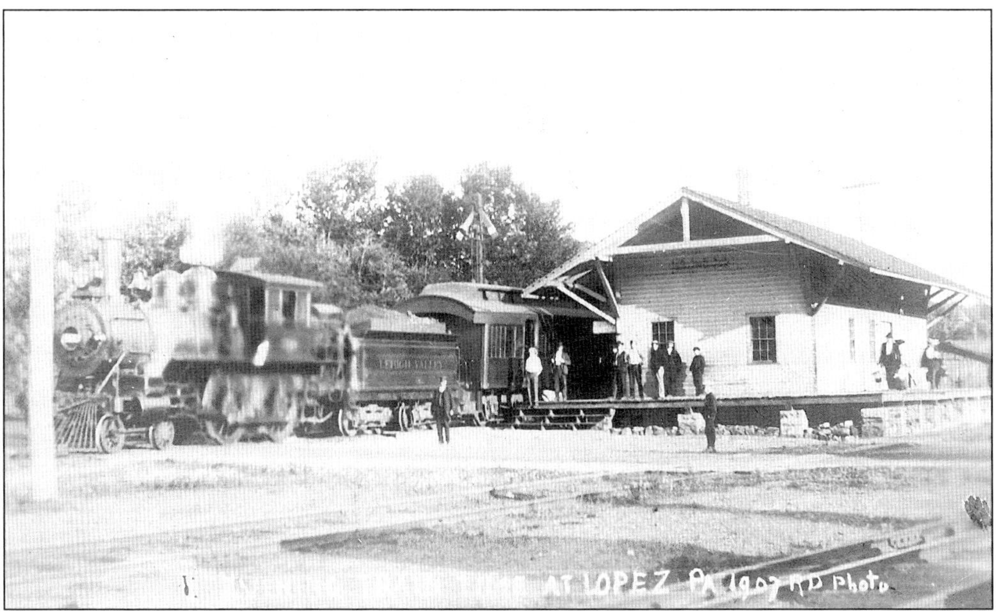

EVENING TRAIN TIME AT LOPEZ, 1907. Postcard photographers often signed their work. This card is signed "RD" for Ranald Douglas. Other names and initials to look for are F.E. Bolles, Wm. A.D., Krumm, and Lent. (Postcard courtesy of Norm Brauer.)

Contents

ACKNOWLEDGMENTS

Many organizations and individuals helped with this project, and I could not have completed it without their aid and kindness. The Susquehanna County Historical Society, the Bradford County Historical Society, French Azilum, Inc., and the Tioga Point Museum generously allowed reproduction of postcards from their collections. At the Susquehanna County Historical Society Betty Smith, Linda Smith, and Debra Adleman answered questions and pulled research files for me. Betty Smith graciously loaned cards from her personal collection. Henry Farley, Bob Veleker, and Doris Hugo from the Bradford County Historical Society patiently answered my questions and pointed me in the direction of other sources. Russell Swody, site manager of French Azilum, was helpful with information and very helpful with his patience, listening to me whine unproductively.

Thanks to Chuck Frisbie for identifying mysterious scenes and to Maryann Friend for helping me make up my mind when I had too many good cards to choose from. Vincent Latini loaned helpful railroad books, and Everett Howard inspired me with postcards of the Nicholson Bridge.

Almost 25 percent of the cards in this book are from the personal collection of Norm Brauer, whose generosity in loaning them is truly appreciated. Some of the finest and most unusual postcards are his, and he found cards for many of the spots that I was afraid I would never fill.

Finally, I wish to acknowledge the help of my husband, Ned Margie. He put up with me without complaint throughout the process of doing this book. He re-photographed many of the cards, helped in their selection, and proofread the text. Of course any errors are entirely his fault.

Bonnie Stacy
Athens, Pennsylvania
January 1999

INTRODUCTION

The Endless Mountains region of northeastern Pennsylvania, for the purposes of this book, consists of the counties of Wyoming, Susquehanna, Sullivan, and Bradford. Each town in this area has its own unique character, but the history, industry, and recreational activities are similar for all four counties. They also have in common the Susquehanna River and the hilly terrain. I will use postcards printed, for the most part, in the first four decades of the 20th century to show the cohesiveness of the region.

The four chapters address different aspects of the history of the area. The first is an overview of the historical events that occurred through World War I, as seen through postcards published by historical societies and museums. It also has cards that show some of the local history organizations that are open to the public, either year-round or during the summer. Chapter Two chronicles the work life of the Endless Mountains, from agriculture through logging and the railroads. The third chapter focuses on the recreational resources that have always attracted visitors to the area and enhanced the lives of those of us who live here. In Chapter Four, I will take you on a tour of the Endless Mountains. The tour begins in the east and moves westward county by county. If a town is not on the tour either I could not get a card showing anything in it or I thought the card would fit better into one of the other chapters. I am sorry if I left out one of your favorite places.

The cards were either mailed or not, dated or not. Sometimes I had to estimate the date for lack of concrete information, other times I used the postmark. Of course, this only provides a "no-later-than" date. Personally, I often keep postcards lying around in drawers for years before I mail them. I only hope the mailers of these cards did not share my habit.

Occasionally I have incorporated relevant information, written by the mailer of the card, into my caption. The difficult part was leaving out the irrelevant stuff. Most of the messages were to the point: "Will meet you at the fair Saturday."; "Meet me at the station on the 6th." Every once in a while there was a provocative note—this one's my favorite: "Would never let you go if I knew you were going to act the way you did driving to the station. Heard all about you. John." I guess we will never know what Maud did on the way to the station in 1909.

The sources for the captions are 19th- and 20th-century county histories, newspapers, directories, advertisements, early- and mid-20th-century travel books and pamphlets, and oral history. Virtually all of these sources are in the research collections of the Tioga Point Museum or the Susquehanna County Historical Society. I tried to use sources as close to the cards in age as possible, so many of the quotes use language that is unlike the way we write and speak today.

I hope that this book will inspire people to look at the Endless Mountains in a way that they may not have before. Perhaps you will grab your gazetteer and search for some of these unknown or forgotten places. Many of them have changed, many have not. Some are gone. Just remember what the Sullivan County Chamber of Commerce wrote almost 75 years ago: "Words are altogether impotent to paint the beauties of the Endless Mountain Region; photographs fall far short of portraying the grandeur. Only in the visions themselves can one grasp the real picture."

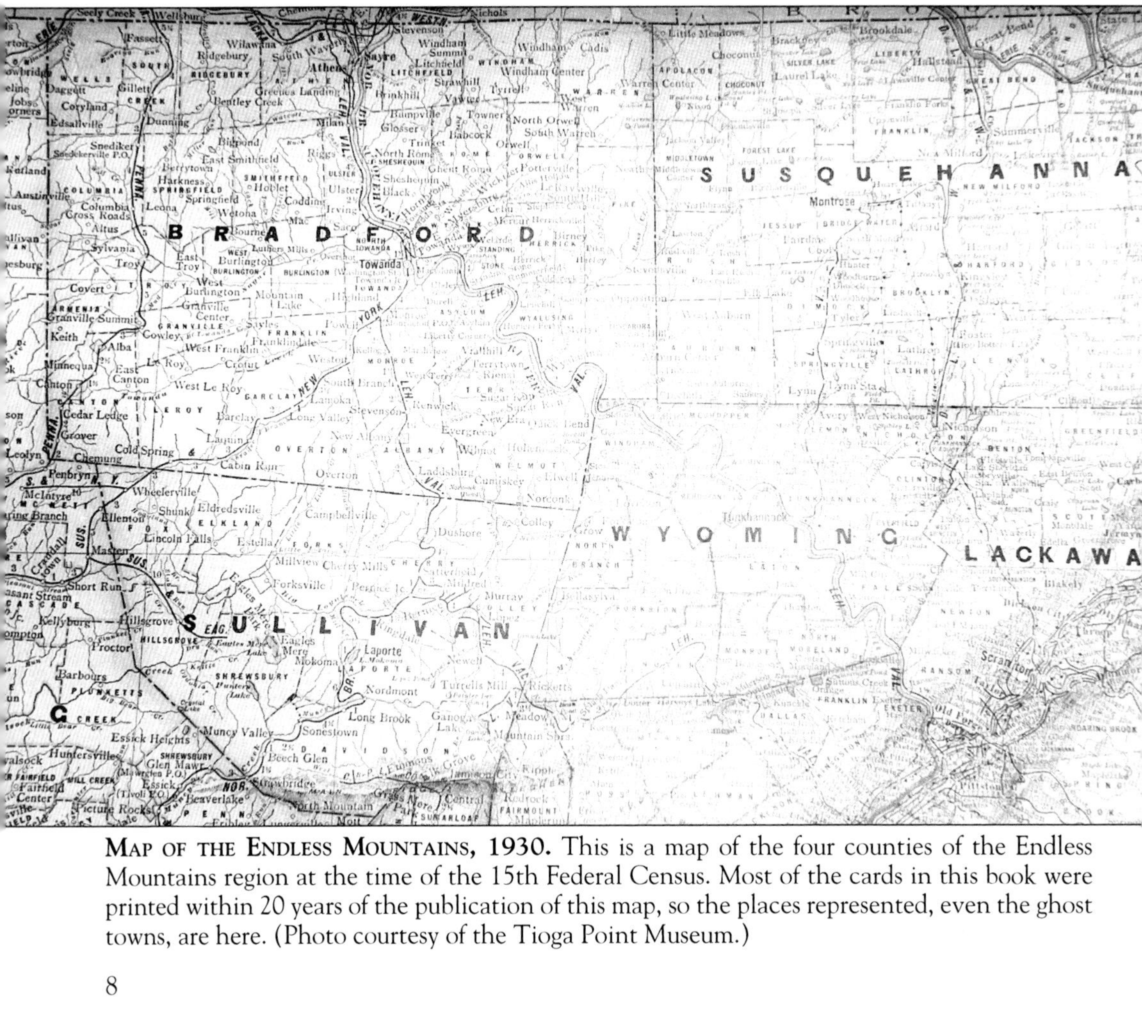

Map of the Endless Mountains, 1930. This is a map of the four counties of the Endless Mountains region at the time of the 15th Federal Census. Most of the cards in this book were printed within 20 years of the publication of this map, so the places represented, even the ghost towns, are here. (Photo courtesy of the Tioga Point Museum.)

One

History

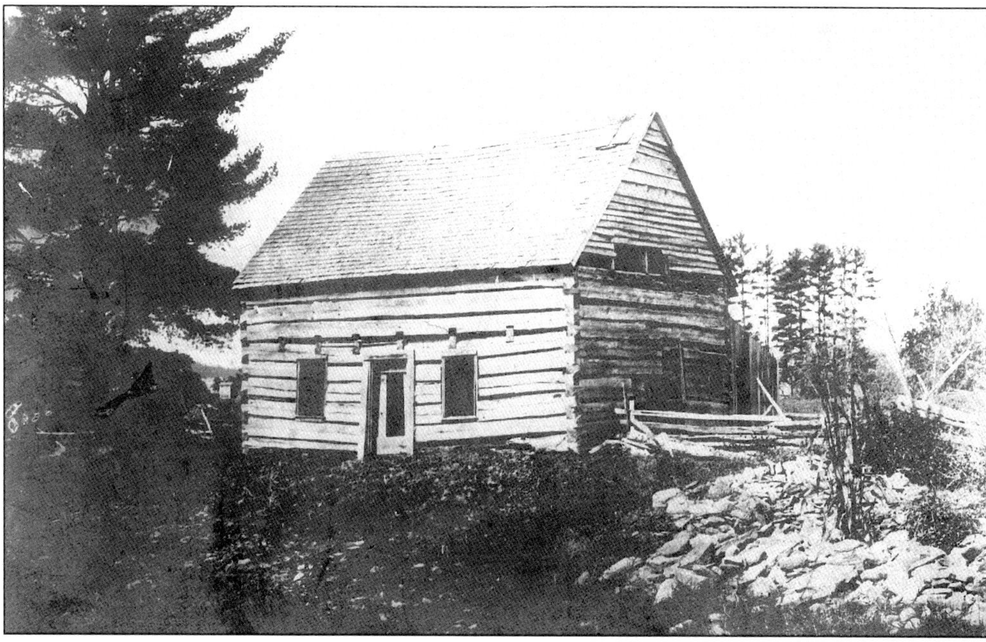

Kingsley House, Wyalusing. This house is identified on the postcard as the oldest in Bradford County, but by 1931 only the walls remained standing. Nathan Kingsley built it, probably before October 1777. Kingsley was a Connecticut man who obtained his land through the Susquehanna Company. The counties of the Endless Mountain region were embroiled, both before and after the Revolution, in a conflict known as the "Yankee-Pennamite War." At the source of the problem were conflicting claims to the same land, with both Connecticut and Pennsylvania asserting their rights to the land between parallels 41 and 42. Shortly after moving to Wyalusing, Native Americans abducted Kingsley and held him for nearly a year. After the Revolution he returned to this house. (Postcard courtesy of the Tioga Point Museum.)

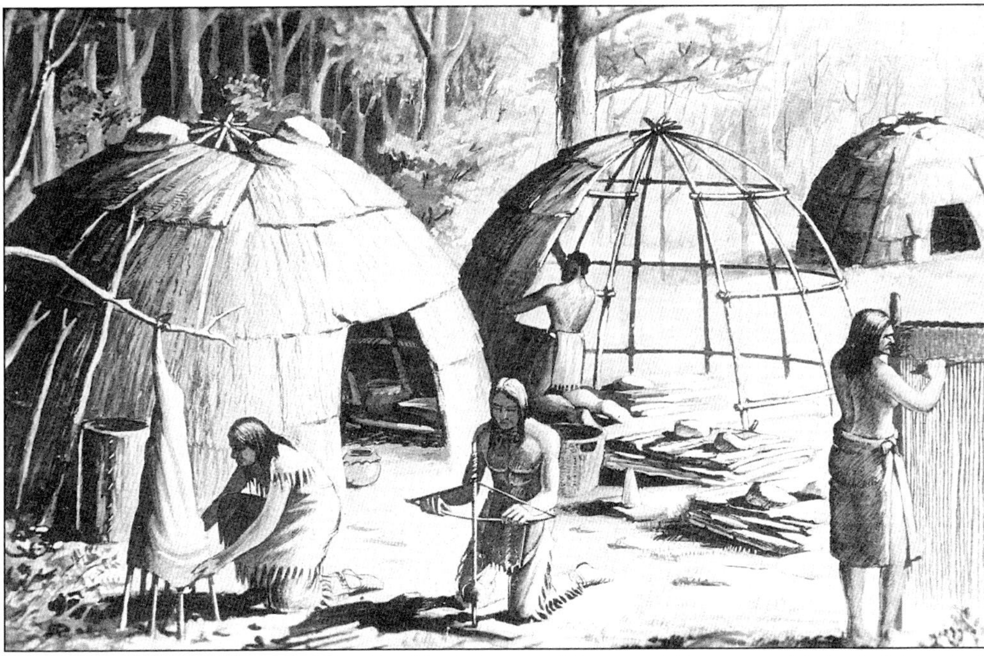

ALGONQUIN ROUND HOUSE. The Bradford County Historical Society published this artist's rendering of typical Algonquin dwellings. Archaeological evidence of Proto-Algonquin and Algonquin occupation abounds in the northeastern region of Pennsylvania in the form of stone tools and pottery. (Postcard courtesy of the Tioga Point Museum.)

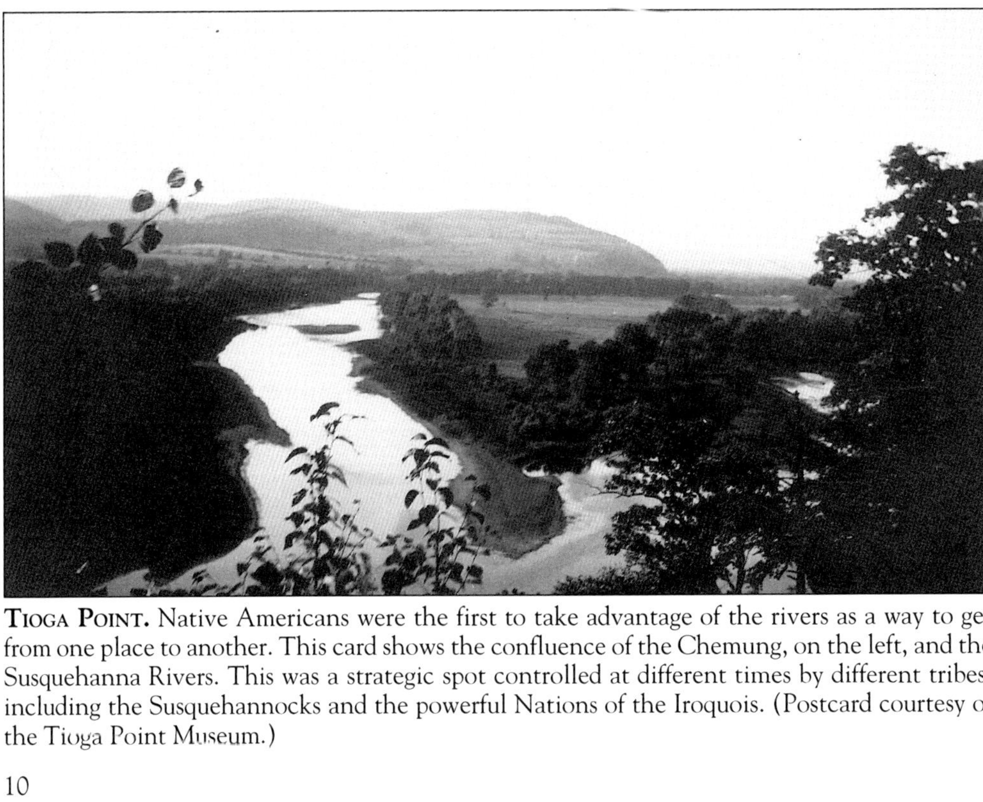

TIOGA POINT. Native Americans were the first to take advantage of the rivers as a way to get from one place to another. This card shows the confluence of the Chemung, on the left, and the Susquehanna Rivers. This was a strategic spot controlled at different times by different tribes, including the Susquehannocks and the powerful Nations of the Iroquois. (Postcard courtesy of the Tioga Point Museum.)

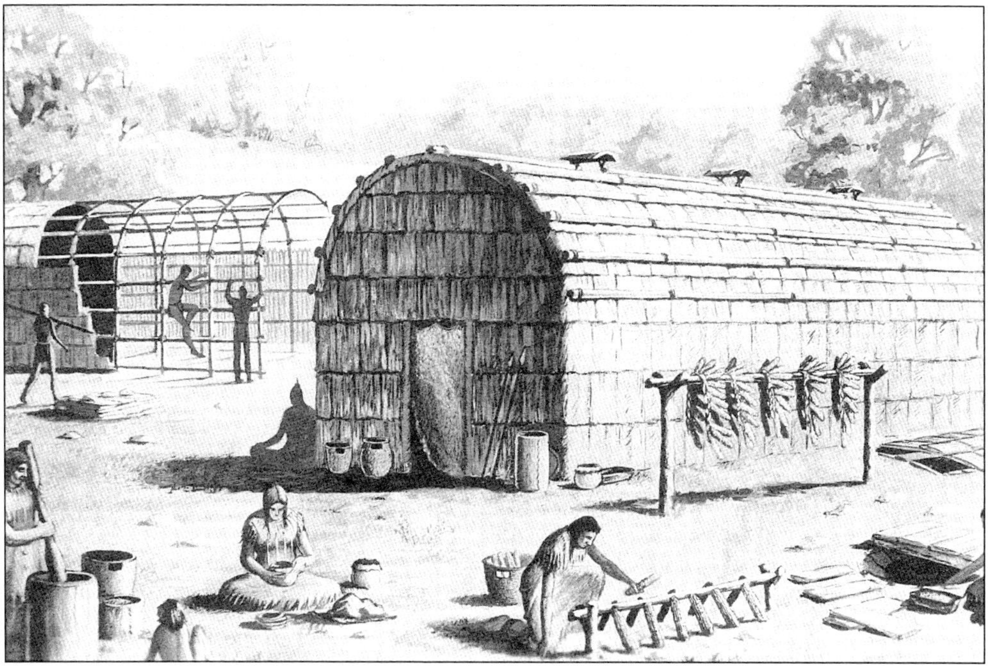

Iroquoian Long House. The Susquehannocks, who spoke an Iroquoian language, and their ancestors lived in this area before 1600. They moved south along the river, leaving the area under the control of the Nations of the Iroquois, who allowed Eghohowin's, later Queen Esther's, band of Munsee (an Algonquin-speaking group) to occupy the area around Tioga Point from 1772 until their expulsion by Colonel Hartley in 1778. (Postcard courtesy of the Tioga Point Museum.)

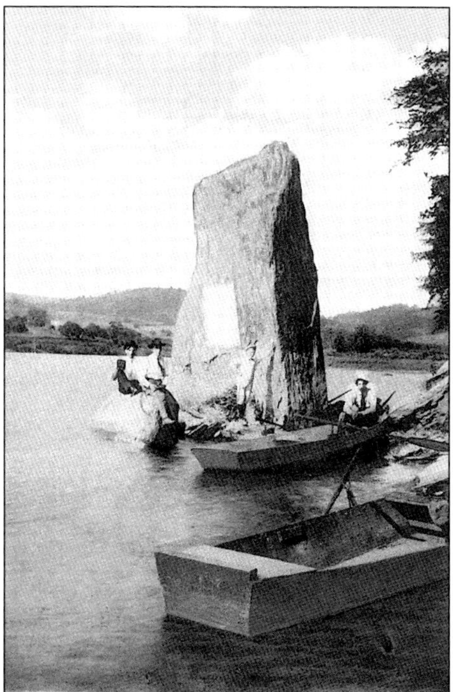

Standing Stone. The Bradford County Historical Society recently acquired this prominent landmark, and is now responsible for its protection as a historic site. Mentioned by virtually every traveler who passed it, the rock was deposited in this position by glacial action long ago. Early travelers noted Native-American pictographs on its surface, but they have long since been washed away by weather. (Postcard courtesy of French Azilum.)

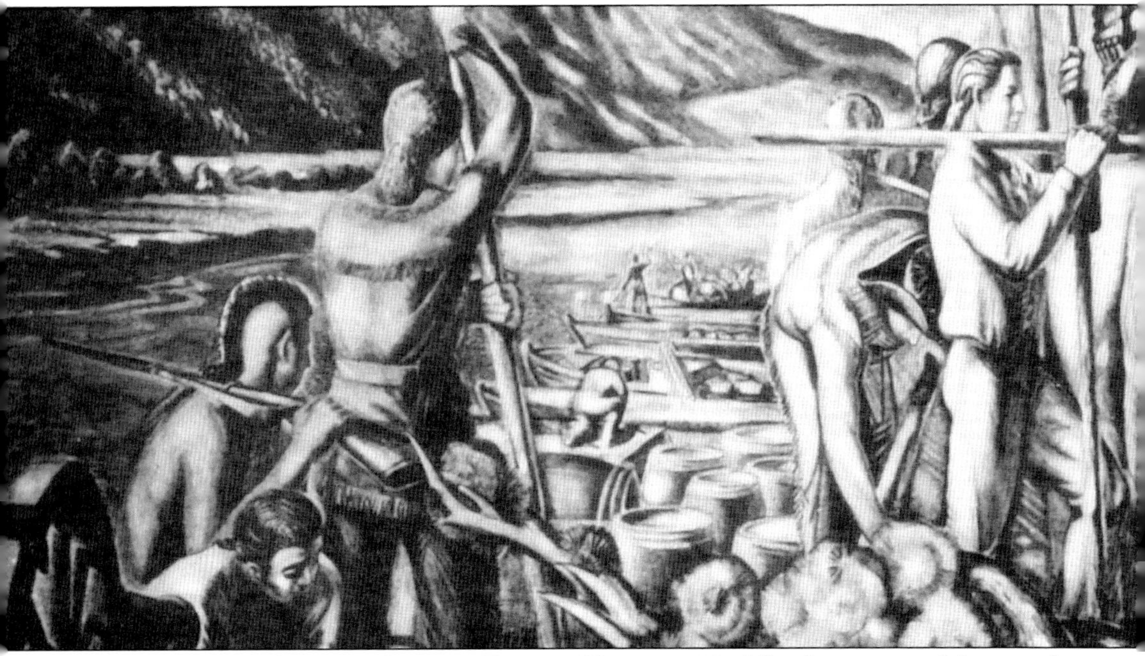

GENERAL JOHN SULLIVAN BUILDS A FORT AT TIOGA, 1779. Allen Jones painted this mural in the Athens Post Office in 1941. It portrays the construction of Fort Sullivan, a structure that only remained standing for two months, but represents the Revolutionary War in this part of Pennsylvania. Sullivan's campaign was mounted as a reaction to the alliance between the Iroquois and the British. Frontier raids by Tories and Natives prompted appeals for help. General

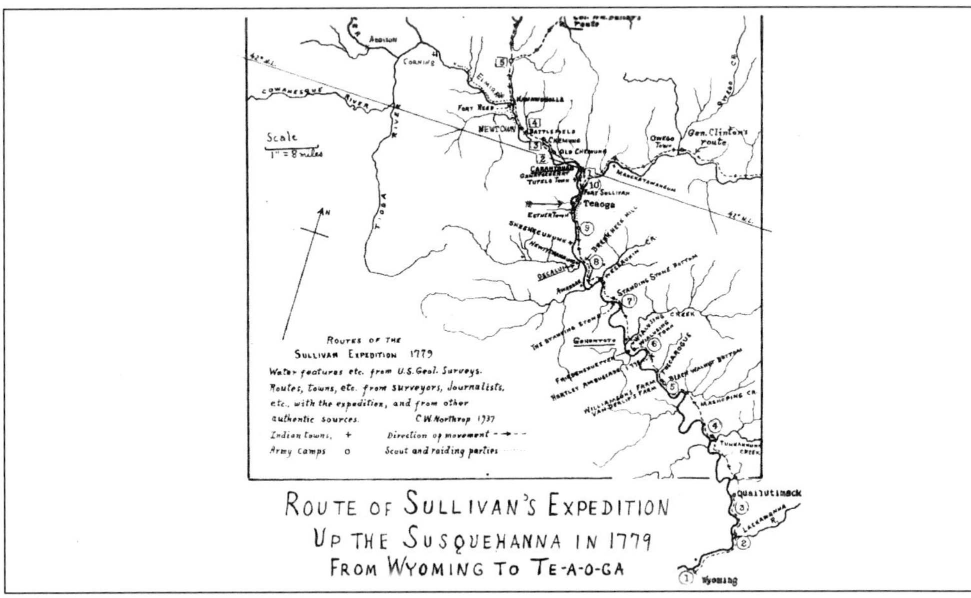

ROUTE OF SULLIVAN'S EXPEDITION. Sullivan's army began in Easton, Pennsylvania, and from there went to Wyoming, where he began to follow the Susquehanna, burning villages and destroying crops along the way. General Clinton's army came down from Lake Otsego in New York, camping for a night in the Great Bend of the Susquehanna River. (Postcard courtesy of the Tioga Point Museum.)

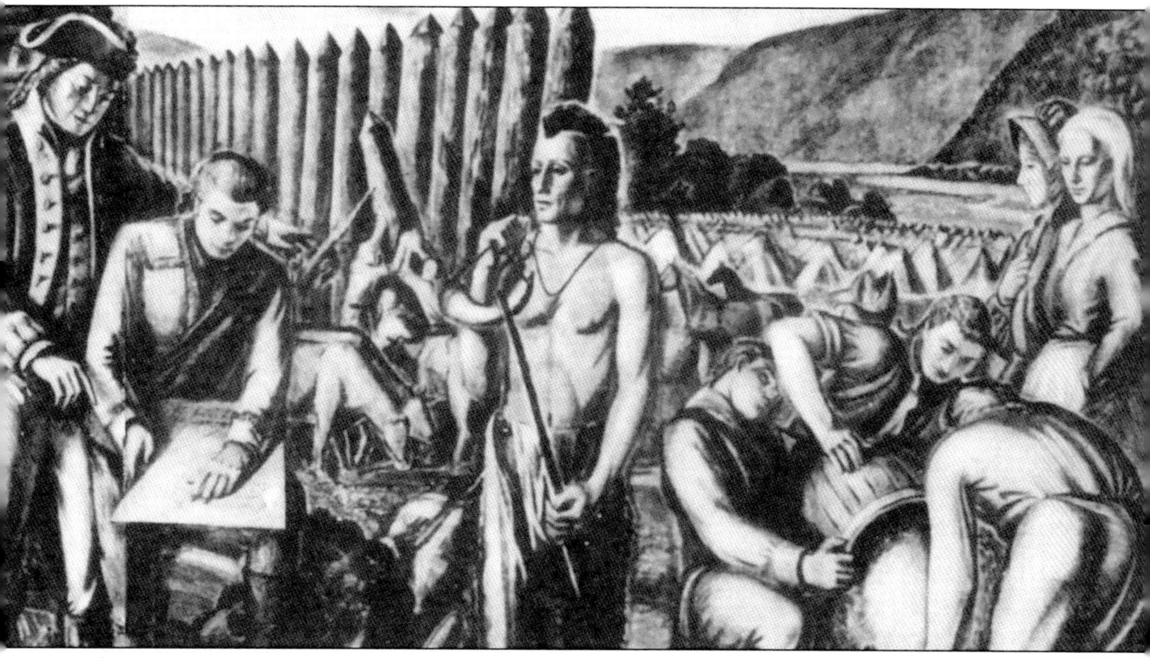

Washington responded by sending Generals Sullivan and Clinton, whose armies met at Tioga Point. The goal of the campaign was to destroy Native-American villages and crops along the Susquehanna and up through the Finger Lakes region of New York, in hopes of removing the Iroquois from the war. They fought only one major battle, at Newtown, near Elmira, New York. (Postcards courtesy of the Tioga Point Museum.)

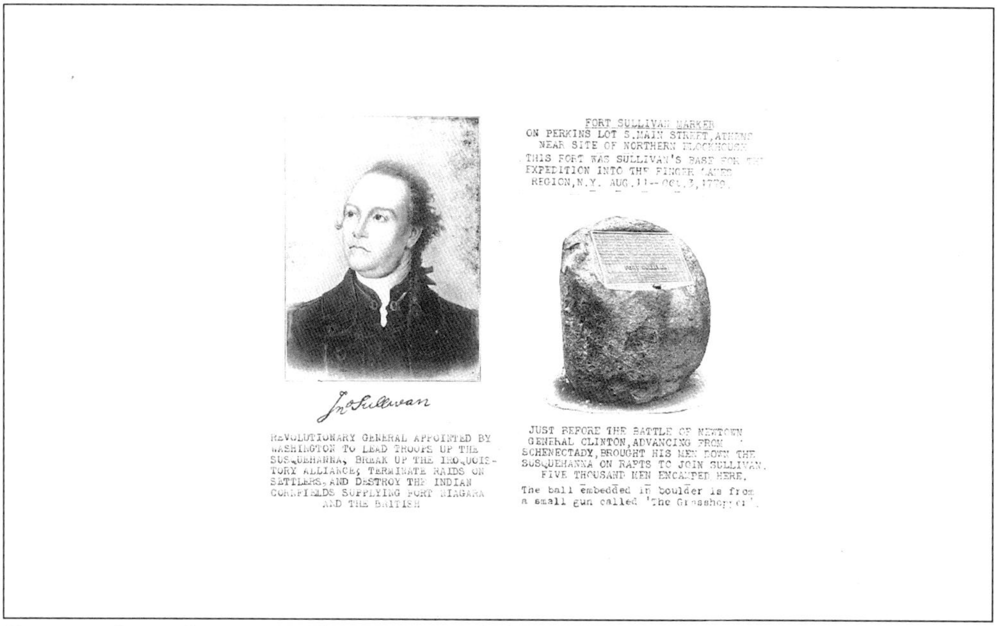

General John Sullivan. The campaign failed to accomplish its goal of removing the Iroquois from the war. The raids resumed the following year and were, if anything, harsher in revenge for the destruction caused by Sullivan's army. (Postcard courtesy of the Tioga Point Museum.)

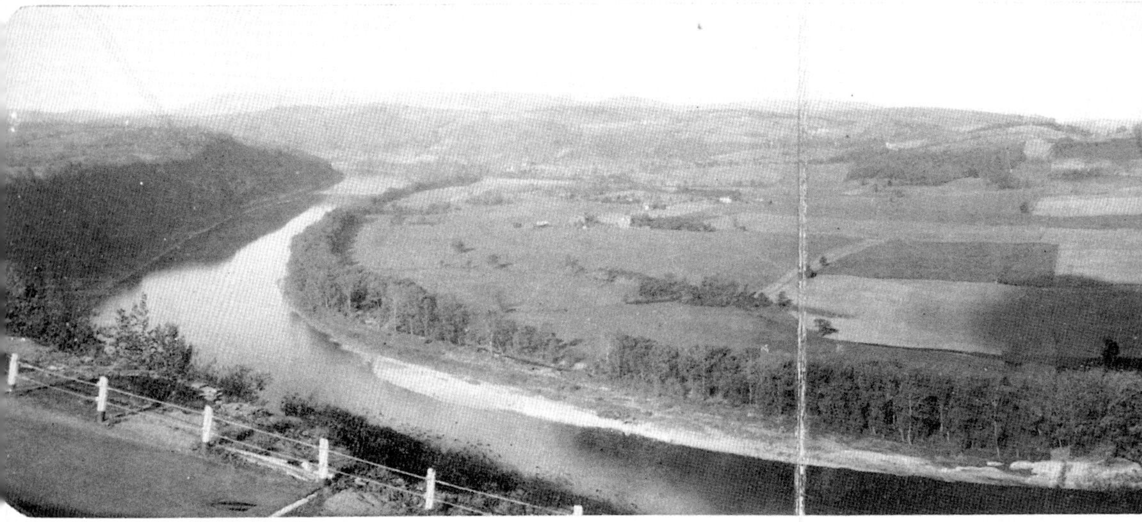

SITE OF FRENCH AZILUM. In 1793 a group of French settlers built a village in rural Bradford County. They found France inhospitable because of the Revolution and San Domingo unsafe because of slave uprisings, so they decided to try their luck in the wilds of Pennsylvania. The settlement only lasted a few years; by 1810 there was no town left, but some of the immigrants remained in the area, lending their names to places on the map (Laporte, Homet). Descendants

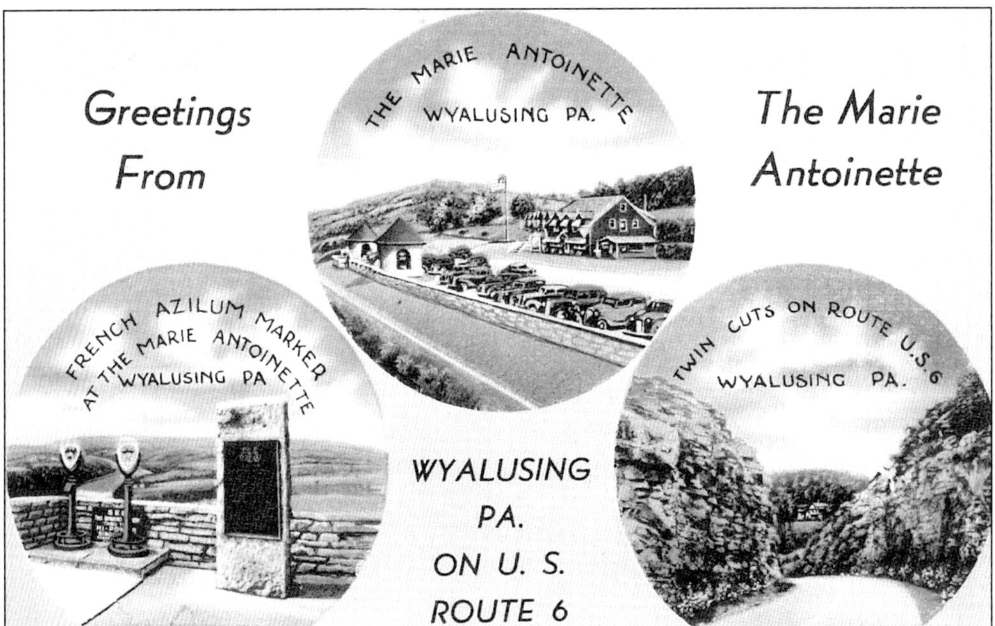

MARIE ANTOINETTE OVERLOOK. Named for the queen who lost her life in the revolution that the Azilum refugees fled, this rest stop off Route 6 gives a fine view of the historic site. The stonework was part of a WPA project. A 1940 travel guide published by the Pennsylvania Writers Project informs us that you can park, picnic, and use binoculars here. (Postcard courtesy of French Azilum.)

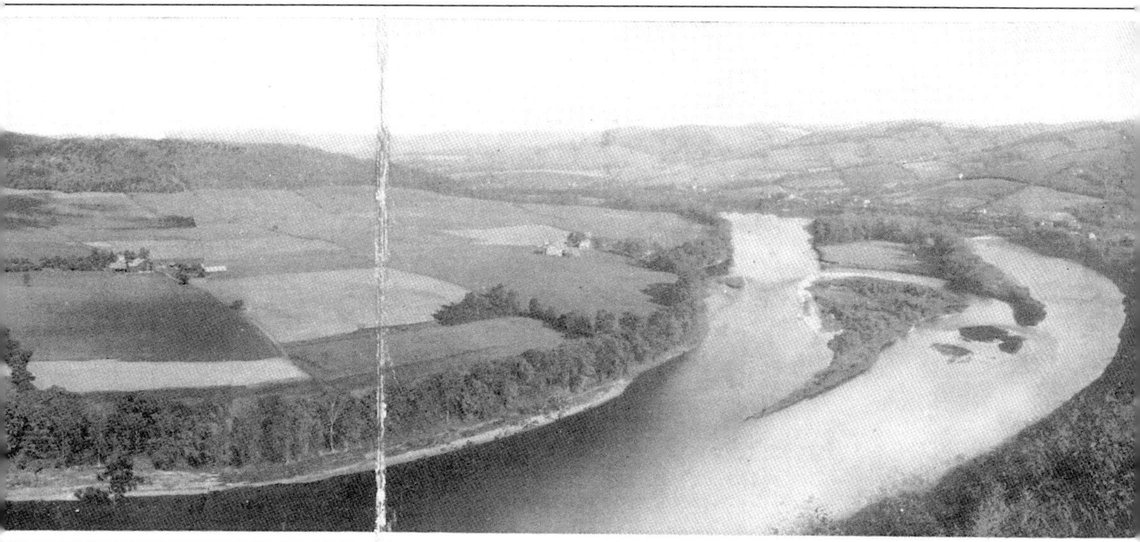

of these settlers kept the memory of "French Azilum" alive along with colorful folklore and legends that persist to this day. The site of the village is now open to the public, along with the Bartholomew Laporte house, built in 1836 by the son of one of the original refugees. It is Bradford County's only museum featuring 18th- and 19th-century decorative arts in a house setting. (Postcard courtesy of the Tioga Point Museum.)

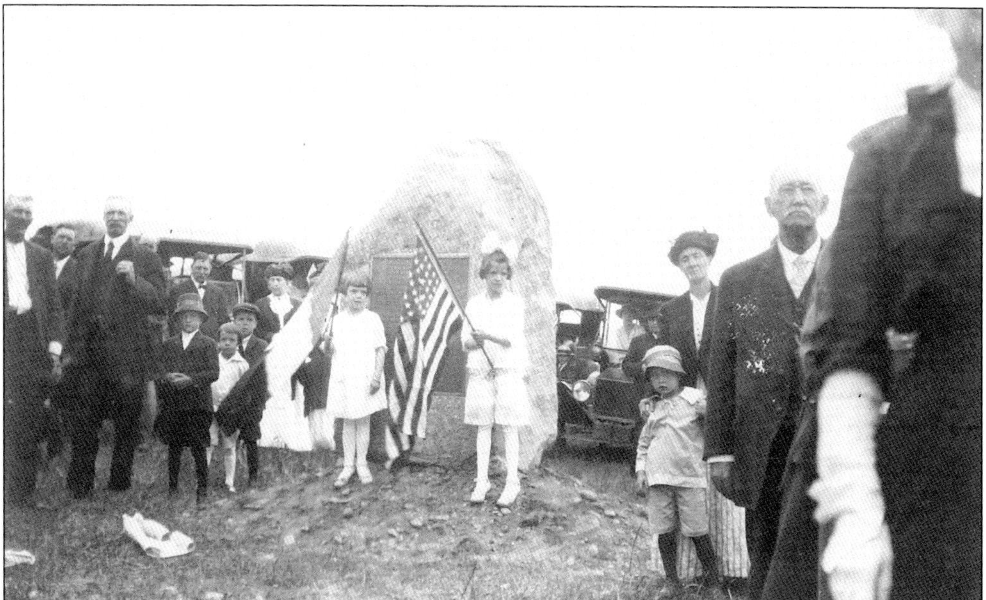

Dedication of the Monument to the Memory of French Royalist Refugees, June 14, 1916. Angelique and Jane Spalding, descendants of Antoine LeFevre, unveiled the monument with great ceremony. The little girls hold French and American flags in front of the boulder, which is located on the way to the historic site. (Postcard courtesy of Norm Brauer.)

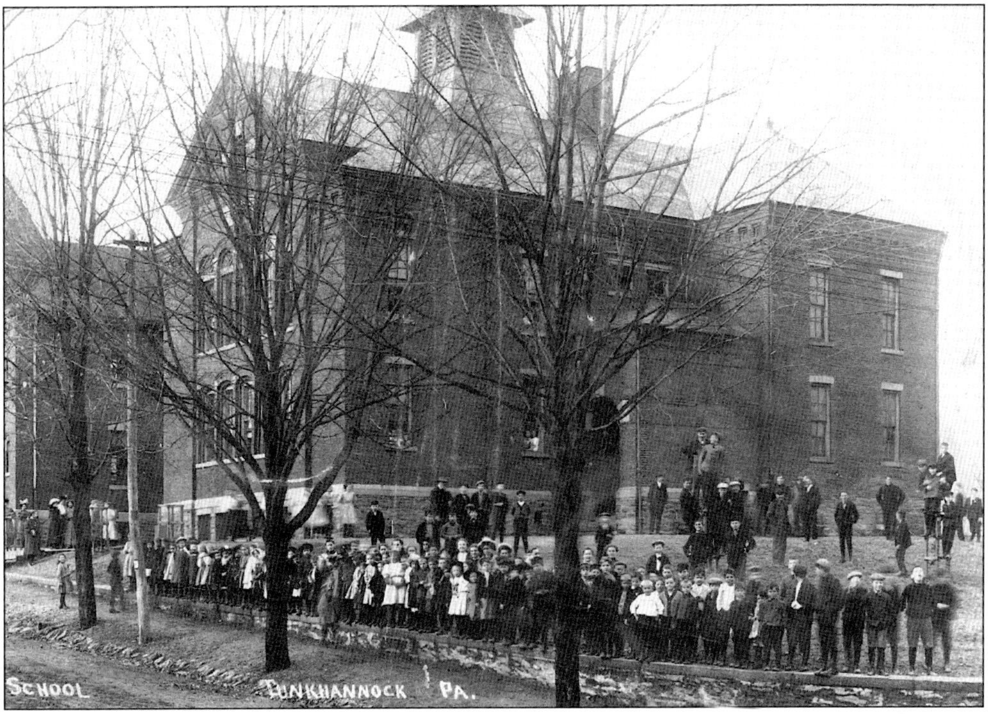

WYOMING COUNTY HISTORICAL SOCIETY. The old high school in Tunkhannock is now home to the historical society and museumfeaturing local history and Native-American exhibits. This postcard shows the building when it was serving its original function. The pupils and their teachers are out for a group portrait; close observation shows that the boys on the right are not taking the exercise seriously. (Postcard courtesy of the Tioga Point Museum.)

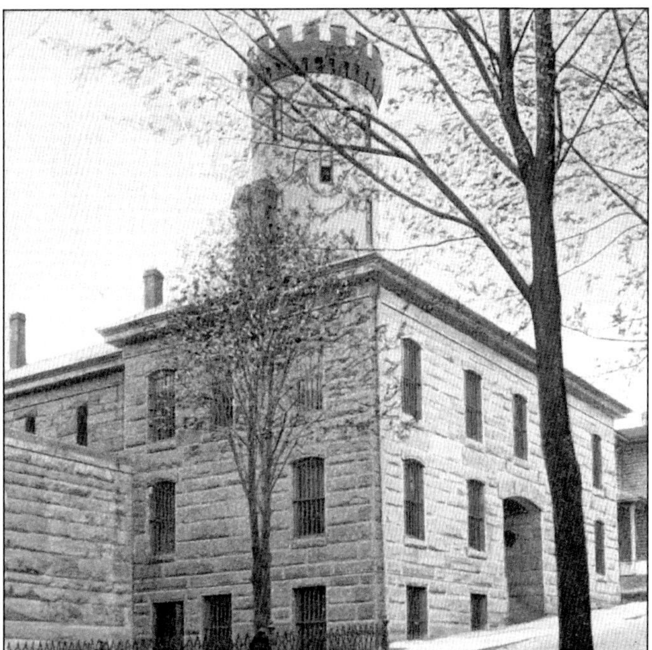

COUNTY JAIL, TOWANDA. The new home of the Bradford County Historical Society (summer 2000), this building stood empty for many years until the county gave it to the society for use as a museum and research center. The historical society was incorporated in 1875 and is the official repository for county historical documents. The museum houses an impressive collection of exhibits from all periods of county history. Particularly interesting are the Civil War, railroad, and pioneer life displays. (Postcard courtesy of the Tioga Point Museum.)

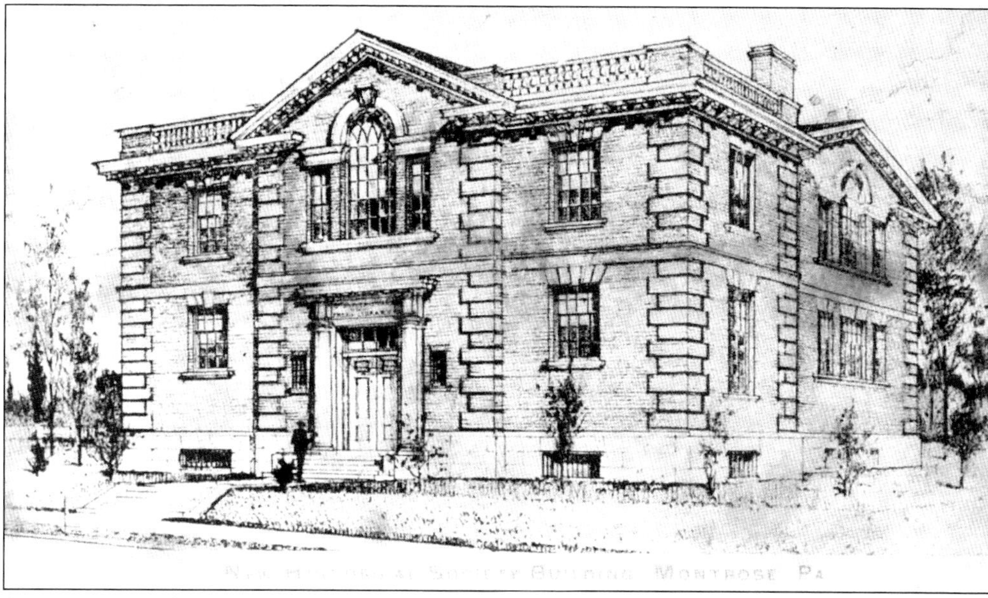

Susquehanna County Historical Society. This building was constructed in 1906 for use as a historical society and library, and continues these functions today. The museum exhibits include portraits of early residents, landscapes, and religious paintings by well-known, local artist Susan Waters, relics of county history, and decorative arts. (Postcard courtesy of the Susquehanna County Historical Society.)

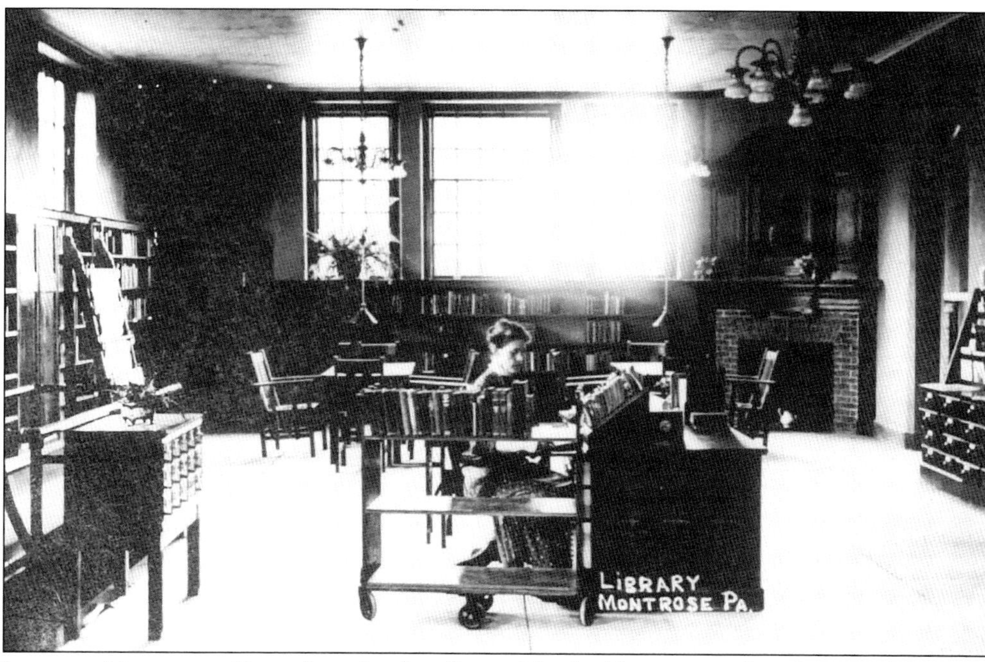

Library, Montrose. Housed on the first floor of the building pictured at the top of the page, the library has served the area for 92 years. When the library was only two years old it owned over 4,000 books. As in many public buildings of this vintage, there is a fireplace (which used to be functional) and many other interesting architectural details. (Postcard courtesy of the Susquehanna County Historical Society.)

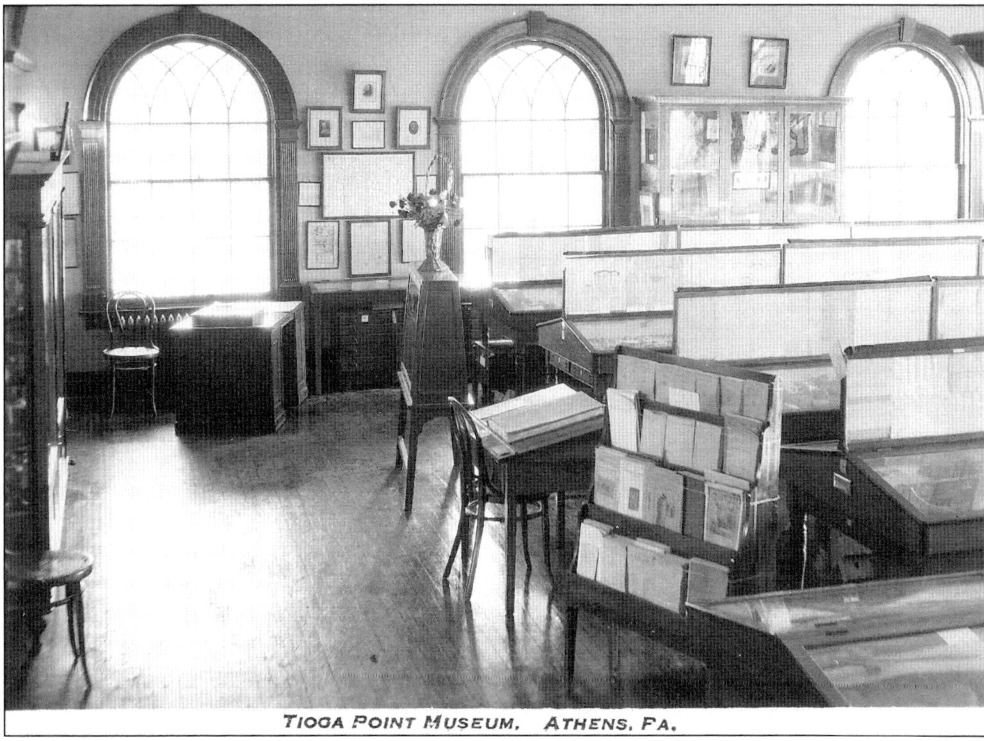

TIOGA POINT MUSEUM, ATHENS, 1928. The four views on these two pages show the interior of the museum as it appeared when an addition was completed. This card shows the main room with its oak display cases, some of which came from the original museum, founded in the Old Academy across the street to display local lore (see p. 2). (Postcard courtesy of the Tioga Point Museum.)

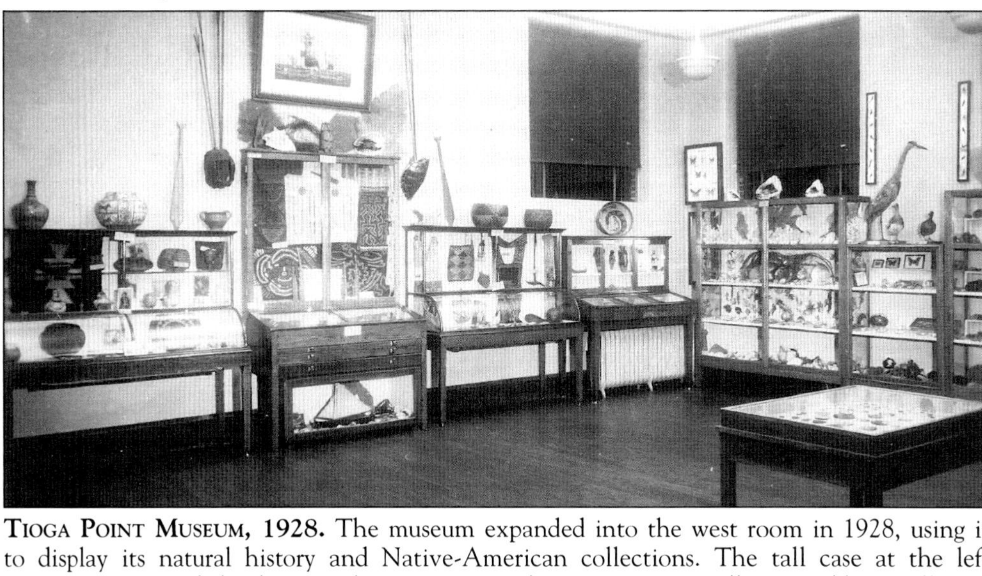

TIOGA POINT MUSEUM, 1928. The museum expanded into the west room in 1928, using it to display its natural history and Native-American collections. The tall case at the left contains items made by the San Blas or Kuna people. Sayre native William Markham collected these things in Panama, where he worked on the railroad. (Postcard courtesy of the Tioga Point Museum.)

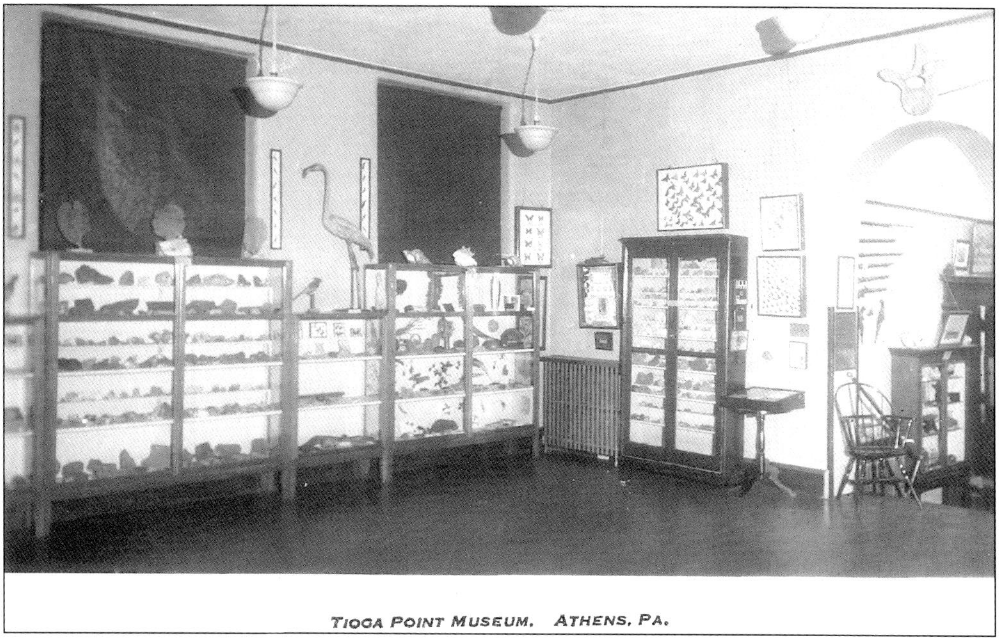

TIOGA POINT MUSEUM, 1928. The early curators of this museum saw it as a tiny Smithsonian, with collections from all over the world, including China, Japan, and Egypt. The curator of entomology in the 1930s was Robert Crandall, who became well known as a film maker. (Postcard courtesy of the Tioga Point Museum.)

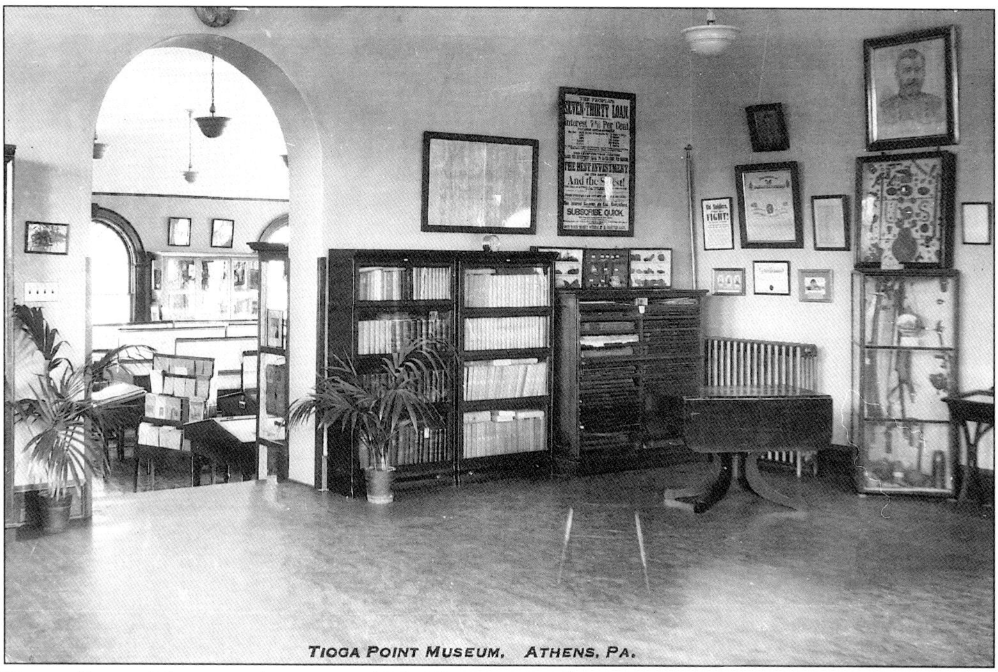

TIOGA POINT MUSEUM, ATHENS, 1928. The museum boasts an extensive research library, as do other museums in the Endless Mountains, including the Bradford, Susquehanna, Sullivan, and Wyoming County Historical Societies. Hundreds of researchers use these facilities each year. (Postcard courtesy of the Tioga Point Museum.)

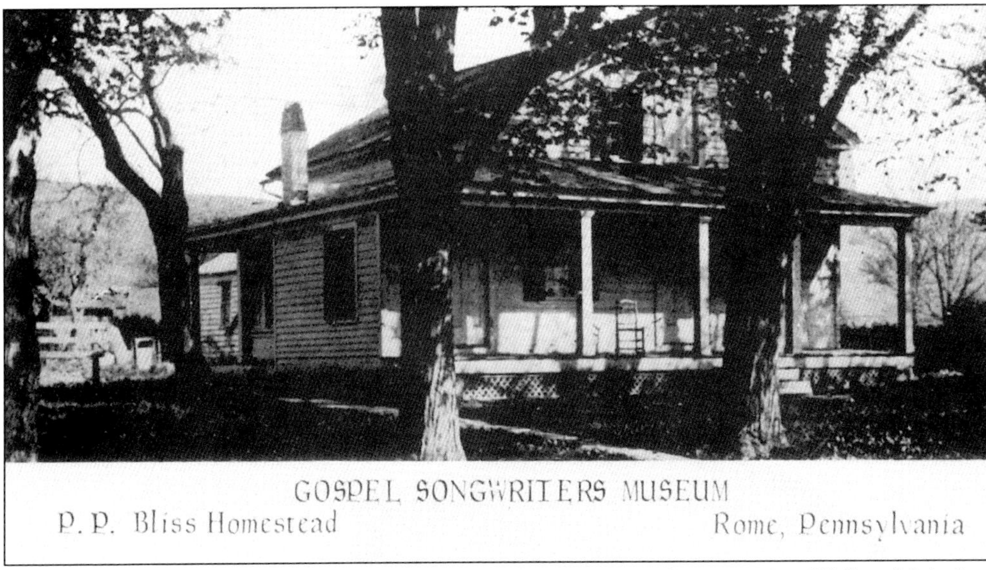

P.P. Bliss Homestead, Rome. The famous gospel songwriter, who wrote *It is Well with My Soul* and many other hymns, lived in Bradford County. His house is on the National Register of Historic Places and is open to the public in the warm seasons. (Postcard courtesy of the Tioga Point Museum.)

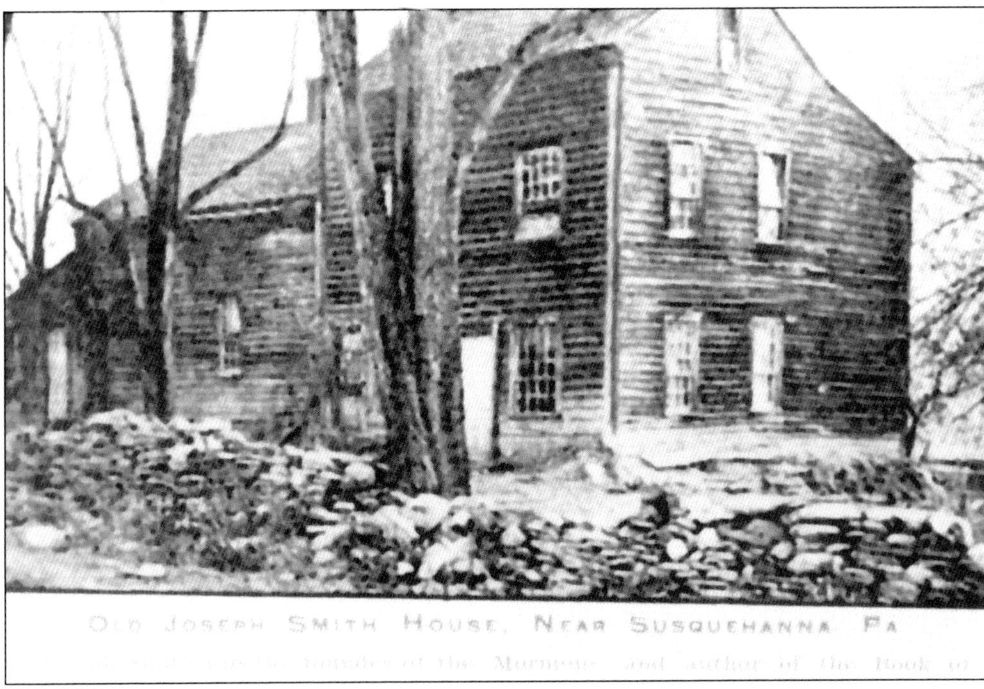

Joseph Smith House, near Susquehanna. The founder of the Mormon faith lived near the town of Susquehanna in the northeast corner of the county of the same name. Joseph Smith and his wife, Emma Hale Smith, inherited this house from her father, Isaac Hale. They lived here from 1828 through 1831. Mormons believe that Smith received a visitation from John the Baptist in the Great Bend area of the Susquehanna River. (Postcard courtesy of the Susquehanna County Historical Society.)

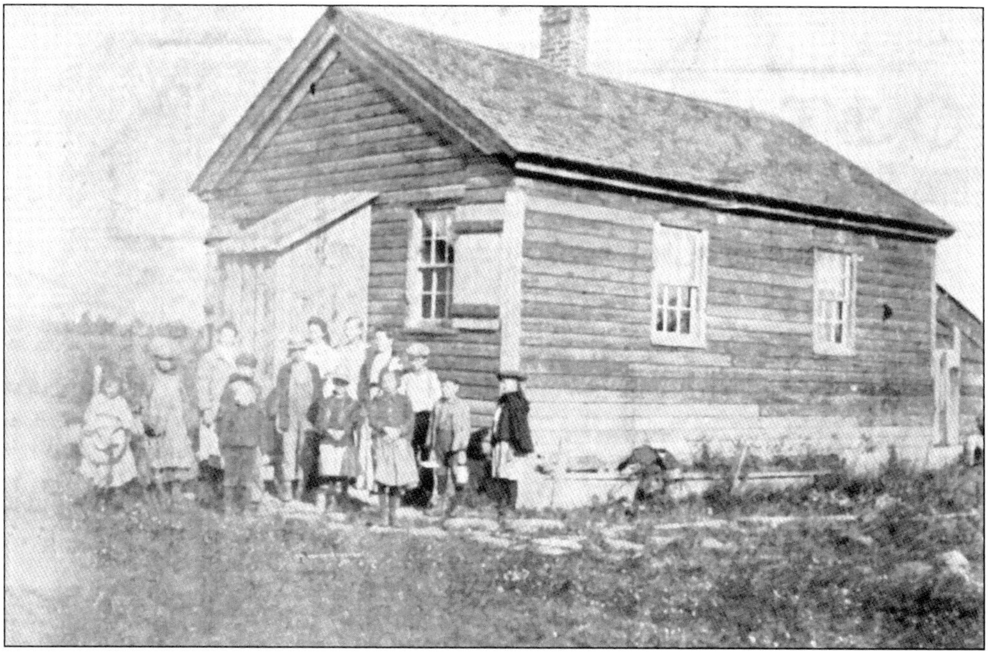

SCHOOL IN LOPEZ, SULLIVAN COUNTY. The Sullivan County Historical Society in Laporte displays articles relating to the history of the county's settlements, including Lopez, a lumber town. The society administers three sites in the Laporte area, the Baldwin House, Celestia, and the Meylert Street museum. Celestia, just outside Laporte, is a former Adventist community founded in 1853 by Peter Armstrong. The community was abandoned after some years, and Armstrong deeded the land to "Almighty God." (Postcard courtesy of the Bradford County Historical Society.)

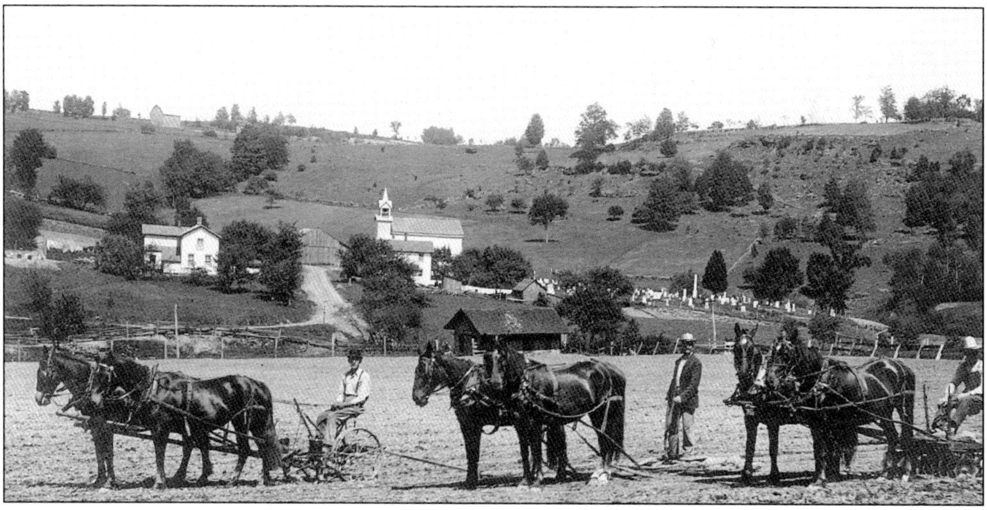

PLANTING CORN IN JOSEPH WATTMAN'S FIELD, LADDSBURG. Agriculture has always been important in this region, and not easy. The river valleys give the best yields because the nutrients in the fertile soil are replenished by frequent floods. In the mountains the farmers had to struggle for subsistence. The soil is rocky and the terrain difficult. The history and tools of farming in the region can be studied at the Bradford County Farm Museum in Troy. (Postcard courtesy of the Bradford County Historical Society.)

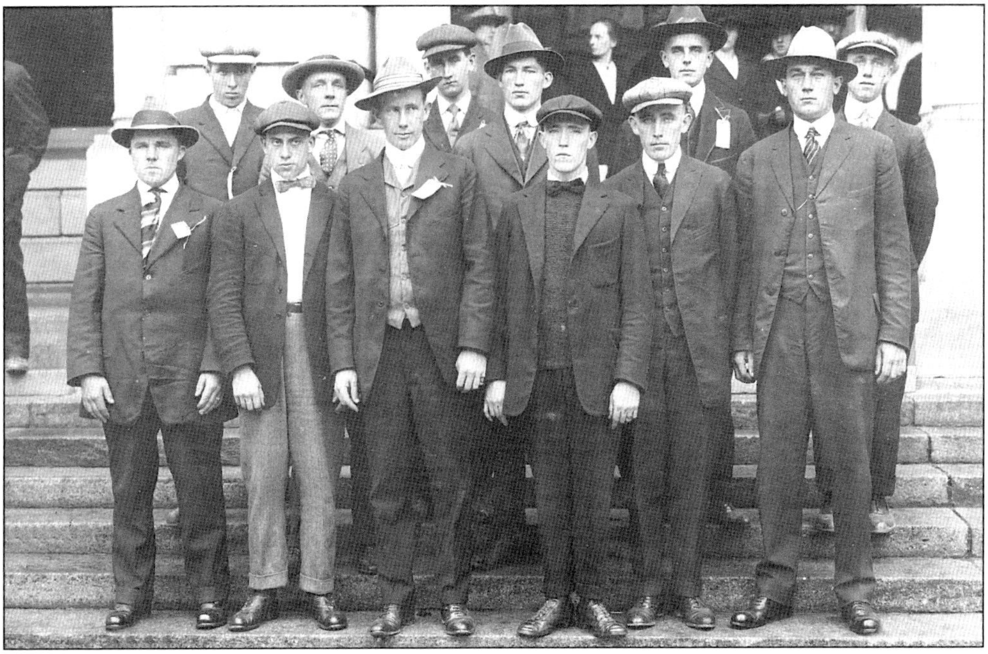

World War I Draftees on the Steps of the Courthouse, Towanda. The four counties of the Endless Mountains sent many soldiers to fight in the war. (Postcard courtesy of the Tioga Point Museum.)

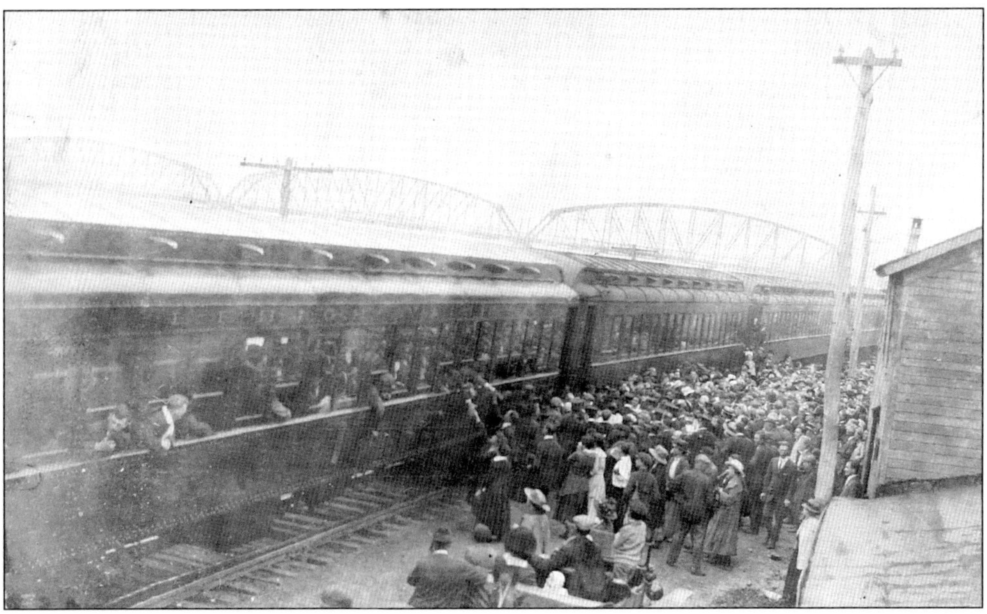

Train Leaving with Draftees, Towanda. The photo for this card was taken from the back of the county courthouse on River Street. Bradford County sent more than 2,000 troops to serve during the war, making this a common scene during the war years. The railroad moved soldiers across the country on a large scale. (Postcard courtesy of the Tioga Point Museum.)

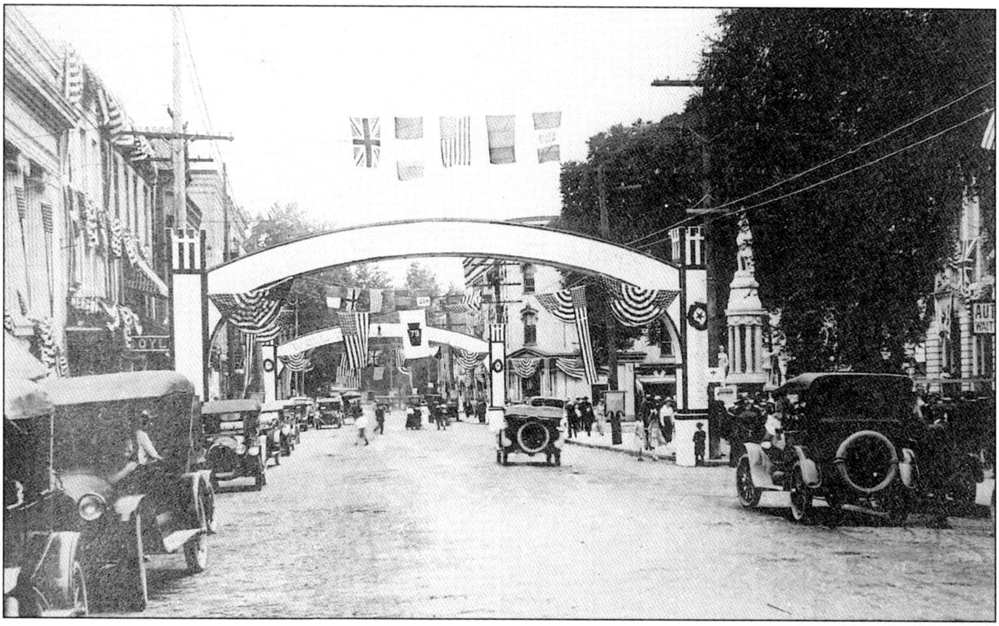

Welcome Home Parade, Towanda, July 26, 1919. When they returned there was a great parade. The flags of Allied nations, including Great Britain, France, the United States, and Italy, are suspended over Towanda's Main Street. Memory of another bloody conflict is present in the Civil War monument in front of the courthouse on the right side of the picture. (Postcard courtesy of the Bradford County Historical Society.)

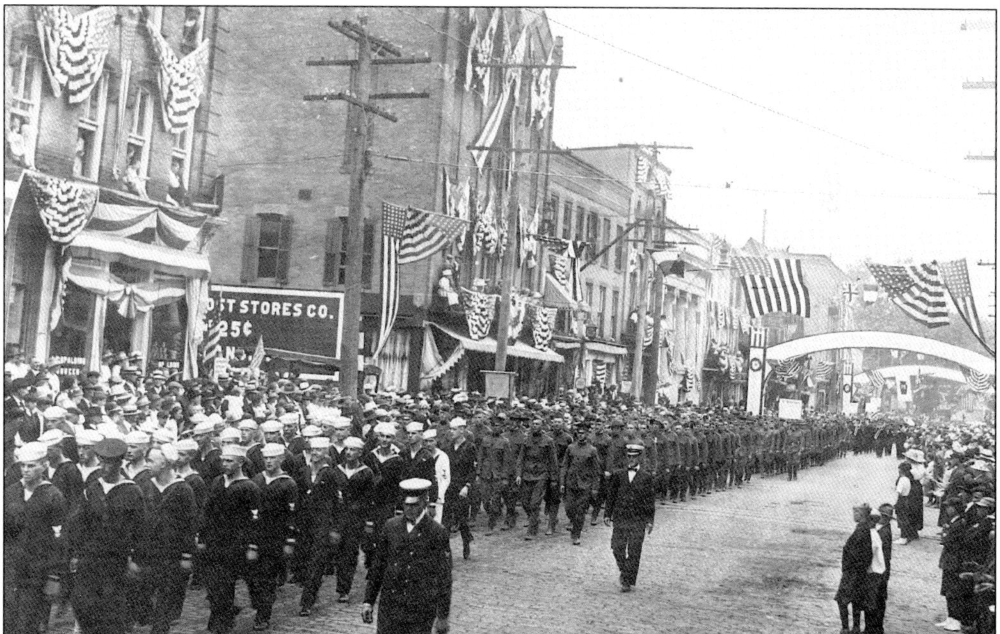

Another View of Parade. In this view of the town at the same time, soldiers and sailors march down Main Street. The buildings are hung with bunting and crowds line the streets. Spectators can also be seen viewing the parade from upper windows along the parade route. (Postcard courtesy of the Tioga Point Museum.)

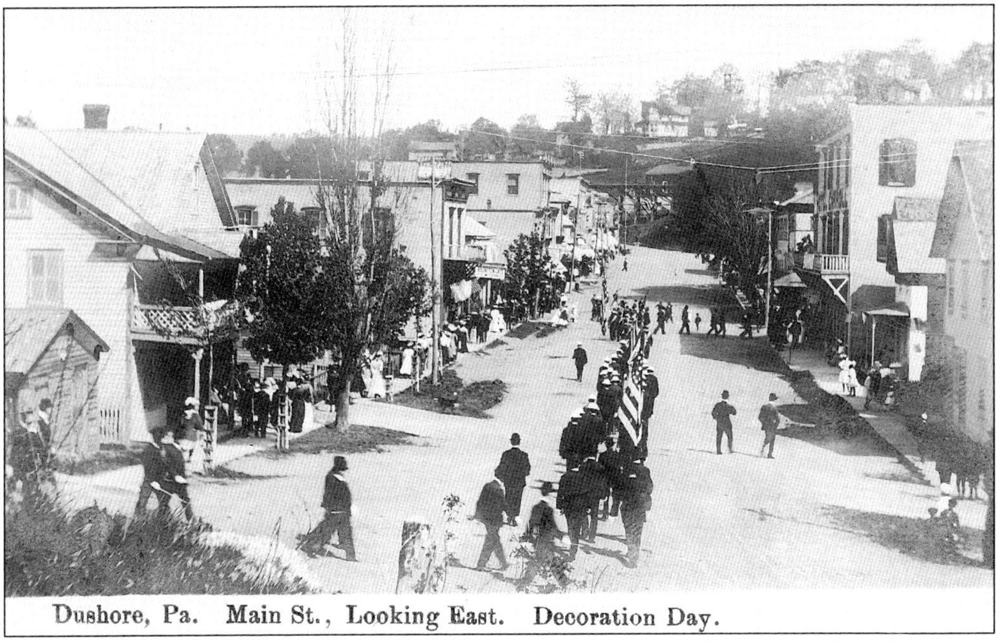

DECORATION DAY, DUSHORE. Every year the Decoration Day parade honored the soldiers who died in World War I. (Postcard courtesy of the Bradford County Historical Society.)

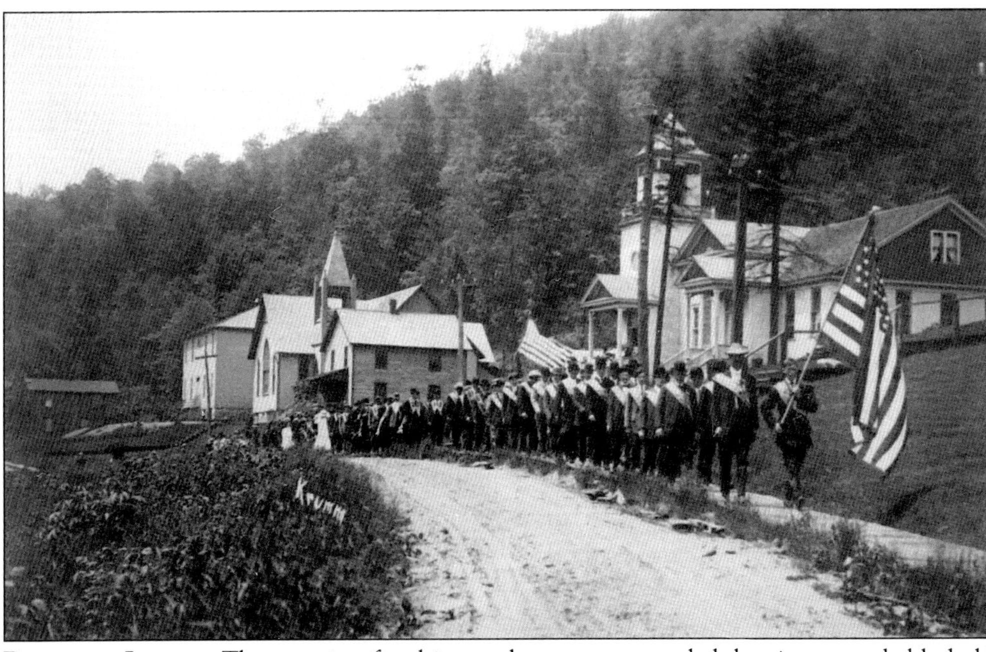

PARADE IN LAQUIN. The occasion for this parade was not recorded, but it was probably held on a patriotic holiday, either Decoration Day or Independence Day. (Postcard courtesy of the Bradford County Historical Society.)

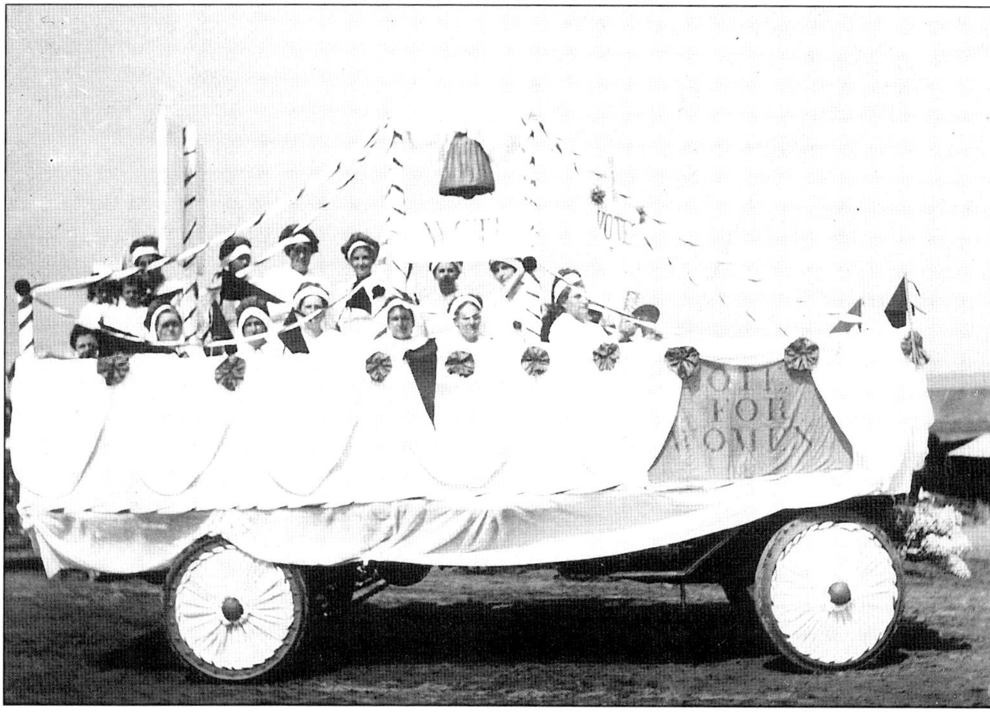

WOMEN'S CHRISTIAN TEMPERANCE UNION FLOAT. This float for a parade, probably in Athens, advocates the vote for women. That places the date for this card before 1922. Both the temperance and suffrage movements were strong in this area. (Postcard courtesy of the Tioga Point Museum.)

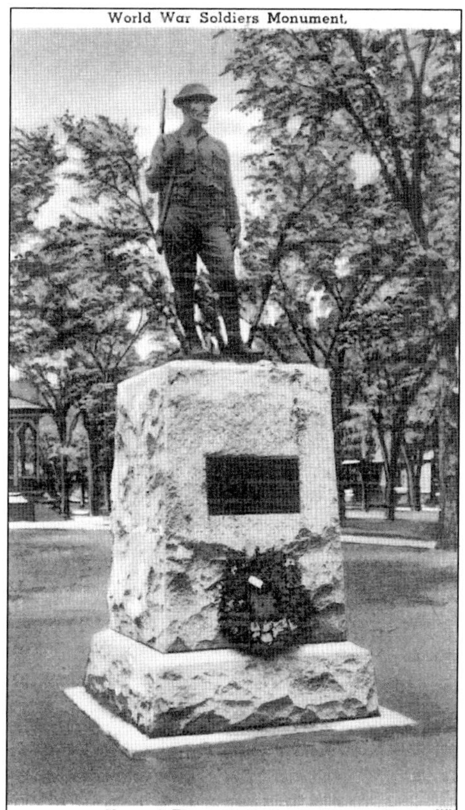

WORLD WAR I SOLDIERS MONUMENT, SAYRE. Known as the Doughboy, this monument is dedicated to the Sayre veterans of the First World War. It stands in Howard Elmer Park. (Postcard courtesy of the Tioga Point Museum.)

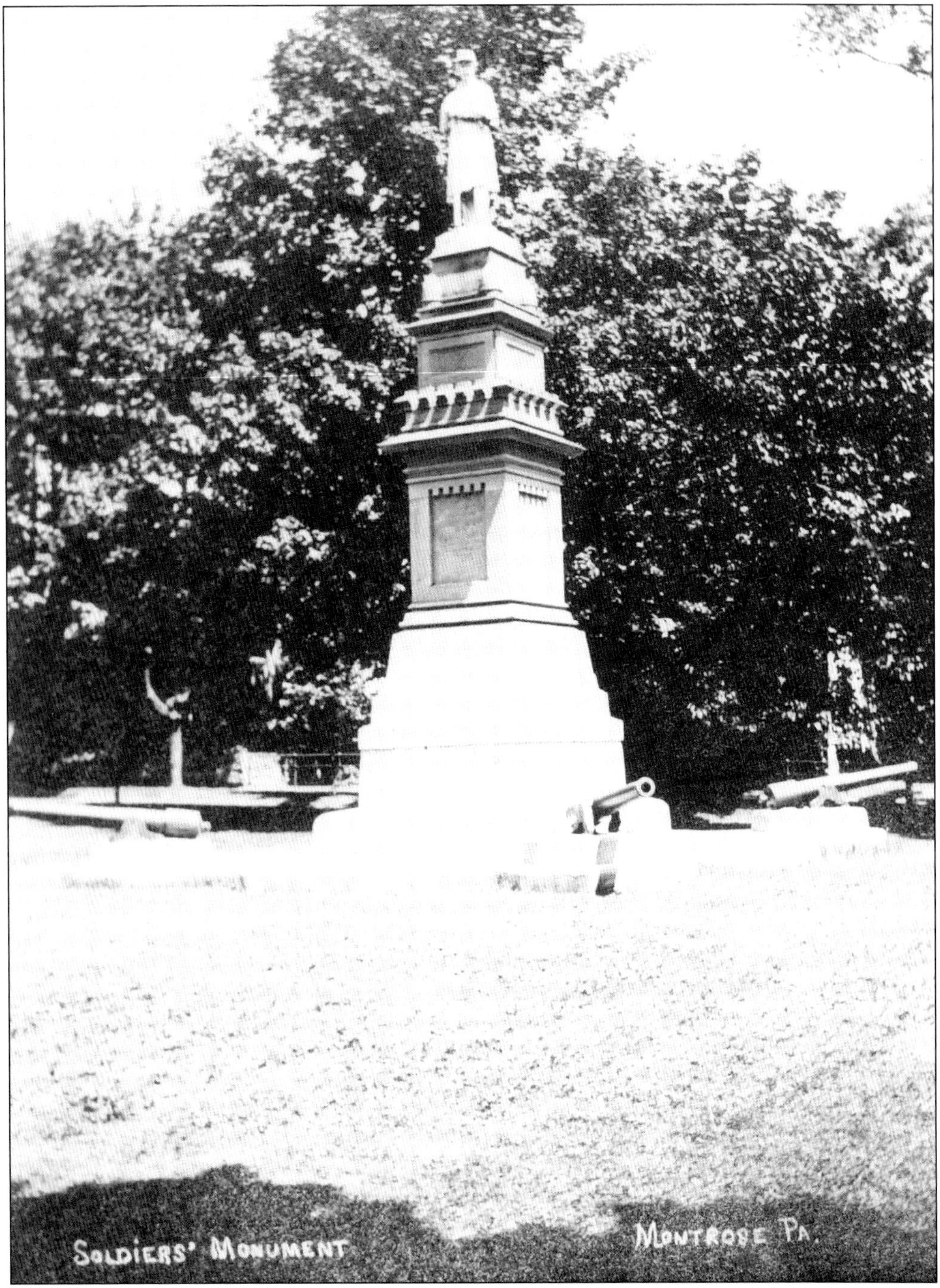

SOLDIERS MONUMENT, MONTROSE. This stone Civil War memorial was unveiled on July 4, 1877. The base of the sculpture is made of stone quarried in Susquehanna County. The Endless Mountain region sent many soldiers to fight in "The War of the Rebellion," and a large number of residents held abolitionist beliefs. The community planned the monument for many years before it was finally able to see the construction completed. (Postcard courtesy of the Susquehanna County Historical Society.)

Two

INDUSTRY

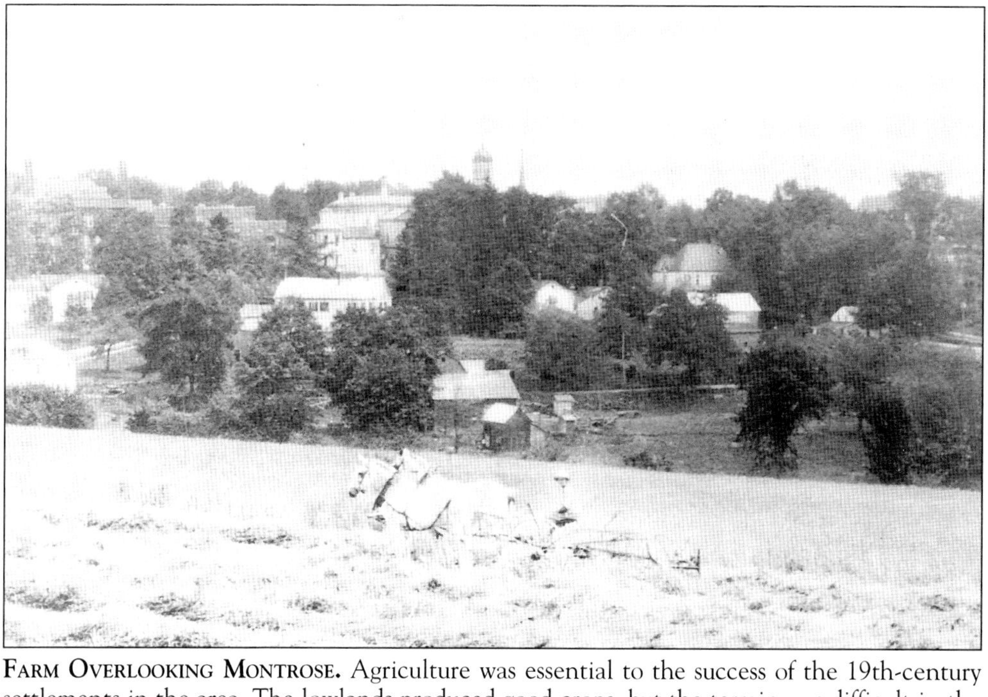

FARM OVERLOOKING MONTROSE. Agriculture was essential to the success of the 19th-century settlements in the area. The lowlands produced good crops, but the terrain was difficult in the mountains, and although cleared and cultivated, the summit farms were not fertile enough for long-term success; erosion was a problem and many farms were abandoned. Agriculture, particularly dairy farming, continues to make a large contribution to the economy and character of the region. (Postcard courtesy of the Susquehanna County Historical Society.)

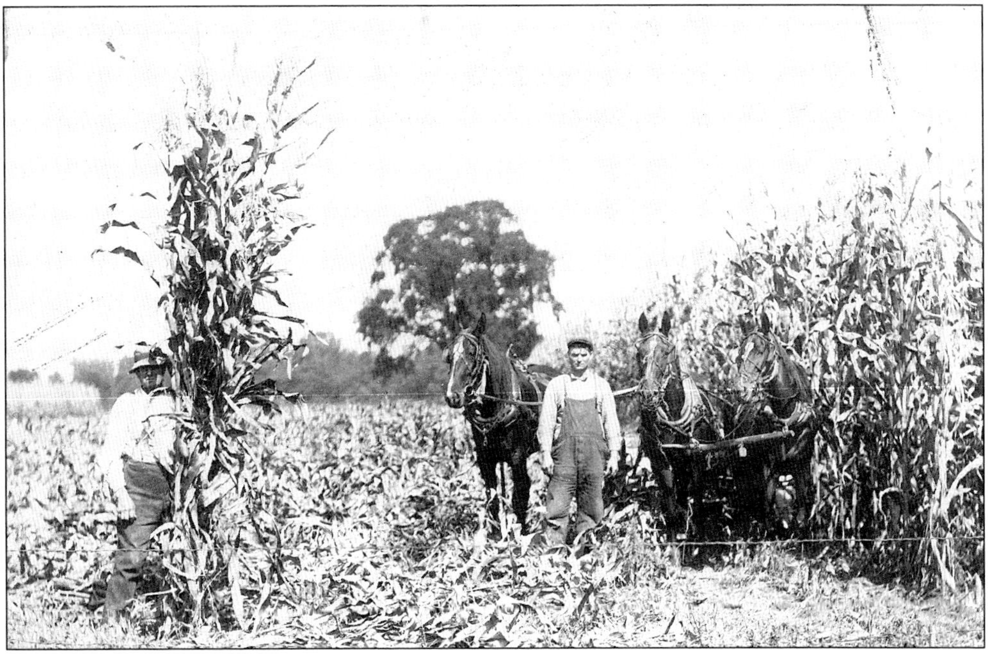

GREAT CORN YEAR OF 1913. Corn was and is grown to feed people and livestock. The Murray farm in West Athens produced this extraordinary crop on the bottom lands west of the Chemung River. Other successful crops grown in the region include hay and potatoes. (Postcard courtesy of the Tioga Point Museum.)

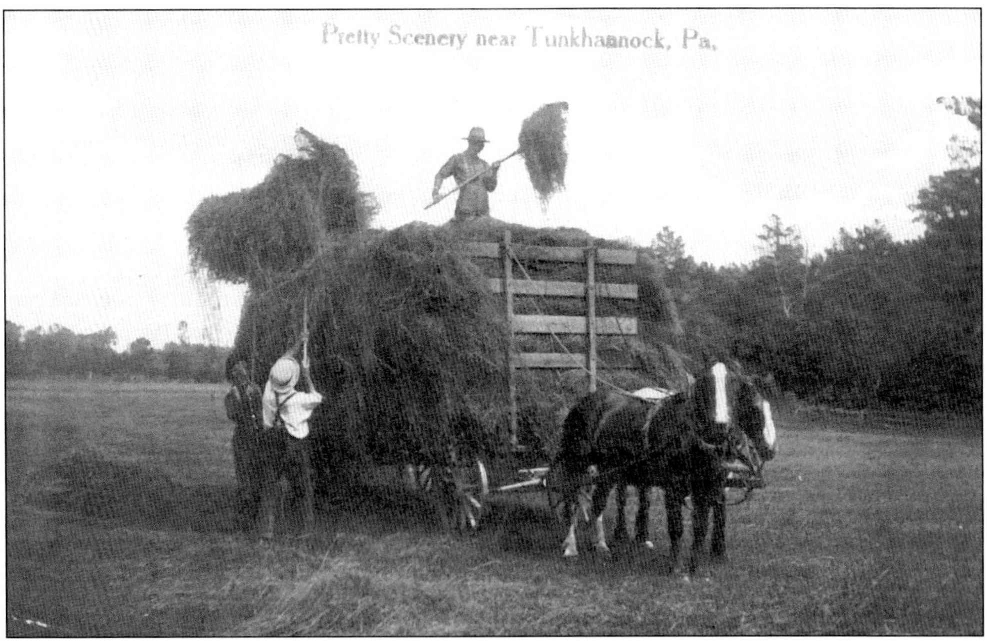

HAYING IN TUNKHANNOCK, 1914. As far back as 1914 postcards featuring the picturesque qualities of the farming communities in the region were being produced. This card shows the essential and difficult haying operation. Farmers needed hay to feed their animals during the winter months. (Postcard courtesy of the Tioga Point Museum.)

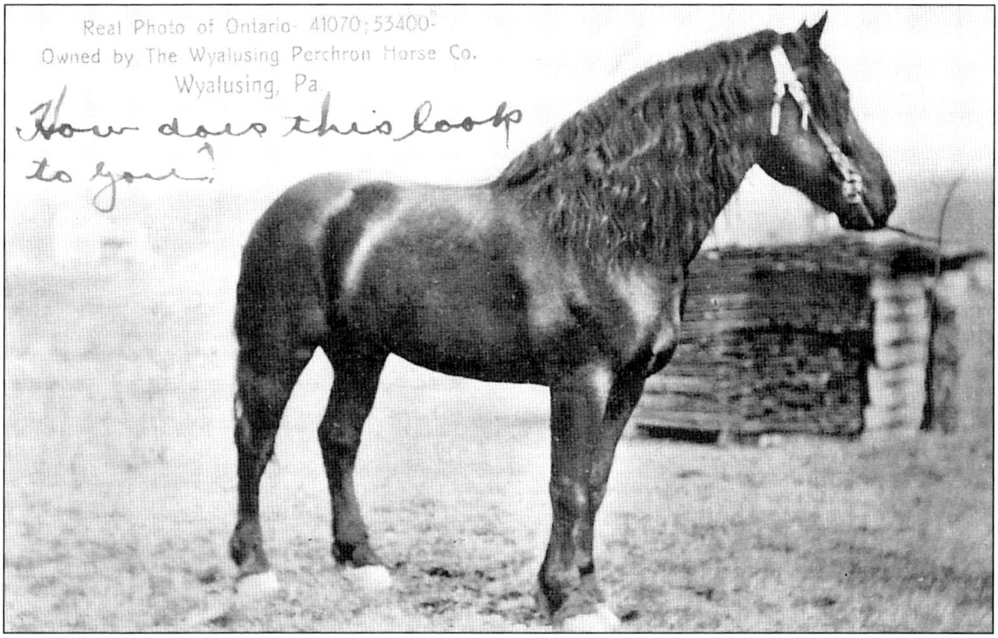

ONTARIO, WYALUSING, 1909. The use of draft animals to pull plows and other farm machinery made the life of the farmer easier. Percherons are working horses, bred for their strength. The Wyalusing Percheron Horse Company boasted their stud, Ontario, foaled April 20, 1901, and imported from France. Ontario stood at the barn of L.H. Marsh in Wyalusing in charge of J.B. Ellsworth.

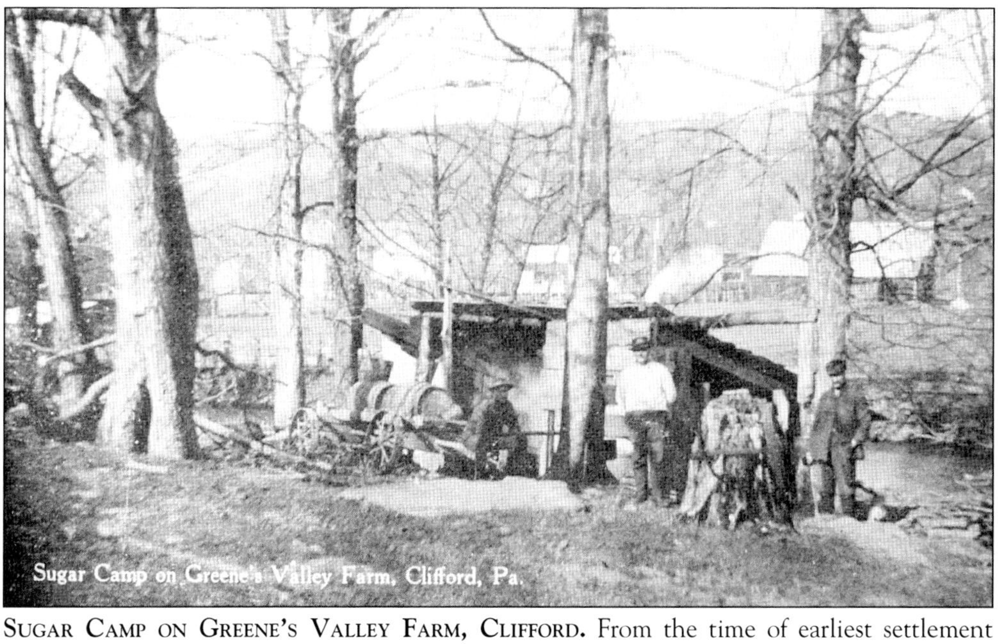

SUGAR CAMP ON GREENE'S VALLEY FARM, CLIFFORD. From the time of earliest settlement people have exploited the natural resources found in the Endless Mountains. Settlers used maple sugar to pay for necessities such as grain and groceries. It is reported that one man could make a ton of sugar in one season. (Postcard courtesy of the Susquehanna County Historical Society.)

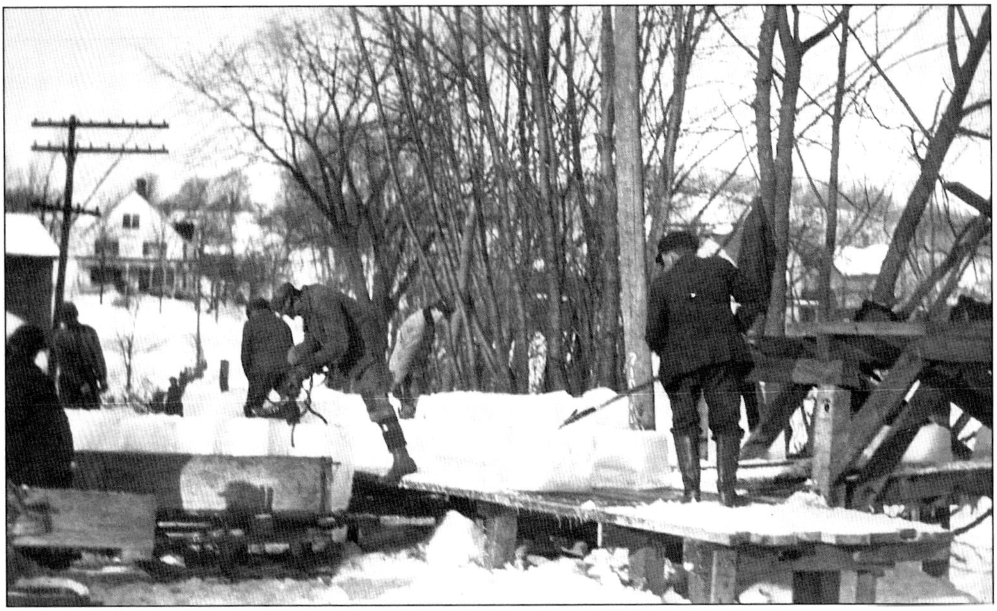

CUTTING ICE IN DUSHORE. Another natural resource to be used was ice. Every winter crews harvested blocks from ponds and lakes. These blocks were stored in ice houses for use during the warmer months before the era of artificial refrigeration. The ice was used in peoples' homes and in railroad cars that transported dairy products to the cities. (Postcard courtesy of Norm Brauer.)

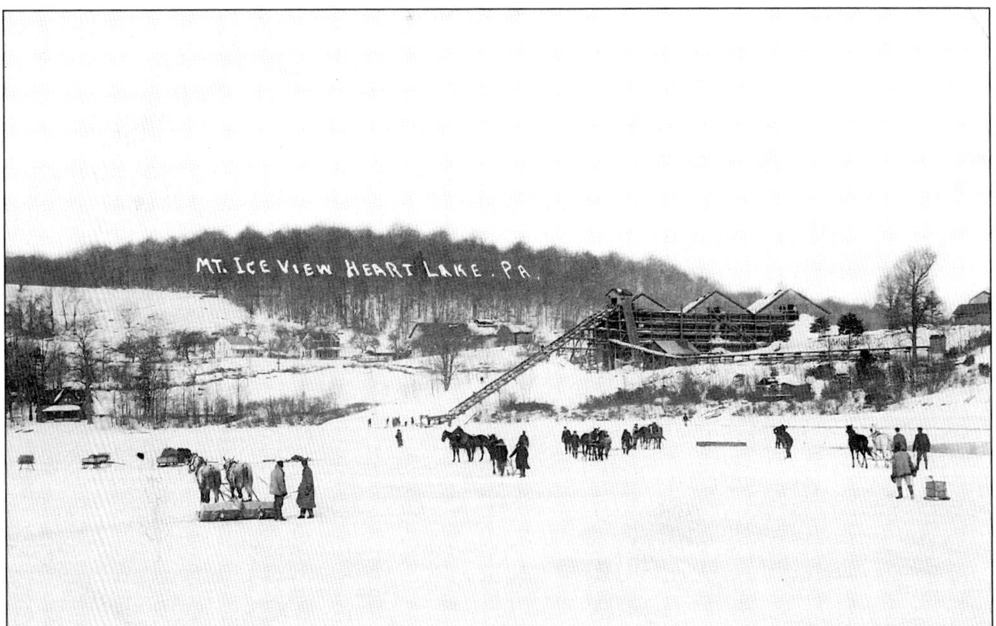

HEART LAKE ICE HARVEST. There were two large ice houses that operated around the lake. The horse teams in the card are scraping snow off the top of the ice; this job was later done by motorized equipment. In the early 1930s a sign posted on the side of one of the ice houses read "A cake of ice never gets out of order." Nevertheless the new technology of artificial refrigeration soon triumphed. (Postcard courtesy of Norm Brauer.)

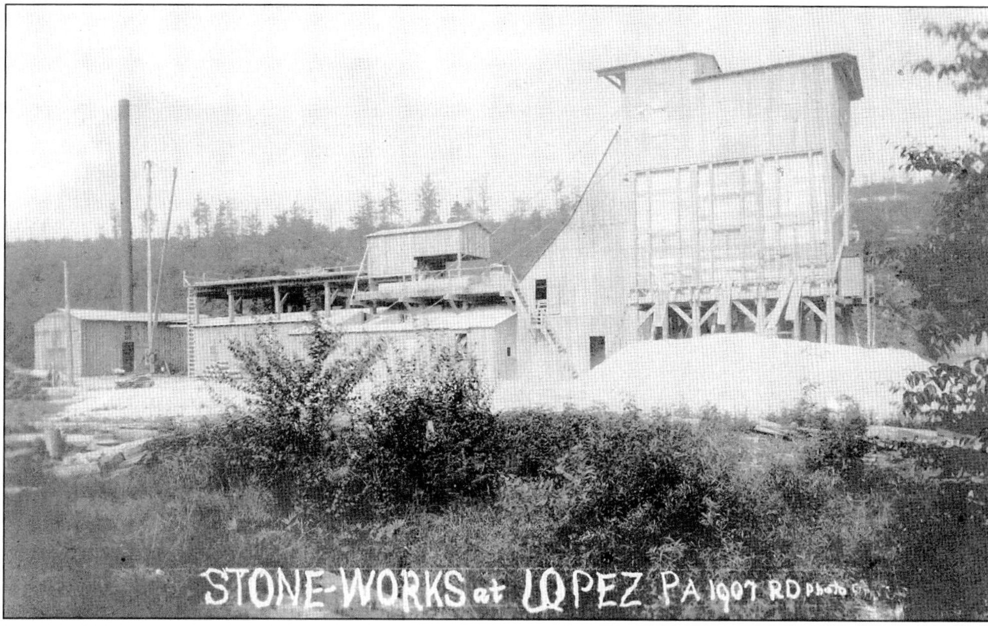

STONE WORKS, LOPEZ. Coal is not the only mineral resource in the area. Slate, shale, and building stones are abundant and continue to be quarried. This facility extracted sandstone. (Postcard courtesy of Norm Brauer.)

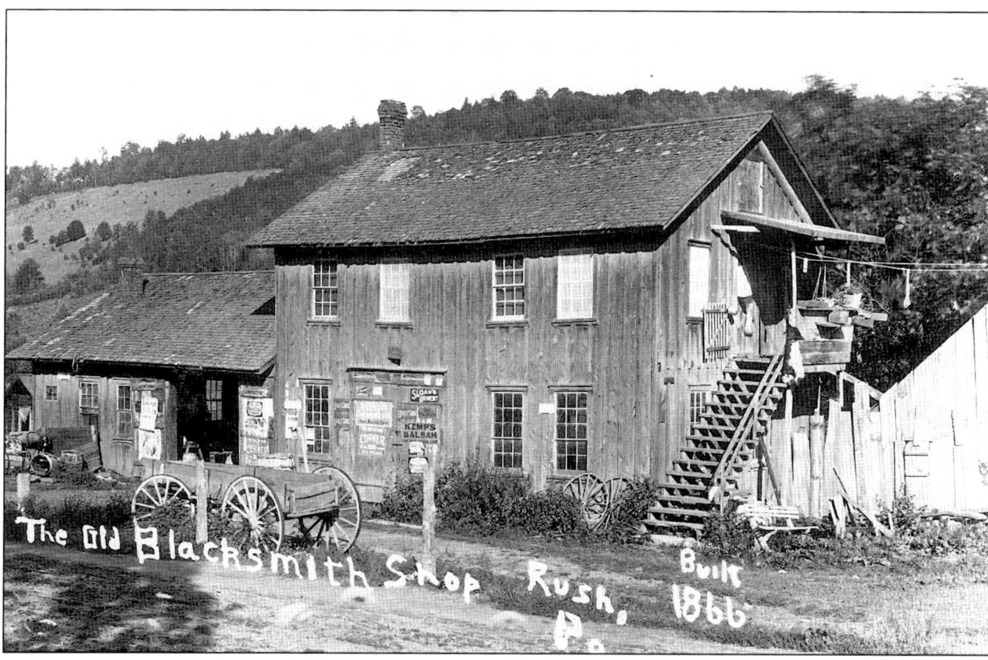

BLACKSMITH SHOP, RUSH. The smith was an essential part of the agricultural community, where horses and oxen required shoes and farmers required tools. (Postcard courtesy of Norm Brauer.)

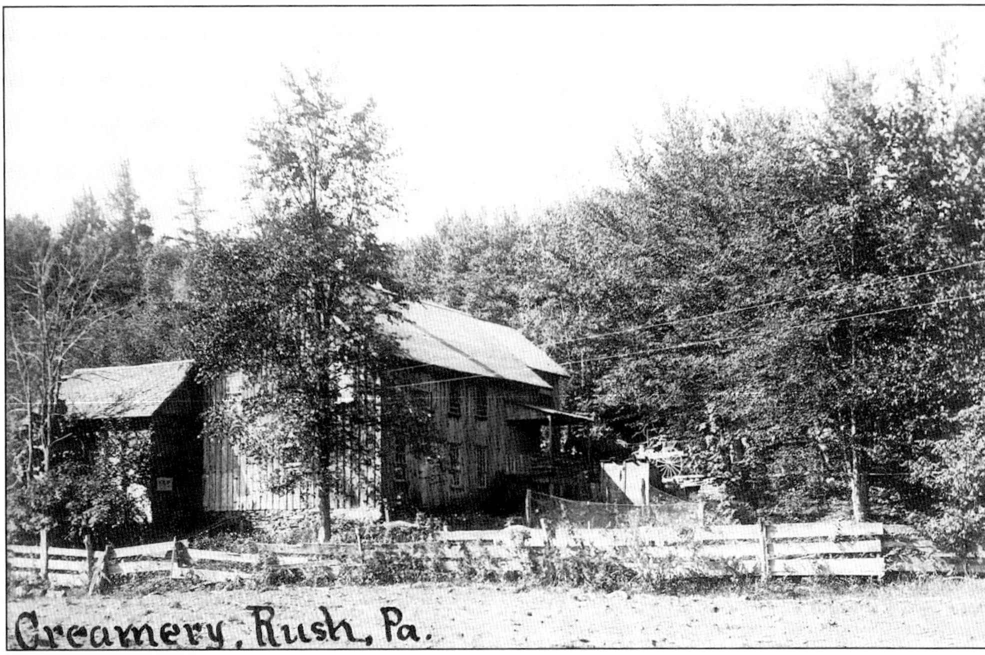

Creamery, Rush. Creameries usually handled milk from many farms. Dairy farmers of the area used the creameries to process their milk and see to the distribution of the final product to market via the railroad, which allowed rapid transport of the perishable dairy goods. The arrival of the railroad caused a surge in milk production. (Postcard courtesy of Norm Brauer.)

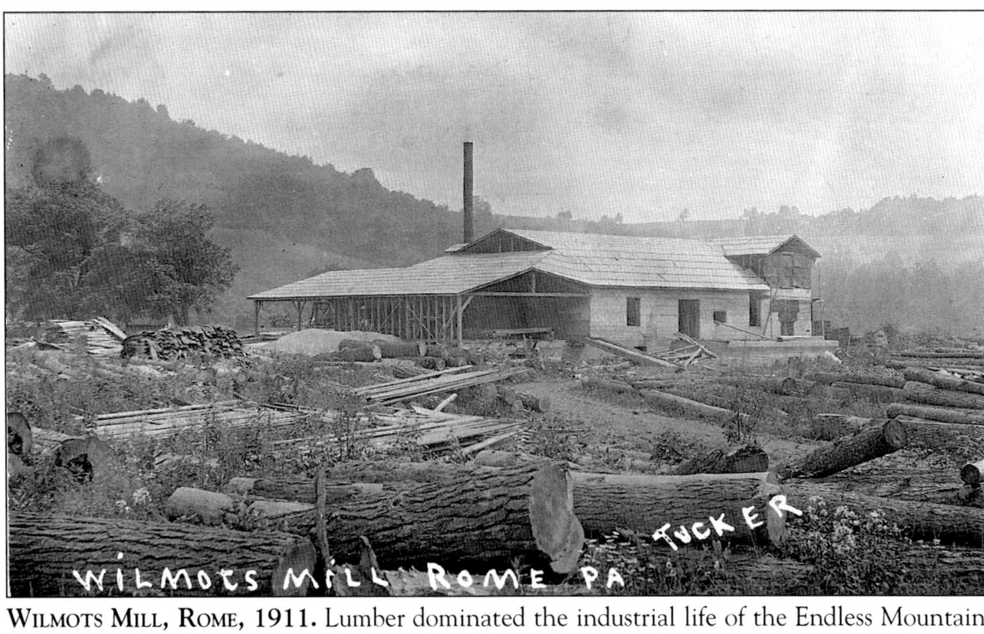

Wilmots Mill, Rome, 1911. Lumber dominated the industrial life of the Endless Mountains from the mid-19th century until the early 20th, with the peak activity occurring in the early 1900s. (Postcard courtesy of the Tioga Point Museum.)

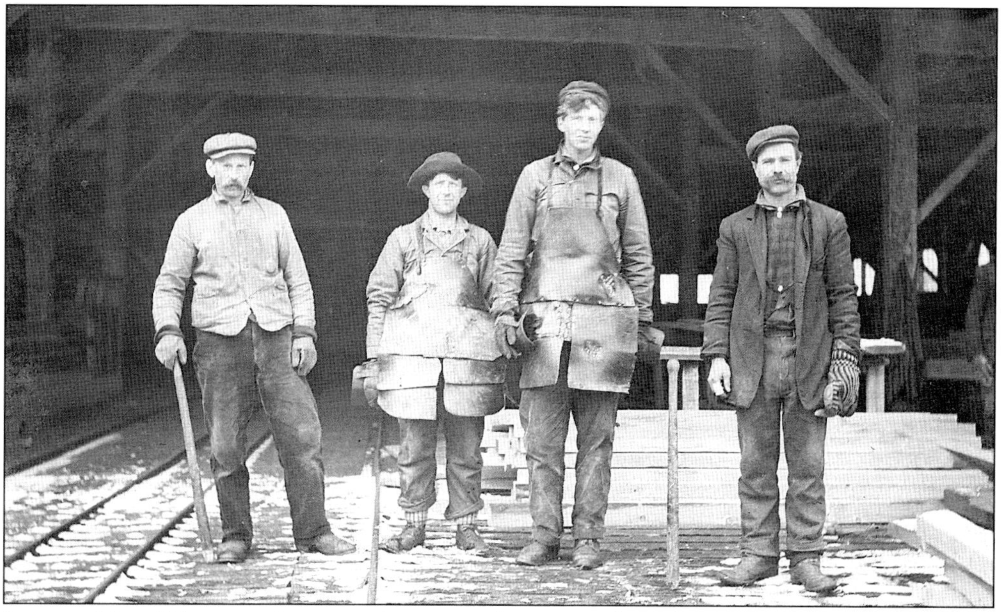

Lumber Mill Workers, Laquin. An extraordinary number of postcards exist that show the thriving lumber town of Laquin (1902–1941). The town had industries that used every part of the tree except for sawdust. There were, in addition to the sawmill, a wood chemical pant, barrel stave plant, and kindling wood factory. Wagon wheel hubs were made and wood chips were sold for use in beer brewing. (Postcard courtesy of Norm Brauer.)

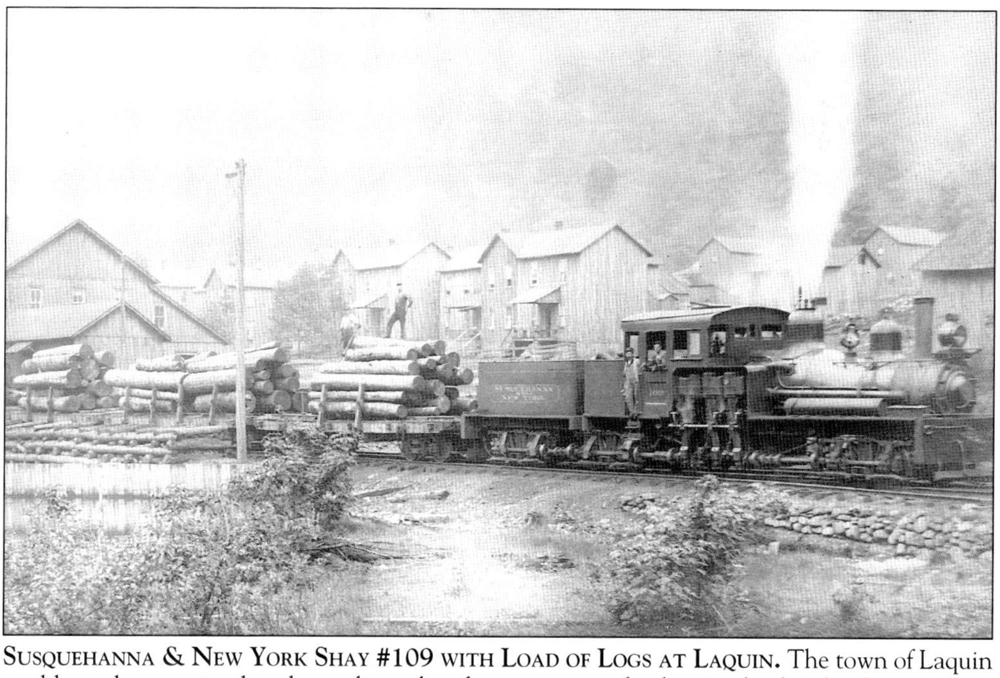

Susquehanna & New York Shay #109 with Load of Logs at Laquin. The town of Laquin could not have existed without the railroad to transport the logs and other lumber products made there. Nestled in the mountains, the town relied on twice-daily train runs as a connection to the outside world. (Postcard courtesy of Norm Brauer.)

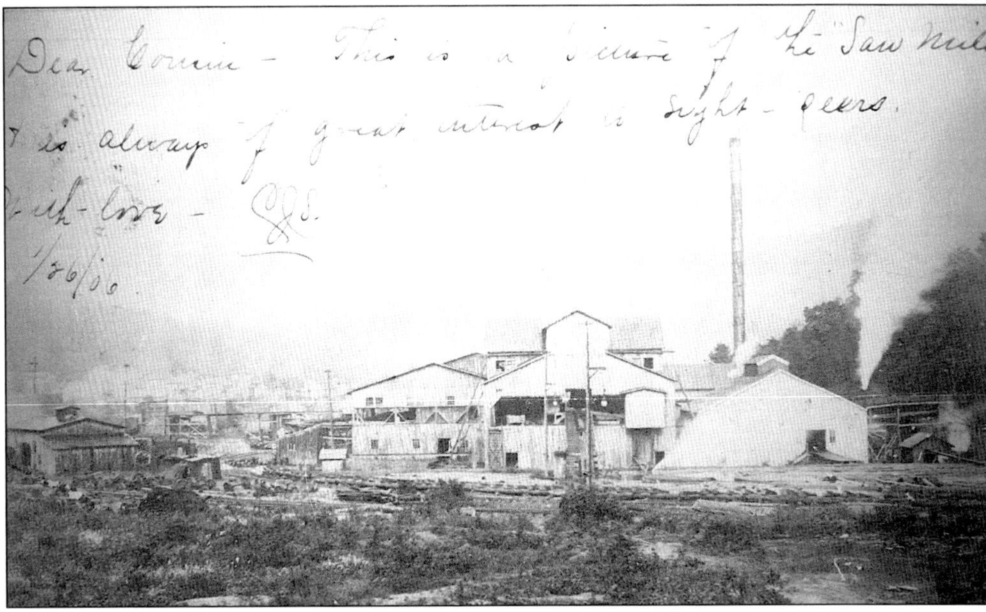

LAQUIN SAWMILL, 1906. The inscription on this card says that Laquin "is always of interest to sight-seers." Perhaps this was because of the enormous size of the operation. The sawmill could cut 135,000 board feet of lumber per 11-hour day, and usually operated at capacity. (Postcard courtesy of the Bradford County Historical Society.)

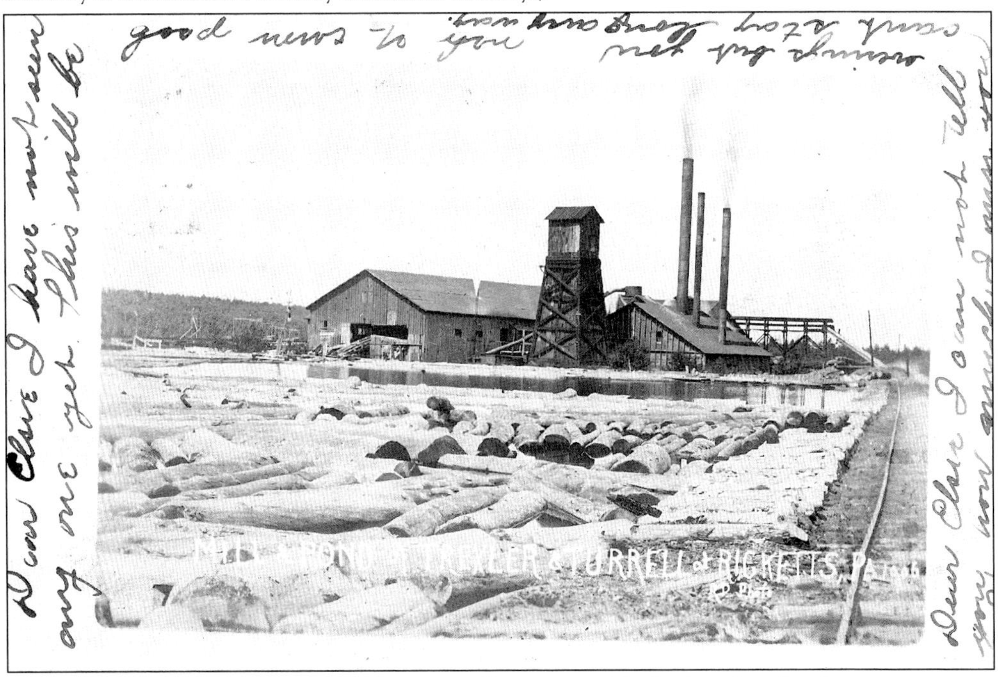

MILL POND OF TREXLER AND TURRELL AT RICKETTS, 1906. Another lumber company in Sullivan County was Trexler and Turrell. Actually, the village straddles the county line with Wyoming. The company constructed this mill in 1891 to process timber that it cut on the land of Colonel Robert Bruce Ricketts, and named the site of the mill after him. (Postcard courtesy of Norm Brauer.)

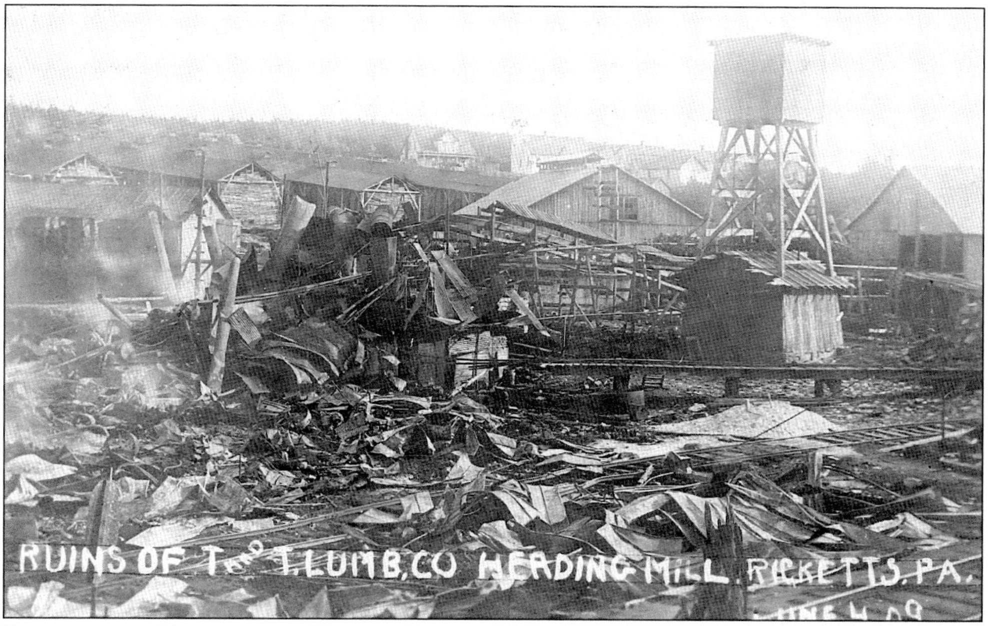

Ruins of the Trexler and Turrell Lumber Company Heading Mill, Ricketts, June 4, 1909. The woman who mailed this card (Lena) describes the cause of the mess here: "This card will show a little of the work of the fire. Eight large sheds, like those on the card, full of 'heading' was destroyed." "Heading" is what barrel tops are called. The mill is closed and has been gone since 1913. (Postcard courtesy of the Tioga Point Museum.)

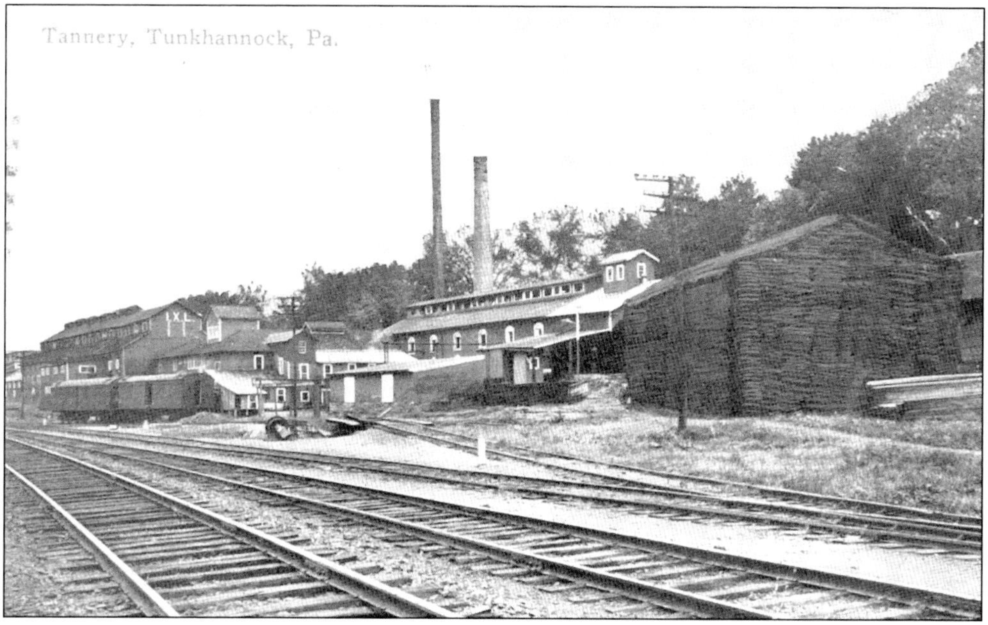

Tannery, Tunkhannock. Leather tanning required tree bark, specifically hemlock, and was often a primary reason for a logging operation to be set up. Tanneries were constructed throughout the region. This one in Tunkhannock is located in the typical spot near the railroad tracks to receive delivery of raw materials and ship out the finished product. (Postcard courtesy of the Tioga Point Museum.)

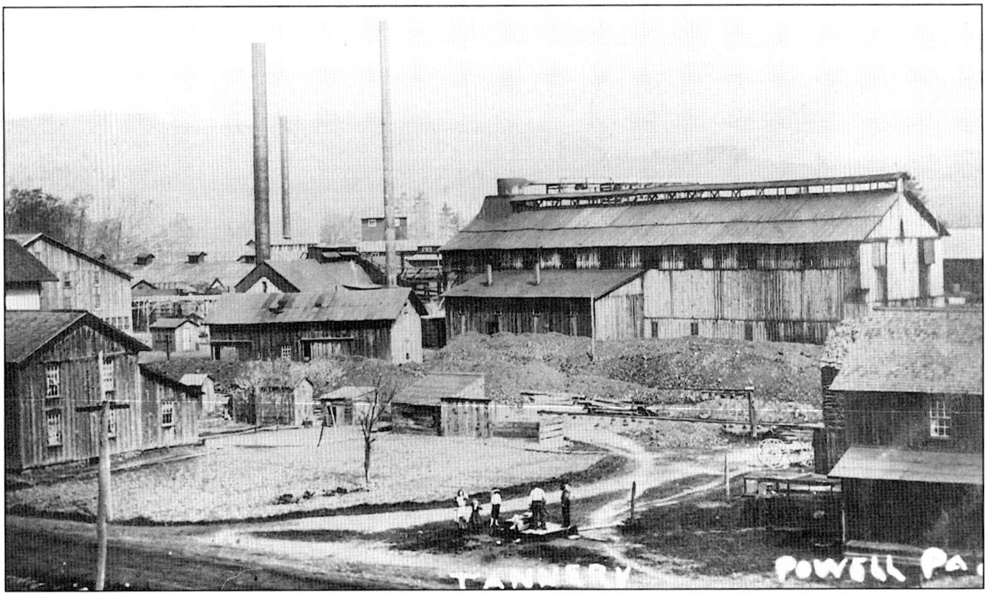

TANNERY, POWELL. This tannery operated from 1867 through 1929 and processed an enormous number of skins. In the beginning it employed about 80 men and turned out approximately 60,000 "sides" a year. A side is one half of the skin of the animal. In 1885 Thomas Proctor purchased the business and expanded output to more than double the previous amount. (Postcard courtesy of the Bradford County Historical Society.)

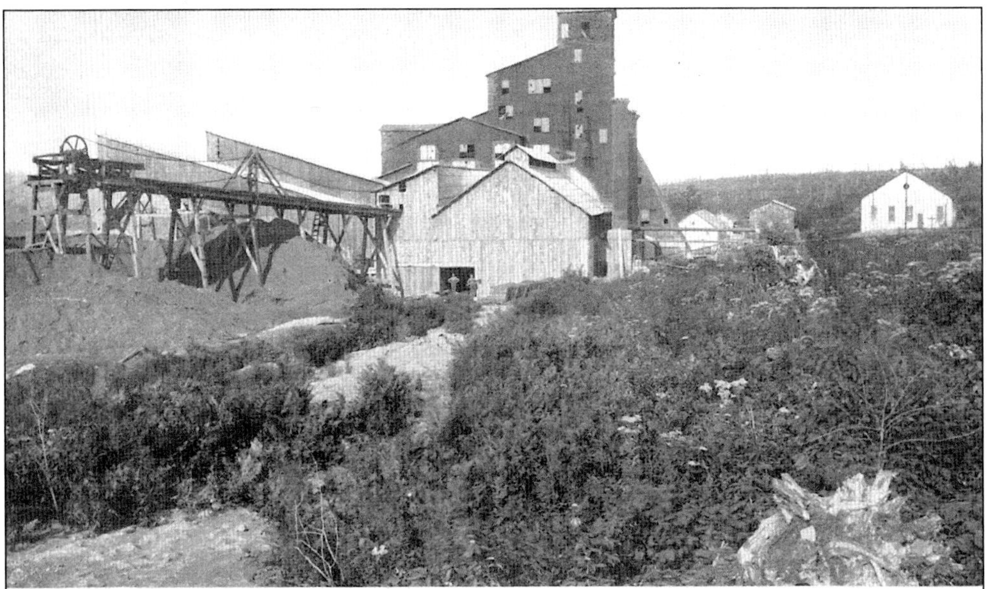

CONNELL COLLIERY, BERNICE, 1912. Coal was not as prevalent in the Endless Mountains as it was in the nearby anthracite regions in Luzerne and Lackawanna Counties, but the few deposits that existed were exploited. The Connell Colliery processed the semi-anthracite coal found in the Sullivan County deposits. The coal mined here ". . . ignites easily, burns with a very pale blue flame, and has the reputation of holding fire under conditions which would cause most other anthracite to 'go out.' " (Postcard courtesy of Norm Brauer.)

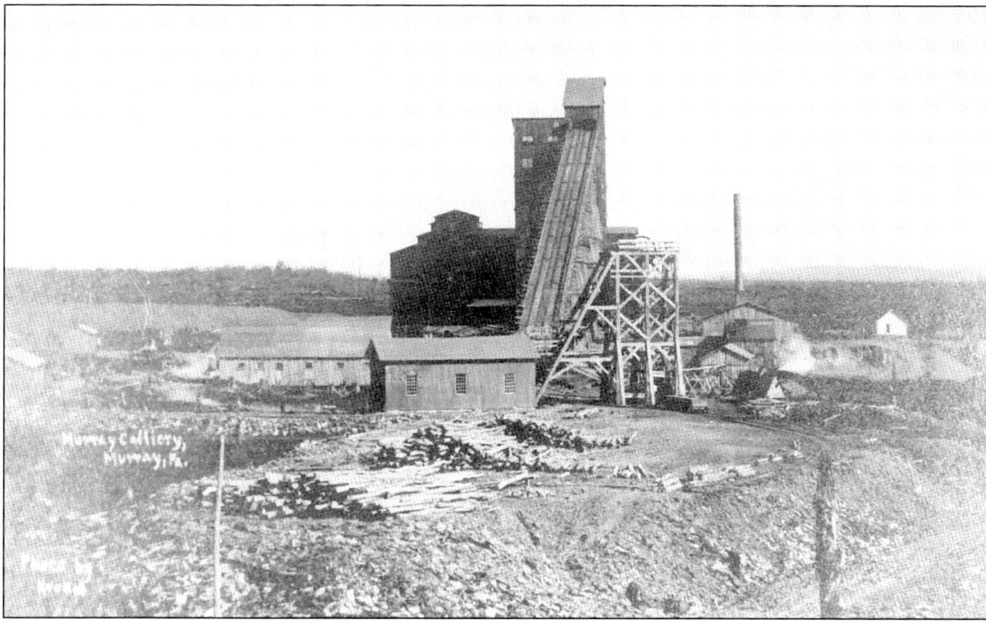

MURRAY COLLIERY, MURRAY. Just one town over from Bernice, this colliery also processed semi-anthracite coal. Bradford County, only a little to the north, produced low volatile bituminous coal at Barclay, now a ghost town. (Postcard courtesy of the Bradford County Historical Society.)

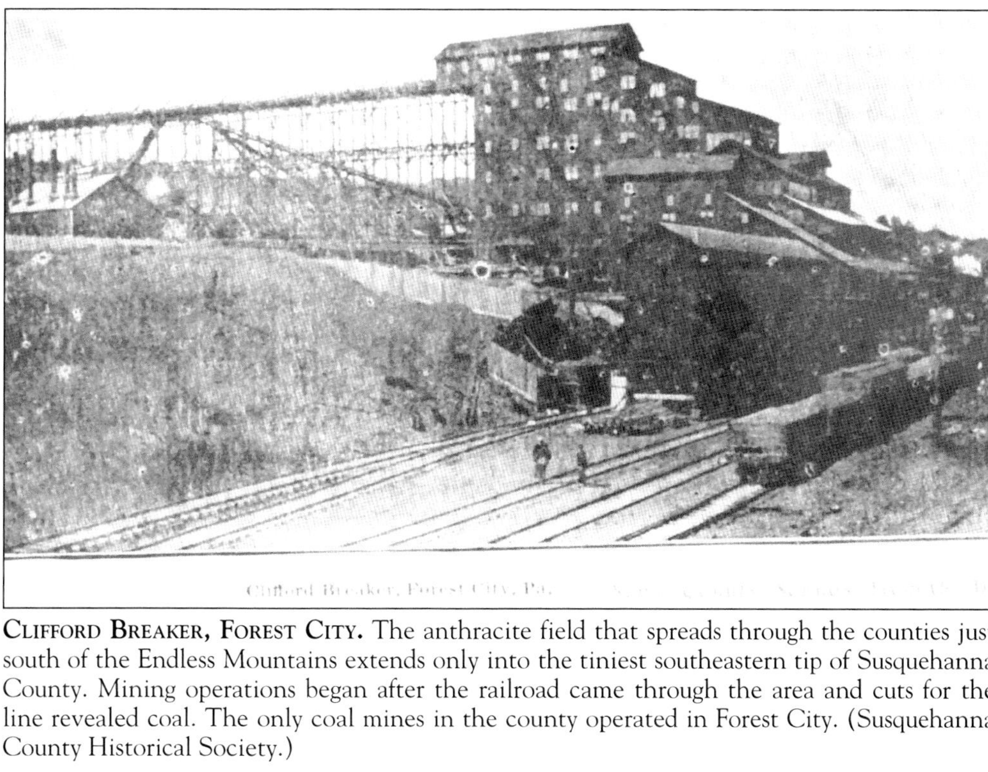

CLIFFORD BREAKER, FOREST CITY. The anthracite field that spreads through the counties just south of the Endless Mountains extends only into the tiniest southeastern tip of Susquehanna County. Mining operations began after the railroad came through the area and cuts for the line revealed coal. The only coal mines in the county operated in Forest City. (Susquehanna County Historical Society.)

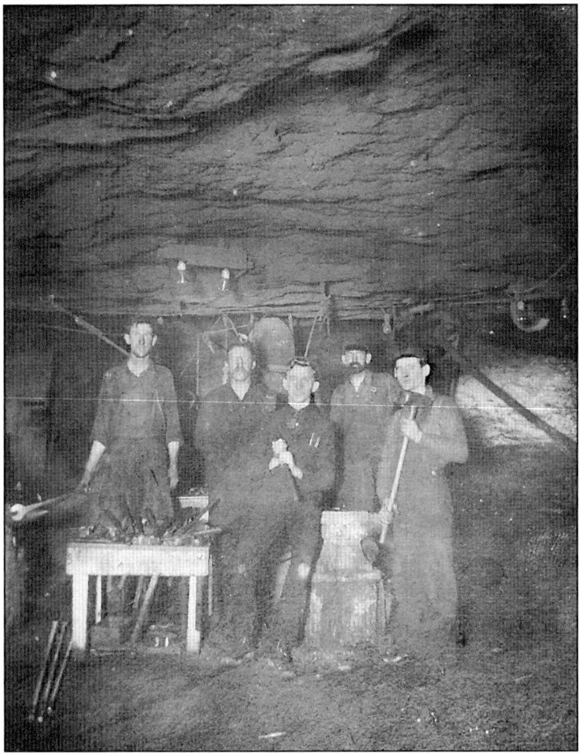

Forest City Mine, Blacksmith Shop. Polish and Slavic and Welsh immigrants worked the mines. There were three mines and three breakers. (Postcard courtesy of the Susquehanna County Historical Society.)

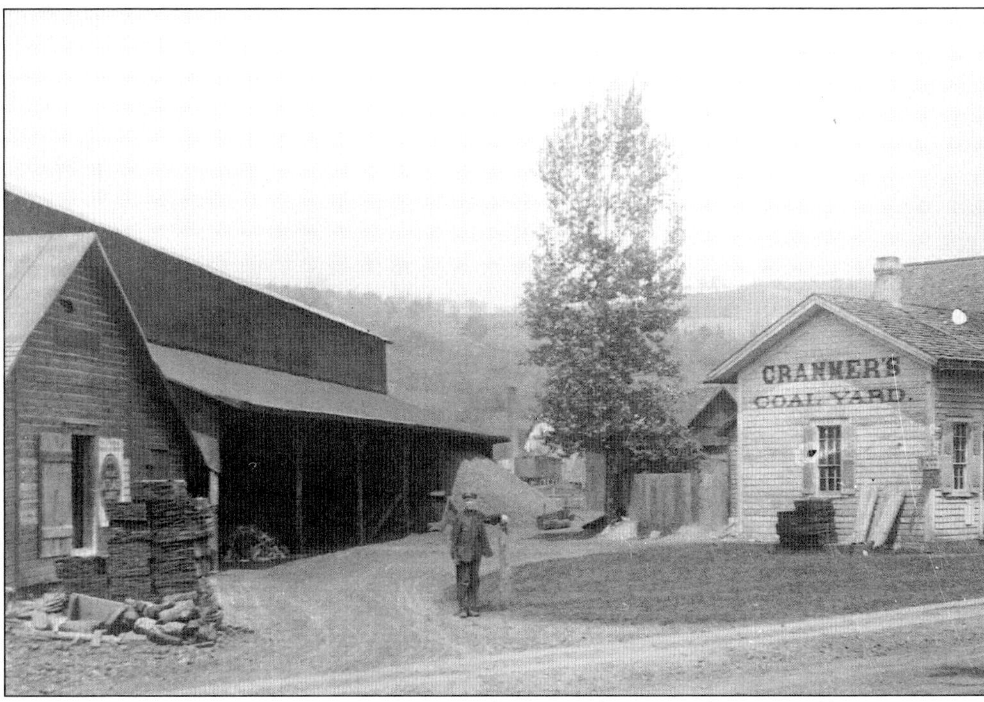

Canmer's Coal Yard, Monroeton. During the time when most houses and businesses were heated with coal, coal yards were common throughout the area. The Cranmer yard was located near the railroad tracks. (Postcard courtesy of the Bradford County Historical Society.)

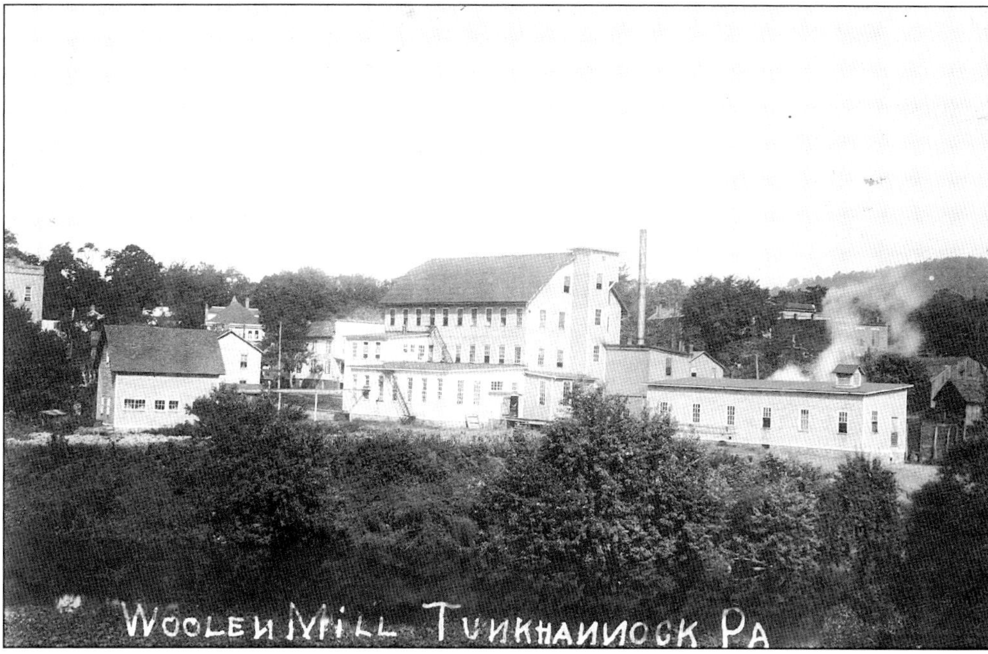

WOOLEN MILL, TUNKHANNOCK, 1908. The textile manufacturing industries were important to the area economy, although they never surpassed agriculture. (Postcard courtesy of Norm Brauer.)

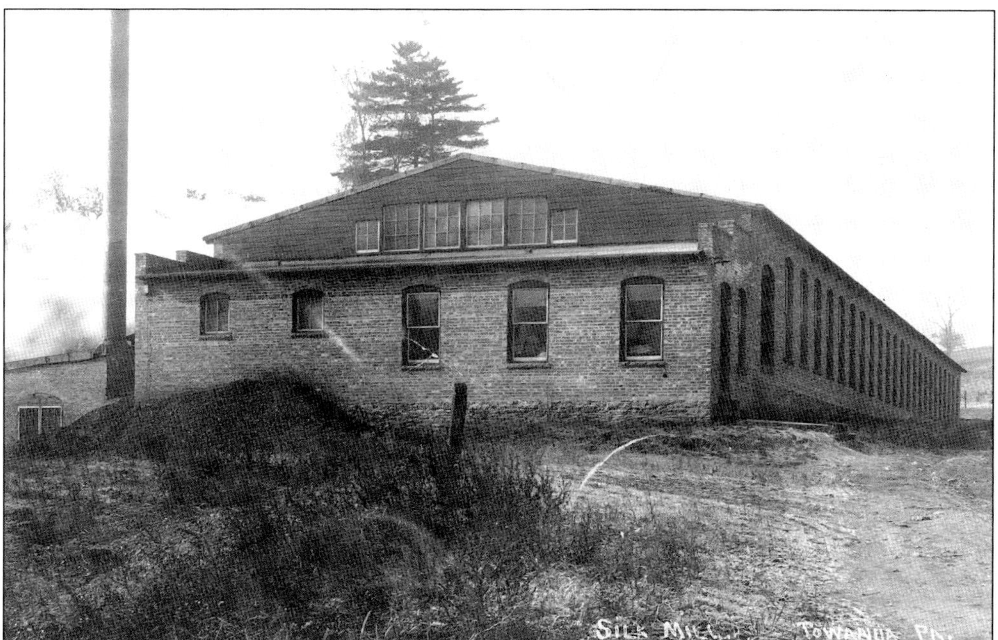

SILK MILL, TOWANDA. This is one of three silk mills that operated in Towanda at various times in the early to middle 20th century. There were many silk mills in the Endless Mountains. (Postcard courtesy of the Bradford County Historical Society.)

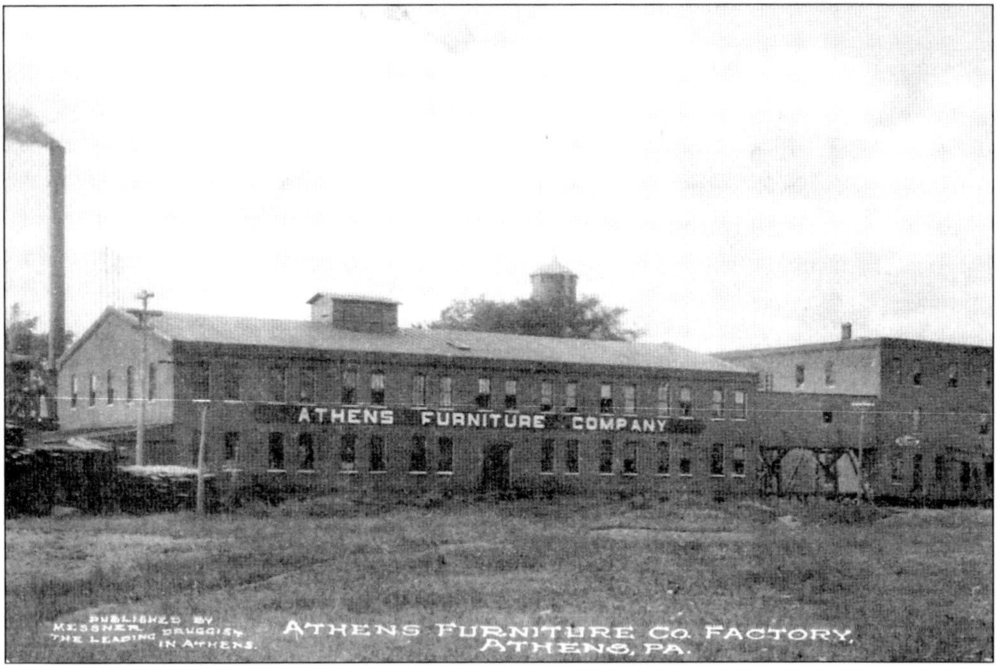

ATHENS FURNITURE FACTORY, 1910. The factory was established in 1870. The company shipped its furniture all over the country and could only thrive because of the presence of the railroad. (Postcard courtesy of the Tioga Point Museum.)

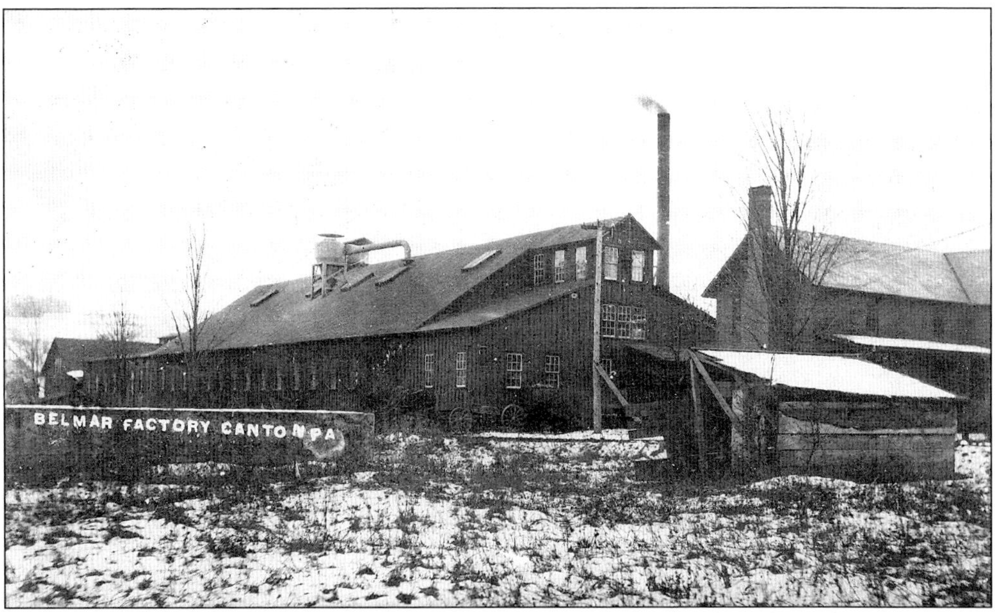

BELMAR FACTORY, CANTON. The 1900 Bradford County Directory lists the Belmar Company, with Louis M. Marble as its president, as a manufacturer of "specialties." The 1907 directory is more specific—the company manufactured clothes hangers. (Postcard courtesy of the Tioga Point Museum.)

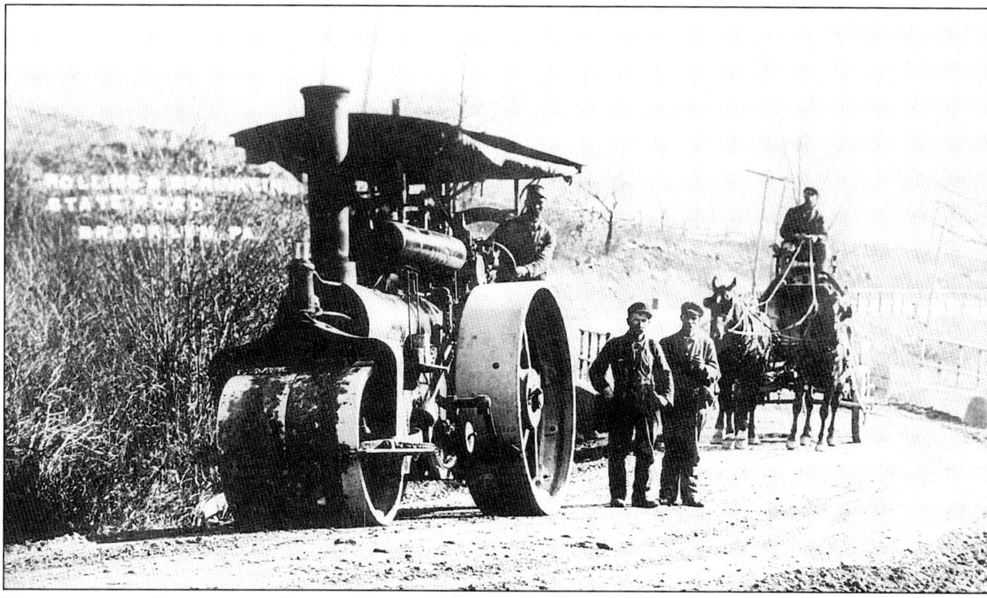

Rolling and Sprinkling State Road, Brooklyn. Few roads at the turn of the century were paved (or "macadamized"). Instead they were flattened with steam rollers, such as this one, and sprinkled with oil to keep the dust down. (Postcard courtesy of the Susquehanna County Historical Society.)

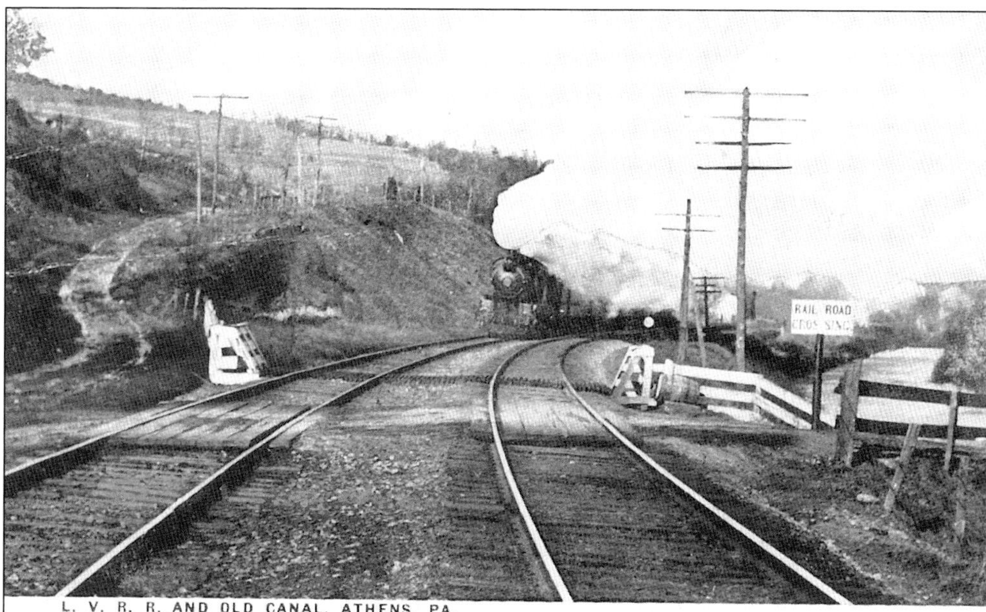

Lehigh Valley Railroad and Old Canal, Athens. From the days when Native Americans were the only inhabitants of the area, the river was an important thoroughfare. In 1854 the North Branch Canal (on the right in the card) was completed. It followed the Susquehanna, then the Chemung from Nanticoke to Athens, and allowed easier transport of industrial materials. The railroad superseded the canal almost immediately after it was completed, using the canal right-of-way to lay many of its tracks. (Postcard courtesy of the Tioga Point Museum.)

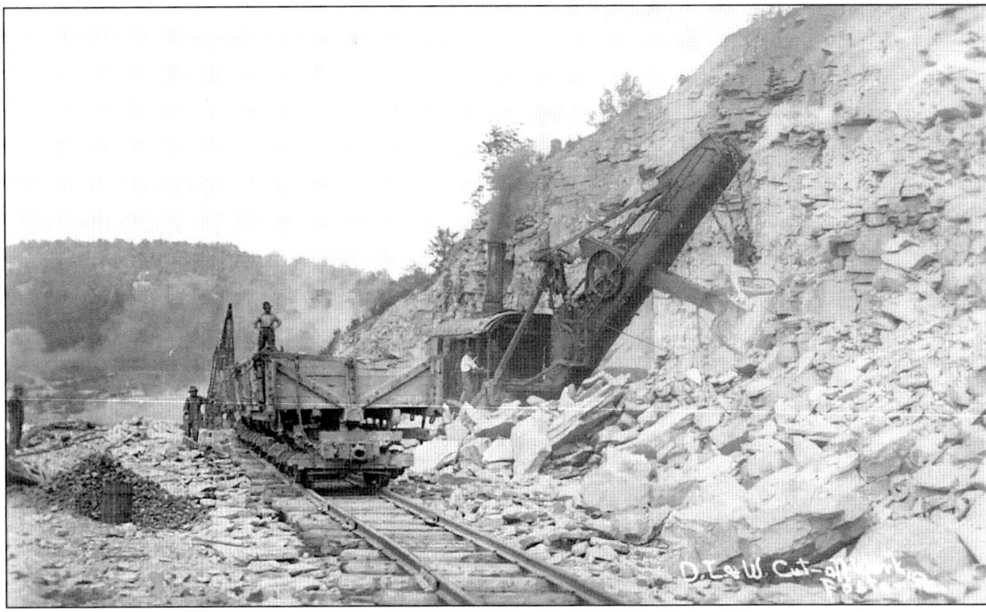

DELAWARE LACKAWANNA & WESTERN CUT-OFF WORK, FOSTER. The postcards on pp. 42 through 47 all show various scenes of the construction of the DL&W line from Clarks Summit to Hallstead. The line replaced an earlier route and was built to allow for increased capacity and reduced costs. (Postcard courtesy of Norm Brauer.)

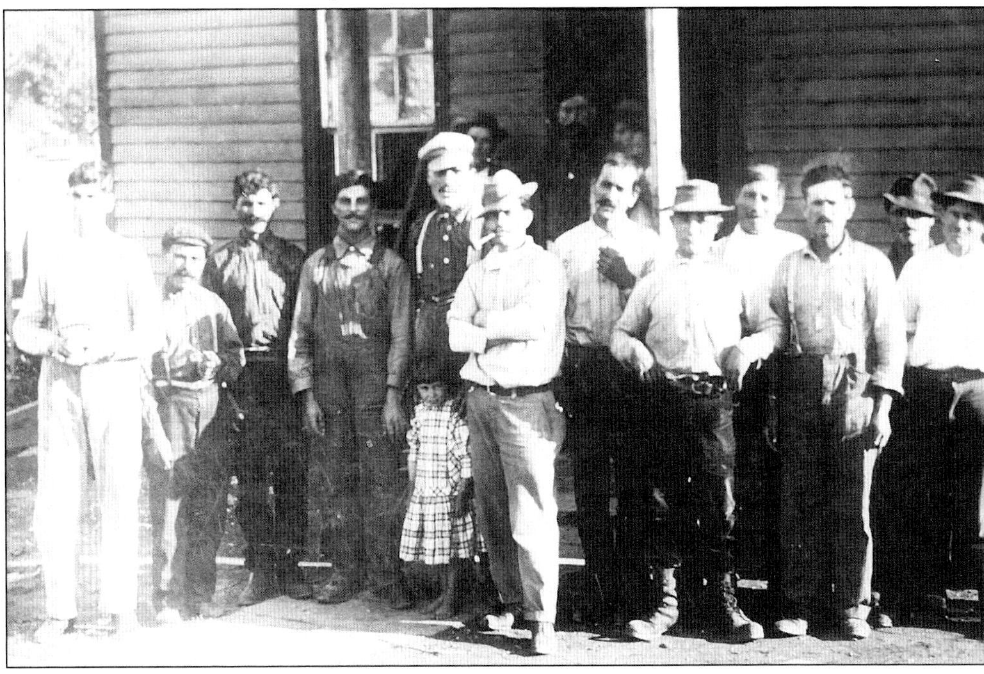

RAILROAD WORKERS FROM ITALY, NEW MILFORD. The railroad industry provided employment for thousands of Italian and Irish immigrants. Besides the initial construction work, there were jobs building the equipment and running it. In addition the tracks and equipment required constant maintenance. (Postcard courtesy of the Susquehanna County Historical Society.)

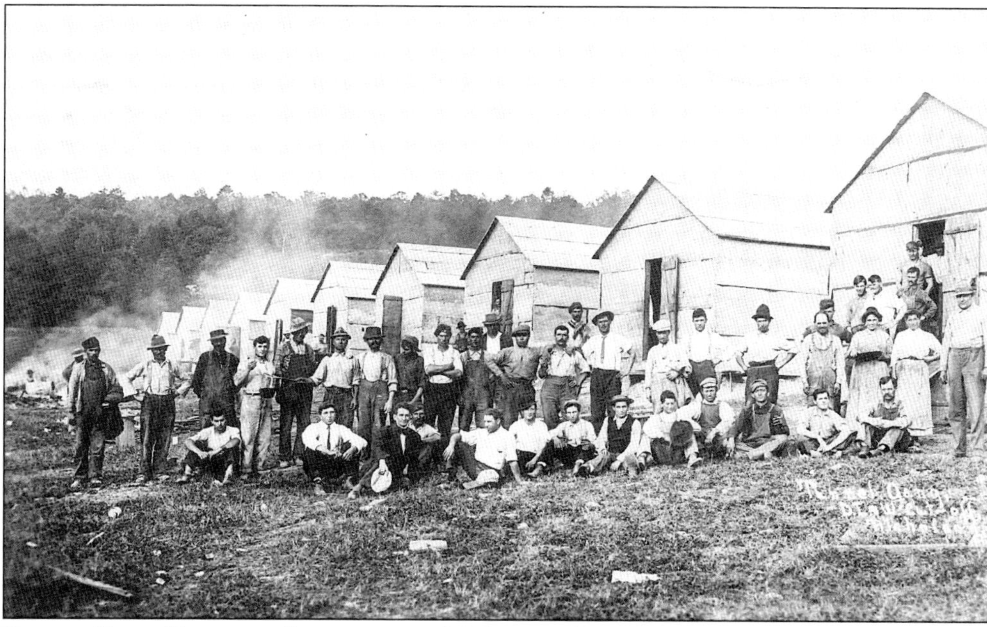

TUNNEL GANG, DELAWARE LACKAWANNA & WESTERN CUT-OFF, NICHOLSON. Living conditions for the workers were often primitive, although in this case the accommodations were probably temporary, only existing until the job was finished. (Postcard courtesy of Norm Brauer.)

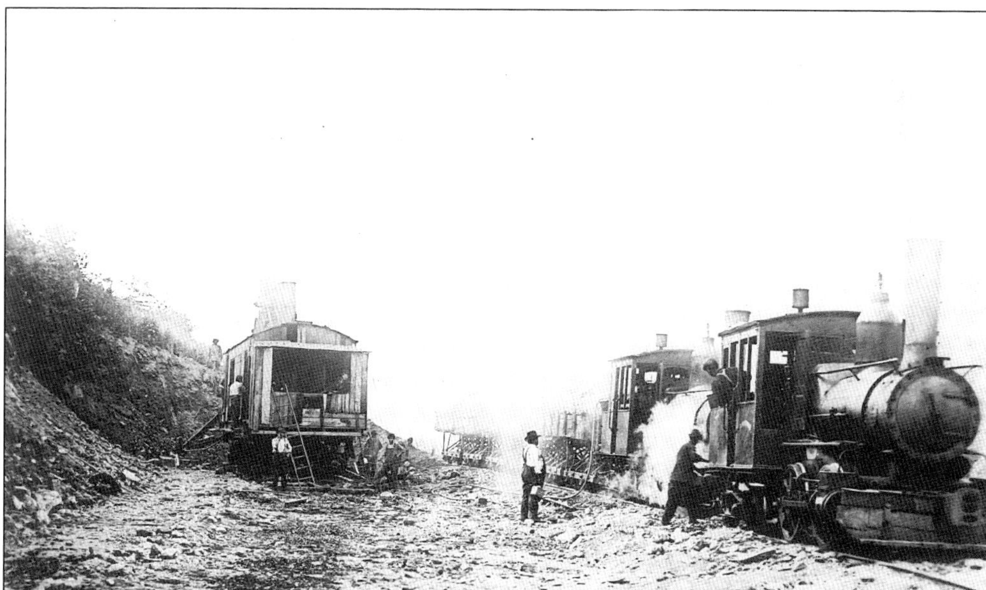

CREAMERY CUT, ALFORD. Railroad travel does not deal well with sudden ups and downs, hence the need for viaducts and cuts. The creamery referred to may be the F.E. Moore Dairy Farm. About 400 quarts of milk bottled on the farm left Alford station for Brooklyn, New York, every day in 1909. (Postcard courtesy of Norm Brauer.)

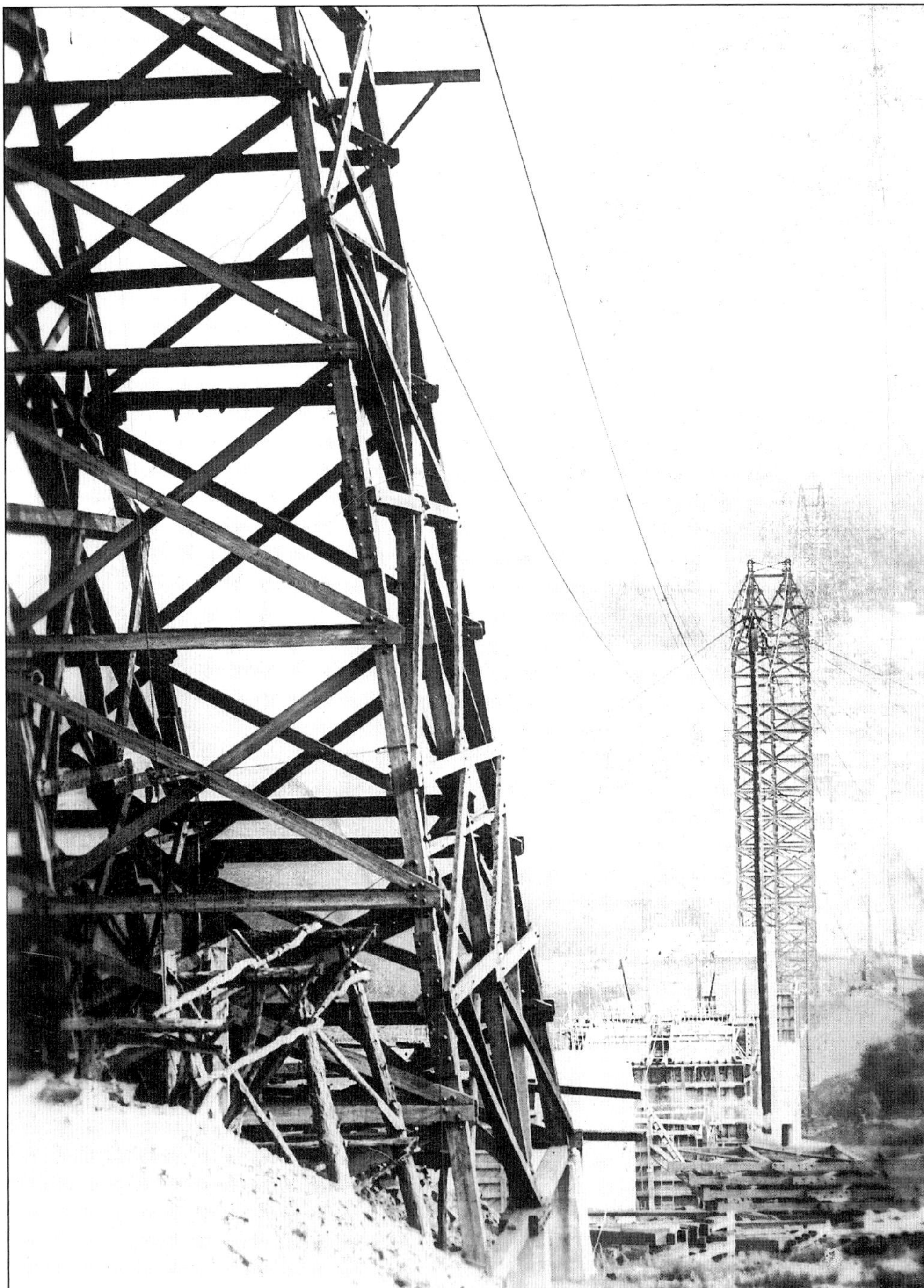

CONSTRUCTION OF THE NICHOLSON BRIDGE, 1915. Also known as the Tunkhannock Viaduct, this massive reinforced concrete structure was the largest of the engineering works on the Clarks Summit-Hallstead line. Construction on the line began in 1912 and took three years to complete. Footers for this bridge were sunk 60 feet below ground. (Postcard courtesy of the Bradford County Historical Society.)

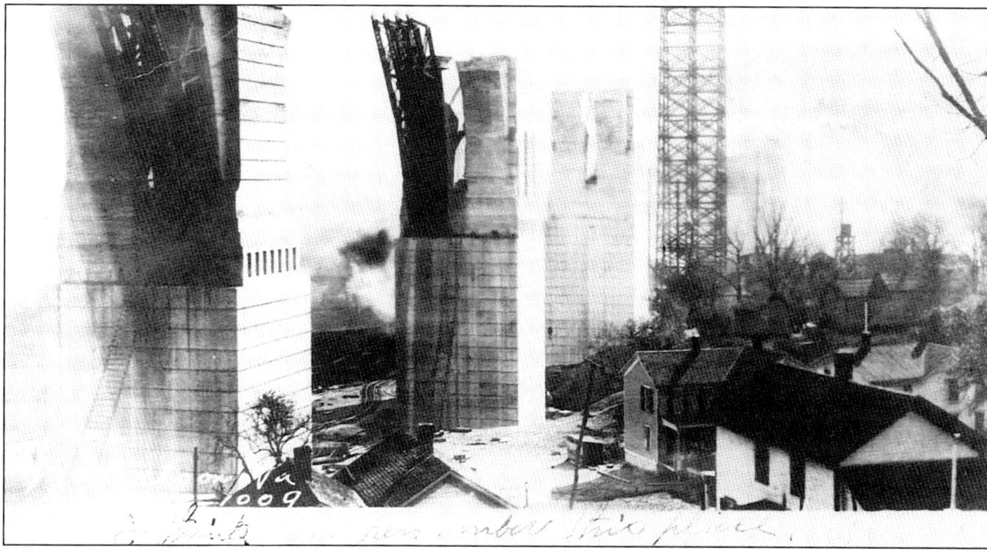

NICHOLSON BRIDGE, 1915. The bridge construction dwarfs the houses built in its shadow. It is easy to see why postcards of its construction were popular. This one reads "I think you remember this place." (Postcard courtesy of the Susquehanna County Historical Society.)

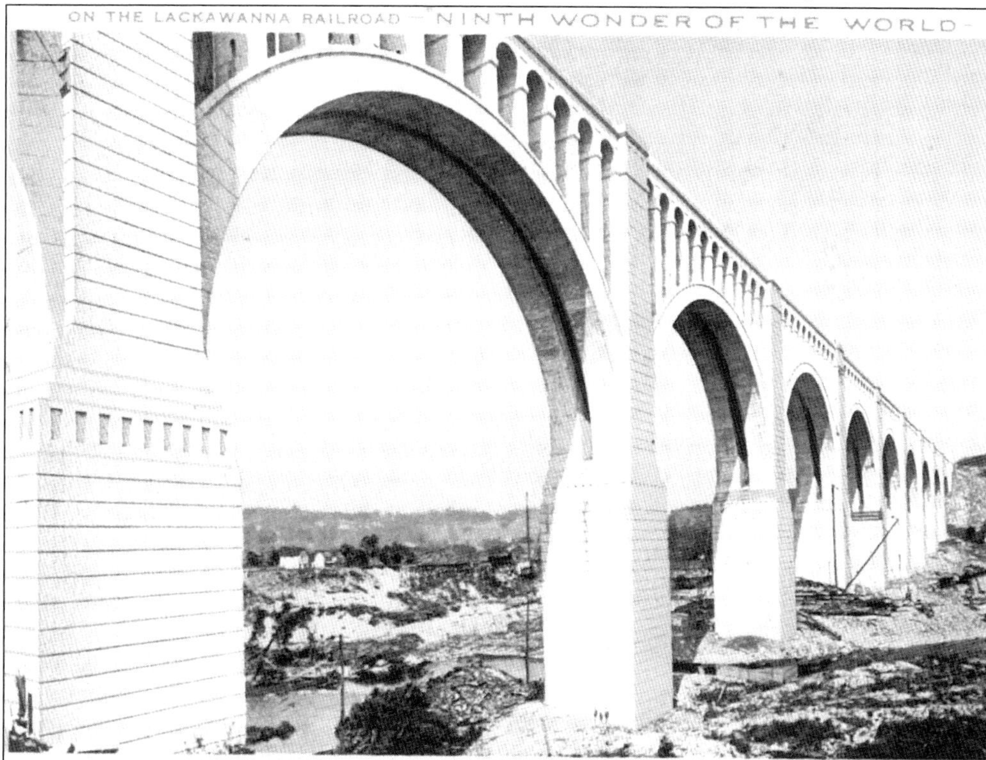

NICHOLSON BRIDGE. The finished structure is .5 miles long and stands 240 feet above the creek. Each span is 180 feet long. Construction required a huge amount of concrete, approximately 350,000 tons. The tiny people at the base of the second support give an idea of the scale. (Postcard courtesy of the Bradford County Historical Society.)

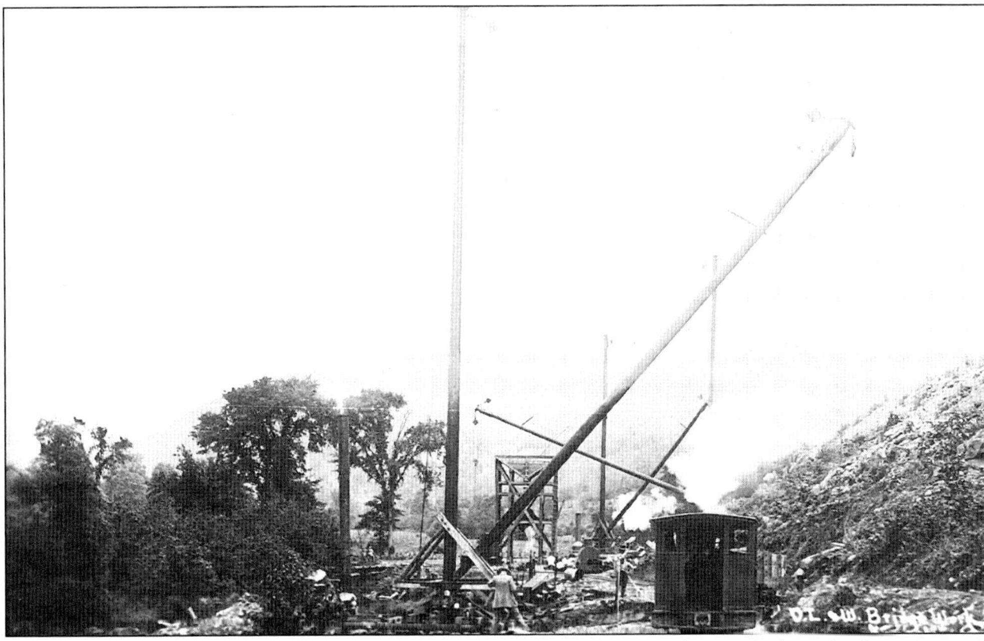

Kingsley Bridge. The Kingsley Bridge was on the same line as the Nicholson bridge. In 1910, before the new line was built, an average of 800 cars ran over the route in each direction. This included both freight and passenger trains. (Postcard courtesy of the Susquehanna County Historical Society.)

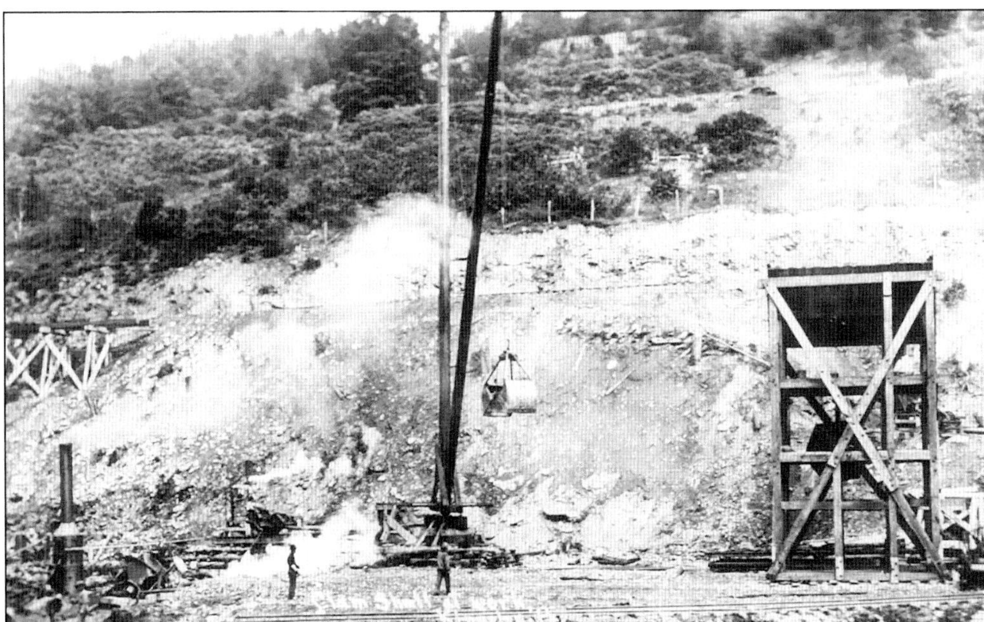

Clam Shell at Work, Kingsley. By making the grade more even, there would be less need for extra engines to push heavy trains up hill, and by straightening the tracks the trains could run faster. (Postcard courtesy of the Susquehanna County Historical Society.)

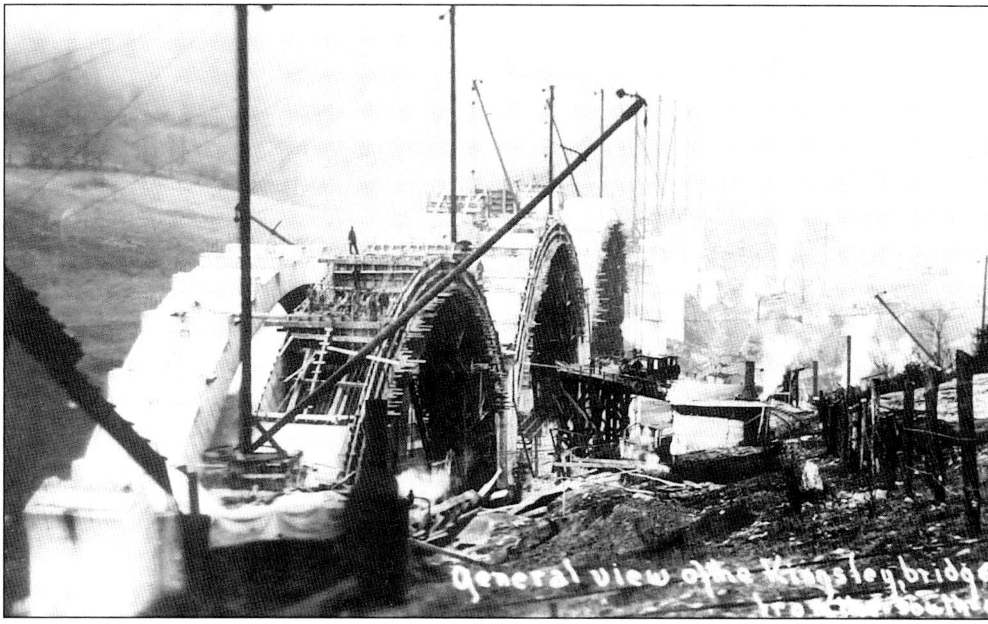

GENERAL VIEW OF THE KINGSLEY BRIDGE FROM THE SOUTHEAST. This bridge is not as large as the Nicholson, but it is still a major engineering feat. (Postcard courtesy of the Susquehanna County Historical Society.)

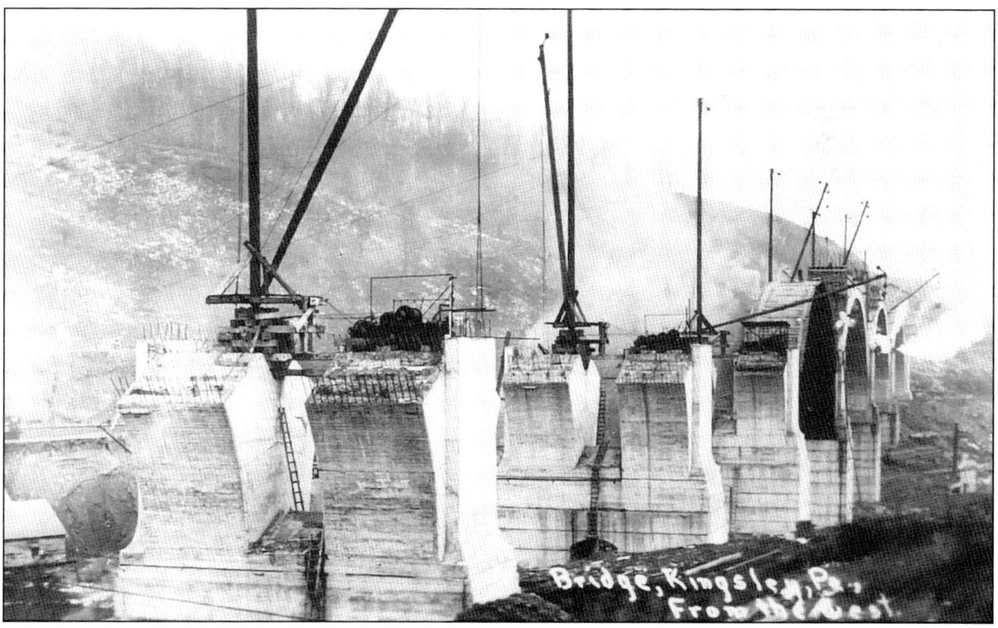

KINGSLEY BRIDGE CONSTRUCTION FROM THE WEST. The total cost of the Clarks Summit-Hallstead line came to $14,275,428, and the DL&W paid for it by selling stock in the railroad. The old line was closed, and the company presented most of the right-of-way to the Commonwealth of Pennsylvania for an improved Route 11. (Postcard courtesy of the Susquehanna County Historical Society.)

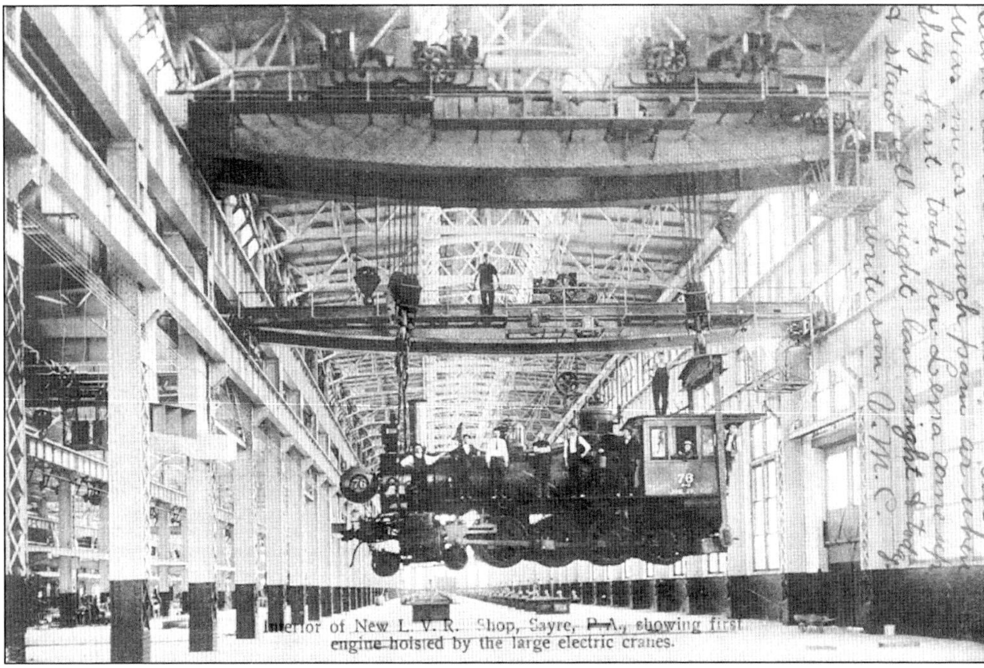

LEHIGH VALLEY RAILROAD SHOP SHOWING THE FIRST ENGINE HOISTED BY THE LARGE ELECTRIC CRANES, SAYRE. This postcard was very popular for obvious reasons. Although it has been published many times, it is the best reminder that Sayre was an extremely important industrial area early in this century. (Postcard courtesy of the Tioga Point Museum.)

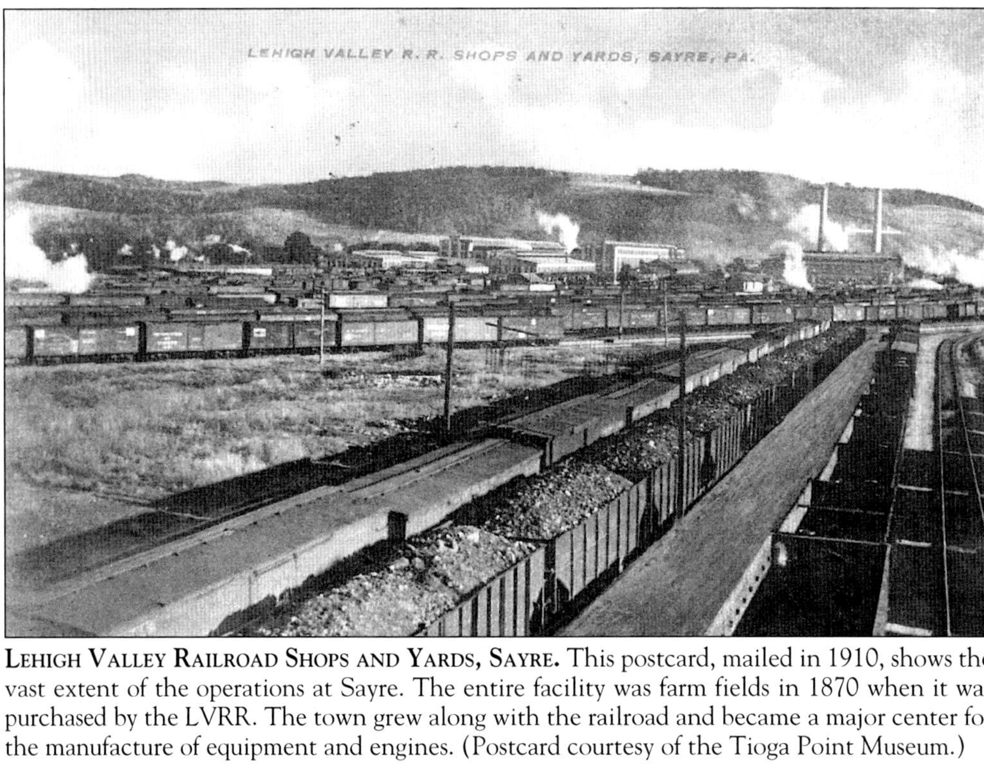

LEHIGH VALLEY RAILROAD SHOPS AND YARDS, SAYRE. This postcard, mailed in 1910, shows the vast extent of the operations at Sayre. The entire facility was farm fields in 1870 when it was purchased by the LVRR. The town grew along with the railroad and became a major center for the manufacture of equipment and engines. (Postcard courtesy of the Tioga Point Museum.)

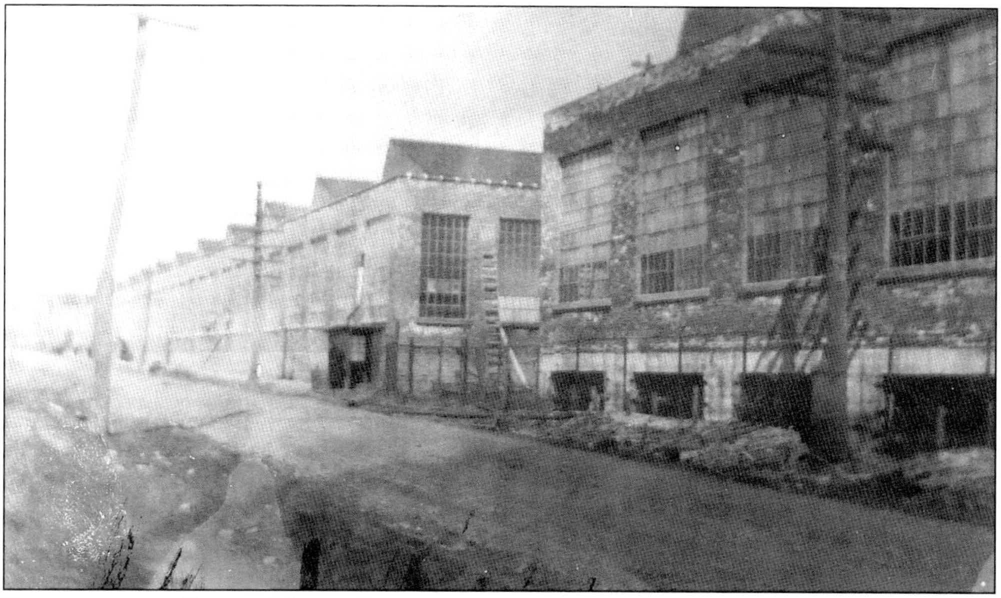

Exterior of the Lehigh Valley Railroad Shops, Sayre. The new main shops for the Lehigh Valley Railroad were constructed in 1904. Sayre's central location on the line between Buffalo and New York City was the primary reason for its selection. Workmen in these shops built and repaired steam locomotives and freight cars. (Postcard courtesy of the Bradford County Historical Society.)

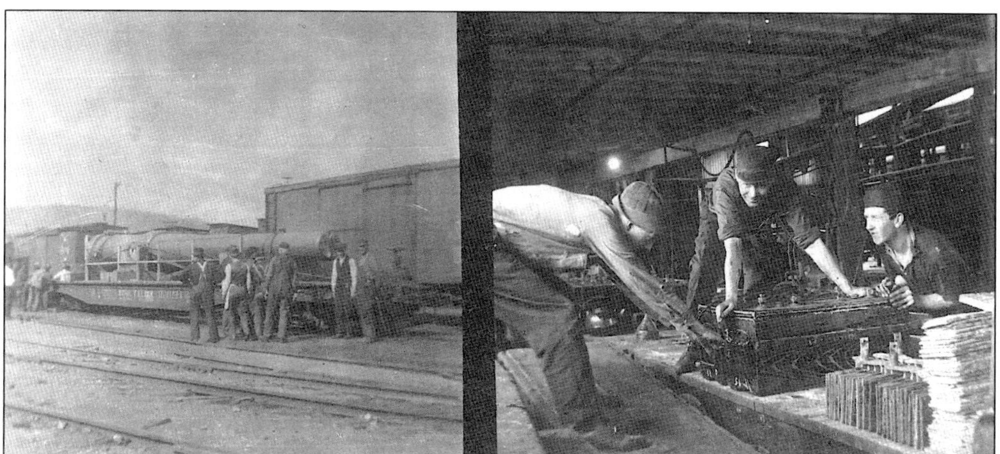

Men Working at the Sayre Shops. These two contact prints reproduced onto a postcard show some of the day-to-day work that went on. On the left is a locomotive boiler; on the right is a signal battery. The man in the center of the right-hand picture is George Cooper. (Postcard courtesy of the Tioga Point Museum.)

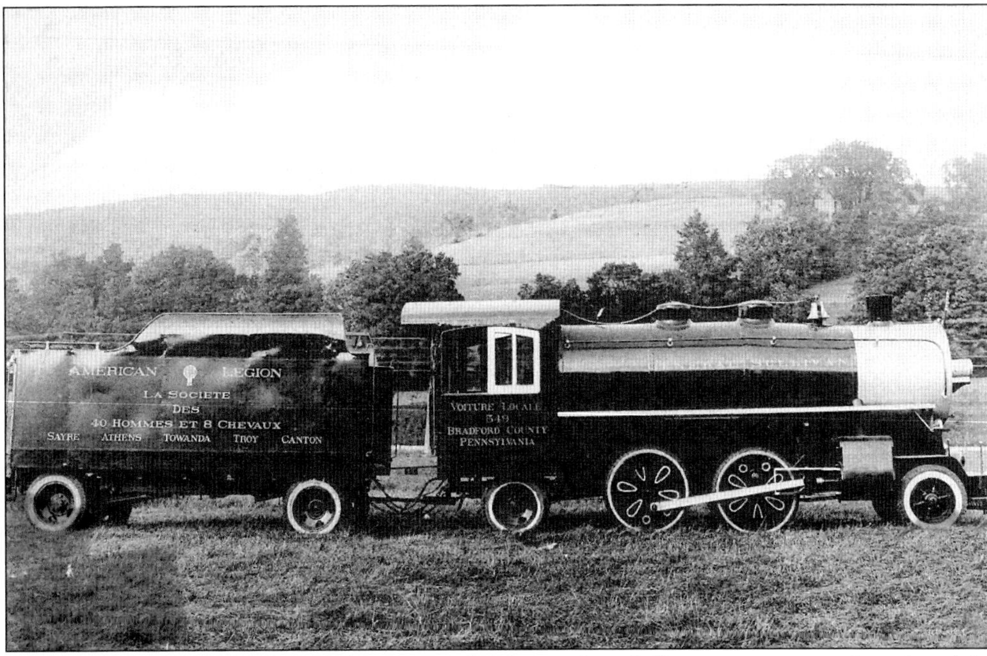

THE *GENERAL SULLIVAN*, 1939. The caption for this card reads "Largest engine and tender of the Forty and Eight in U.S. Weighs ten tons, is 45 feet long. Travels to National American Legion Conventions each year. Built in 1939 at Lehigh Valley Railroad Shops, Sayre, Pa. Valued at $15,000." (Postcard courtesy of the Tioga Point Museum.)

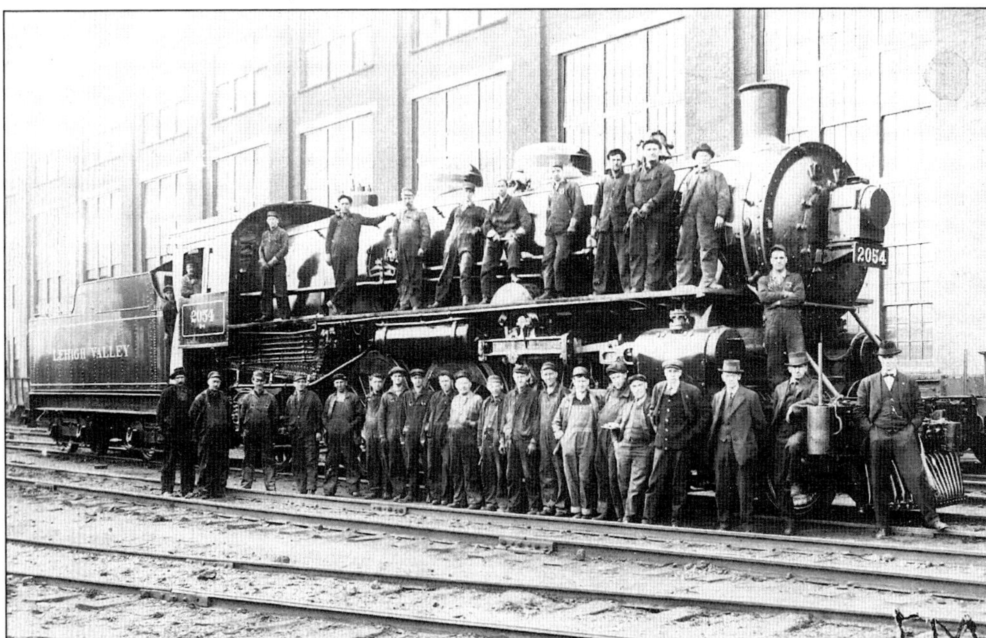

LEHIGH VALLEY ENGINE NUMBER 2054. Often the brand new engines were photographed with workmen and managers in front and on top of them. They were built quickly, but there was always a feeling of accomplishment when one was finished. (Photo courtesy of the Tioga Point Museum.)

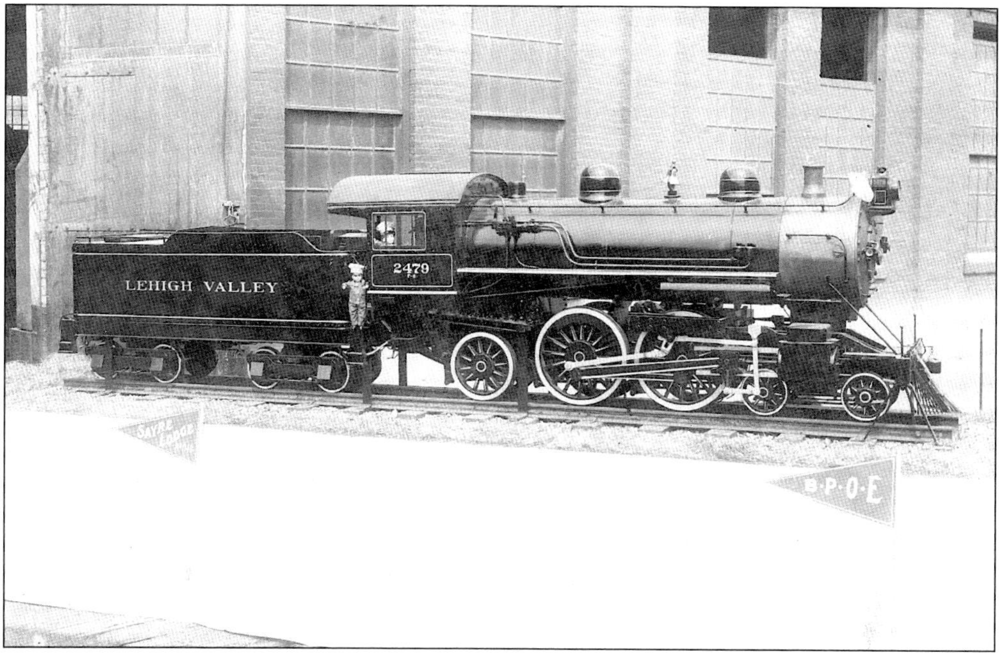

MINIATURE NUMBER 2479. This engine was built in the Sayre shops and used in parades on floats. The engineer and his assistant are dolls. (Postcard courtesy of the Tioga Point Museum.)

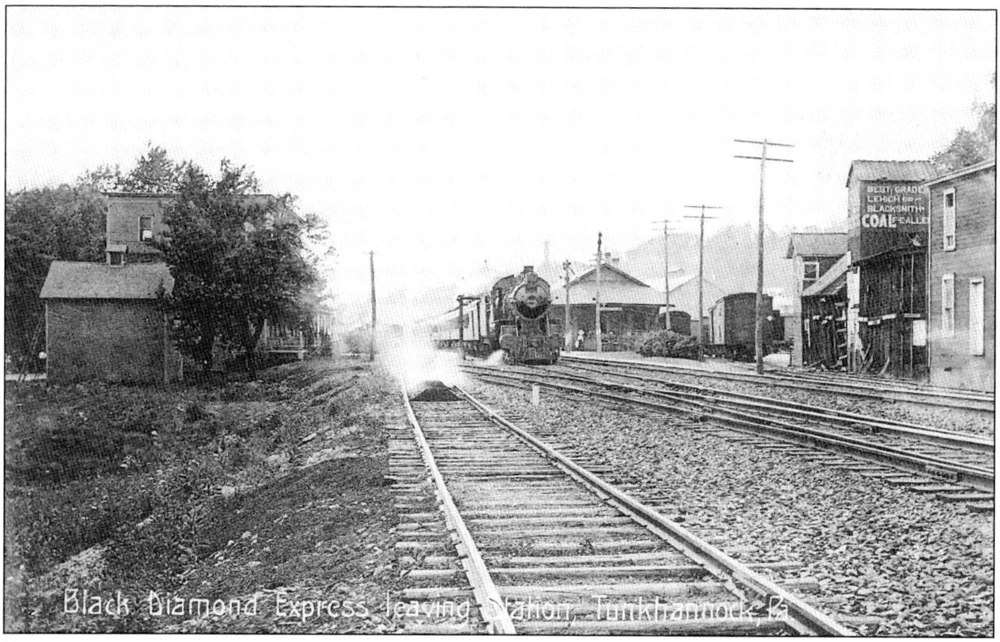

BLACK DIAMOND EXPRESS LEAVING STATION, TUNKHANNOCK. The luxury passenger train, named for the anthracite coal that was responsible for the prosperity of the Lehigh Valley Railroad, ran from 1896 to 1959. Its route took it from Buffalo to Jersey City and back again. The Pullman cars used on the train had elegant furnishings of mahogany and plush upholstery. (Postcard courtesy of Norm Brauer.)

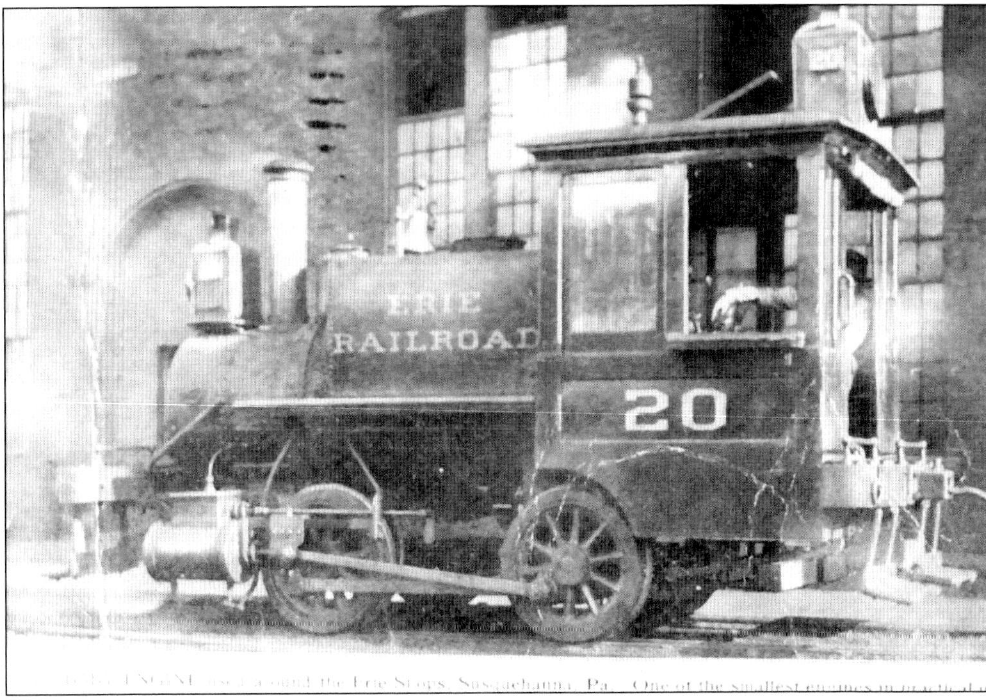

BABY ENGINE USED AROUND THE ERIE SHOPS, SUSQUEHANNA. The Lehigh Valley was not the only railroad company with shops in the Endless Mountains. The New York, Erie & Western Railroad Company constructed its principal motive shops in 1847 in Susquehanna, up at the Great Bend of the river. The company reconstructed the shops in 1865, and they were "formally dedicated by means of interesting and appropriate ceremonies." (Postcard courtesy of the Susquehanna County Historical Society.)

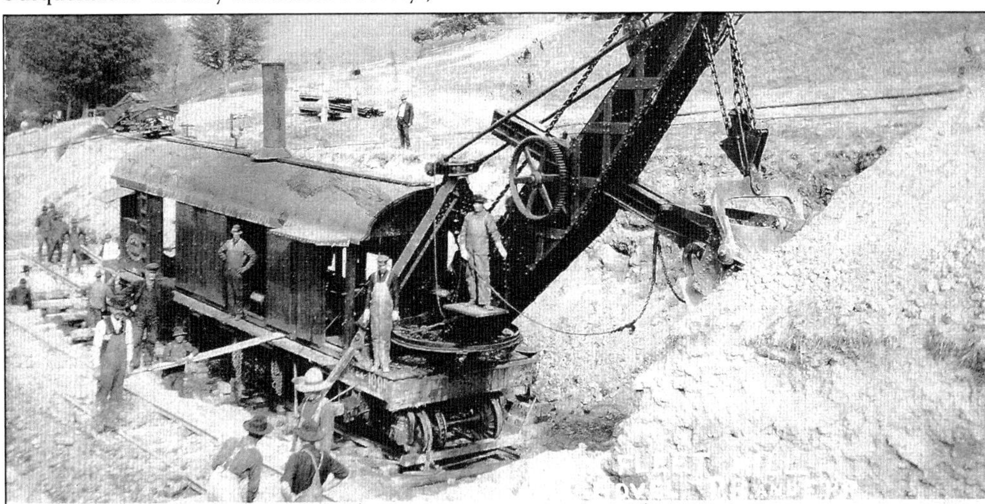

VAN FLEET MILL STEAM SHOVEL, PITTSBURGH, BINGHAMTON & EASTERN RAILROAD, 1906. The PB&E was only partially completed, and never used. In spite of the grand name, the original plan was only for a railroad between Monroeton and Canton. (Postcard courtesy of the Bradford County Historical Society.)

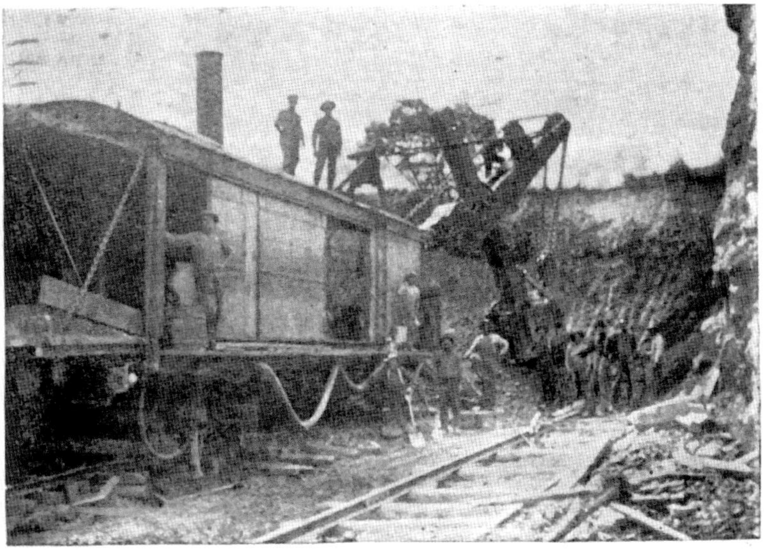

ON THE PITTSBURGH, BINGHAMTON & EASTERN RAILROAD, NEAR POWELL, NOVEMBER 1906. Handwriting on this card identifies this as the "Benedic cut." Italian contractors excavated an 85-foot cut west of Powell at a cost of $500,000, and a 1906 newspaper account reports nearly 1,000 men at work between Canton and Powell, Bradford County. (Postcard courtesy of Norm Brauer.)

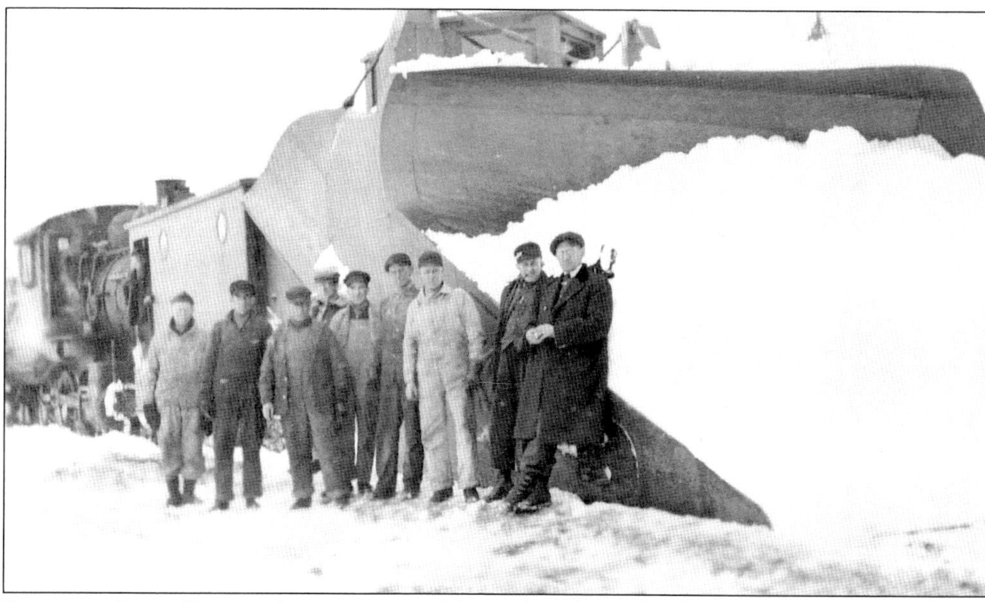

RAILROAD SNOW PLOW. A heavy snow could cripple rail travel. This special plow is mounted on the front of an engine to clear the tracks. The extraordinarily large amount of snow was deemed worthy of a crew photo. (Postcard courtesy of the Susquehanna County Historical Society.)

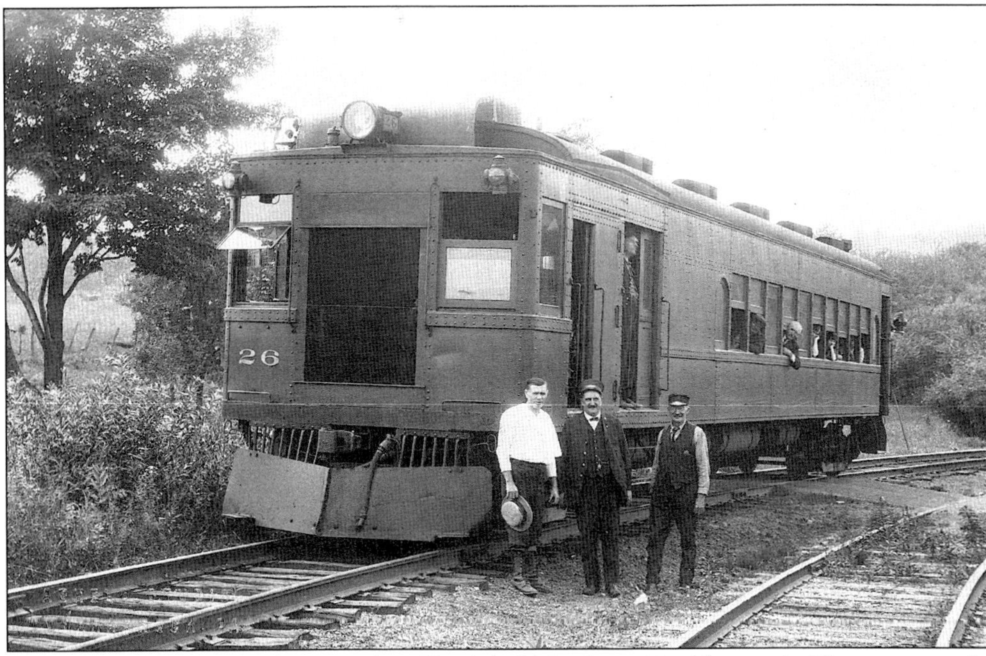

NUMBER 26. This postcard was produced by Asheld Studio in Tunkhannock. The person in the center is Chester Lyman. (Postcard courtesy of the Tioga Point Museum.)

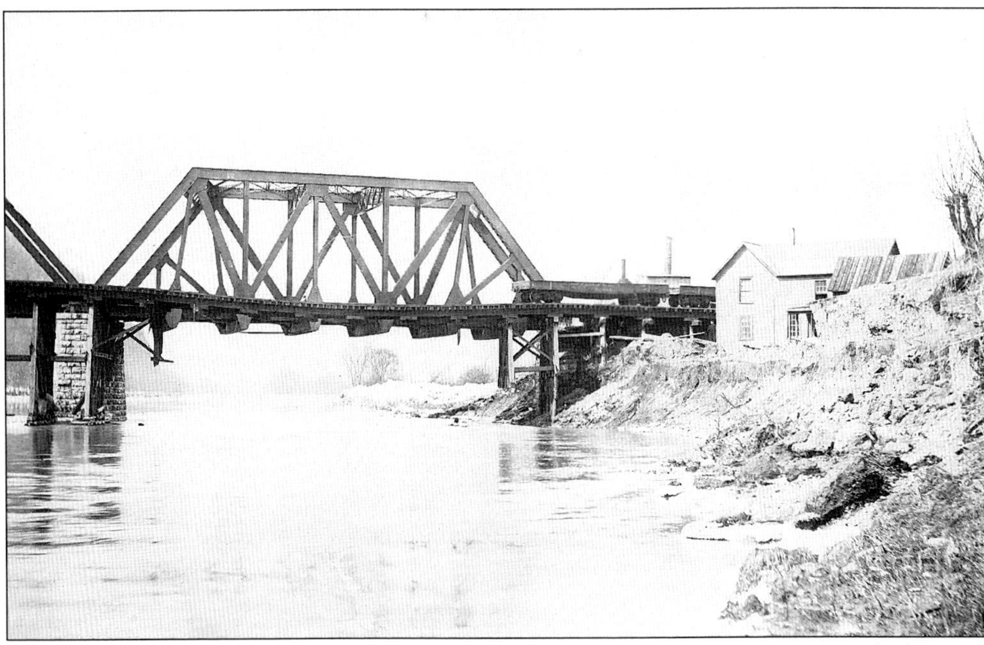

ATHENS RAILROAD BRIDGE, MARCH 1917. This bridge spans the Chemung River. The house to the right was torn down some time after the devastating 1972 flood. (Postcard courtesy of the Tioga Point Museum.)

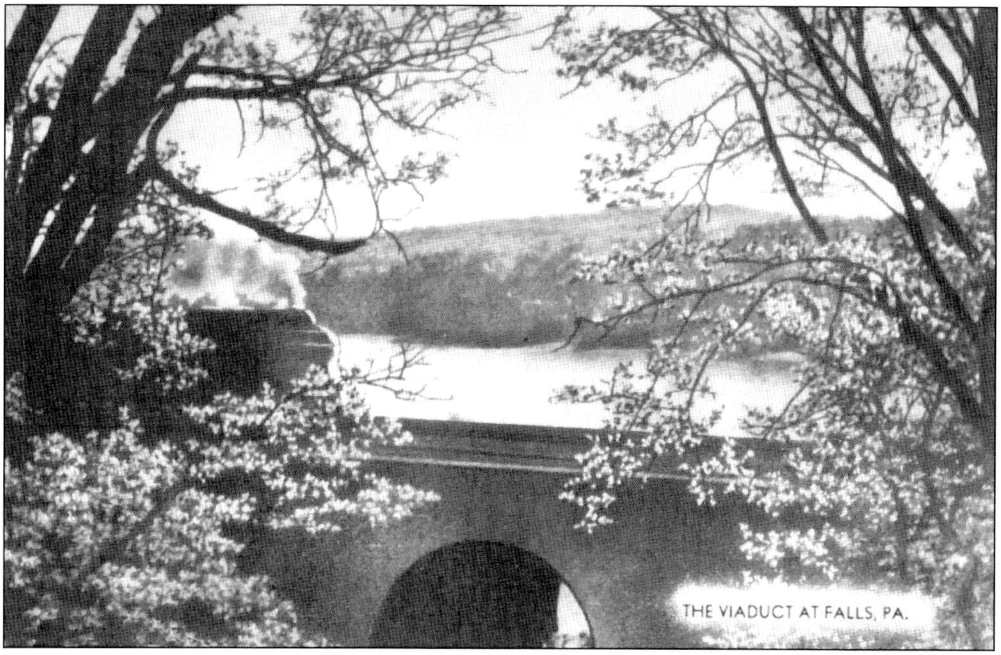

VIADUCT AT FALLS, PA. The caption of this postcard reads "Crack railroad giants roll over this man-made viaduct. Scenes like this are one of many at Falls, Penna." (Postcard collection of the author.)

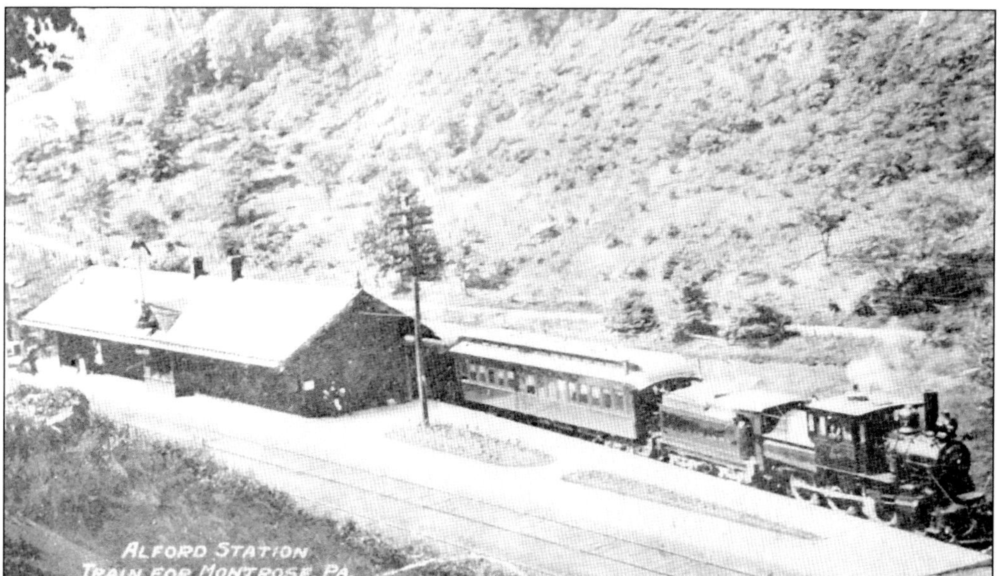

ALFORD STATION, TRAIN FOR MONTROSE. Passenger trains, although never profitable for the railroad companies the way that freight trains were, made travel for the average person much speedier and more comfortable. The Lackawanna Railroad had a spur that took passengers from Alford to Montrose. The main route through Susquehanna County went from Factoryville to Hallstead. (Postcard courtesy of the Susquehanna County Historical Society.)

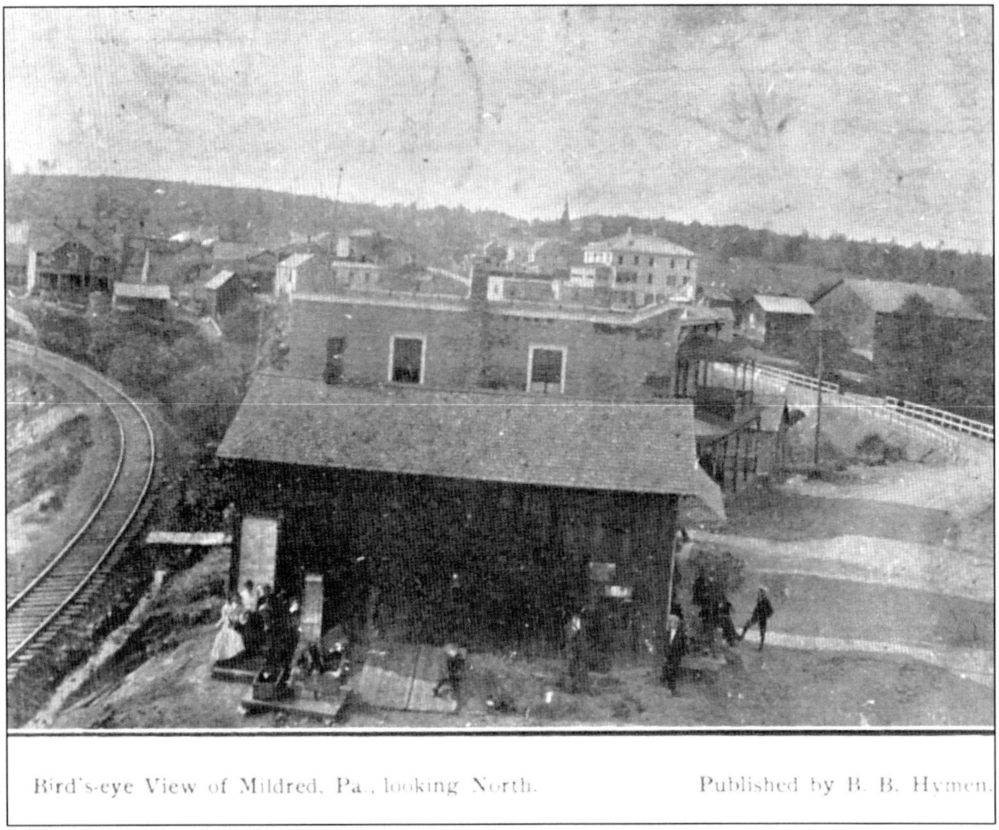

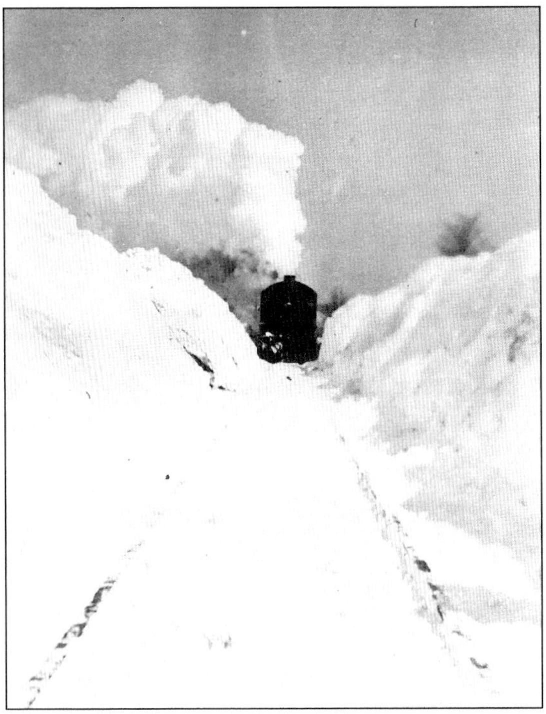

BIRDS-EYE VIEW OF MILDRED, LOOKING NORTH. This 1907 view shows the rail approach to town as well as the road approach. The Lehigh Valley Railroad served Mildred. (Postcard courtesy of the Bradford County Historical Society.)

TRAIN IN A DEEP SNOW. After the plow passed through, the trains were able to run. One cannot help but wonder how the photographer got out of this situation. (Postcard courtesy of the Susquehanna County Historical Society.)

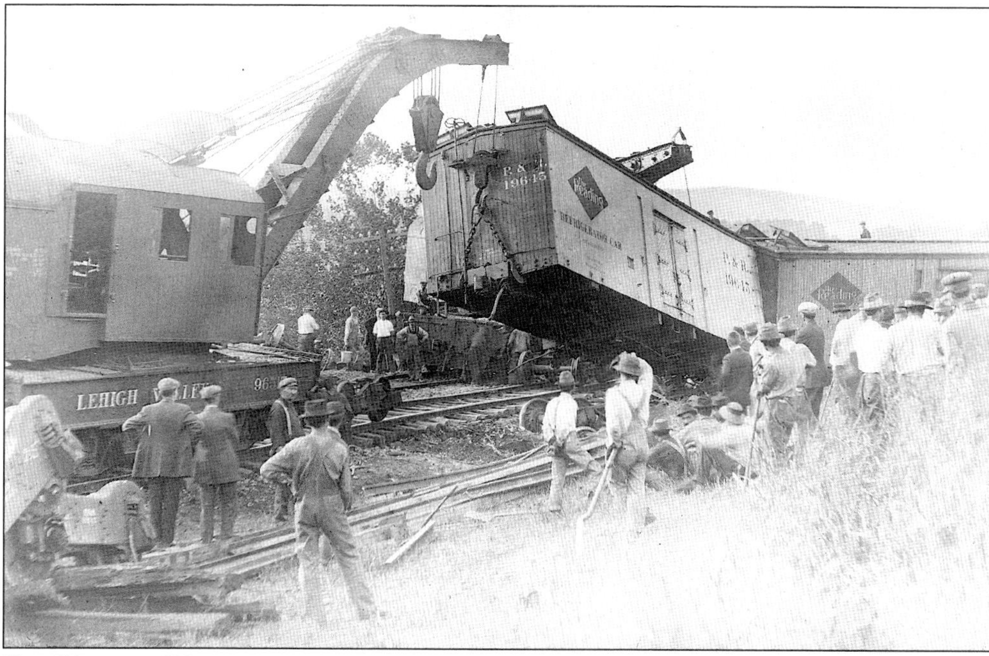

THE "BANANA WRECK," MEHOOPANY, 1913. So called because of the cargo that never made it to market, this Lehigh Valley train mishap provided bananas for the locals for a while, although none of the cars turned over or broke apart. Each car had to be hoisted onto a new truck in order to get back on track. (Postcard courtesy of Norm Brauer.)

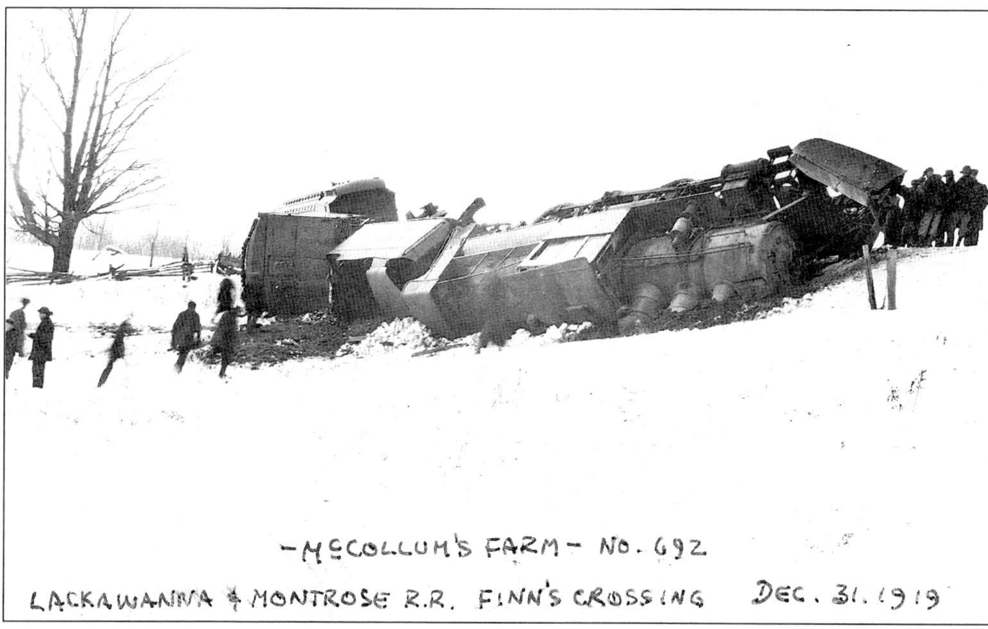

LACKAWANNA & MONTROSE RAILROAD WRECK AT FINN'S CROSSING, DECEMBER 31, 1919. The engineer, A.M. Sliker of Hallstead, died in this Susquehanna County accident. Railroading was a dangerous job, and the newspapers regularly reported accidents and deaths. (Postcard courtesy of Norm Brauer.)

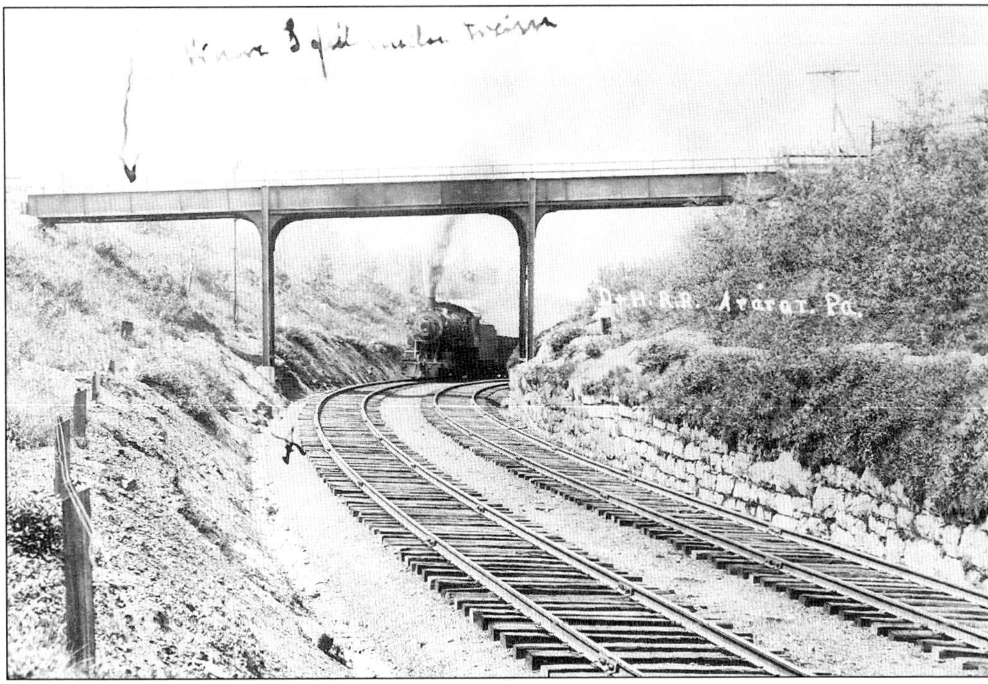

D&H RAILROAD, ARARAT. Not all accidents were fatal. Someone obviously lived to write the message on this card, indicating where he fell under the train. The D&H ran between Wilkes-Barre and Montrose, stopping in Herrick Center, Burnwood, Ararat, Thompson, Starucca, Stevens, Brandt, Jefferson City, and Lanesboro in Susquehanna County. (Postcard courtesy of the Susquehanna County Historical Society.)

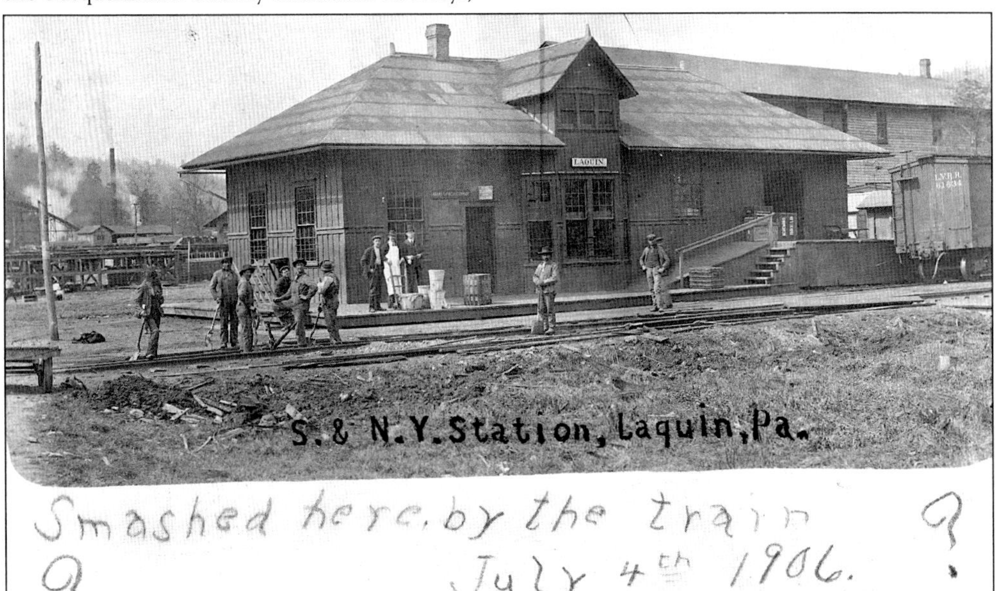

SUSQUEHANNA & NEW YORK STATION, LAQUIN. A similar message to the one above appears on this card, but there is no hint of what, or who, was "smashed." (Postcard courtesy of Norm Brauer.)

Three

RESORTS AND RECREATION

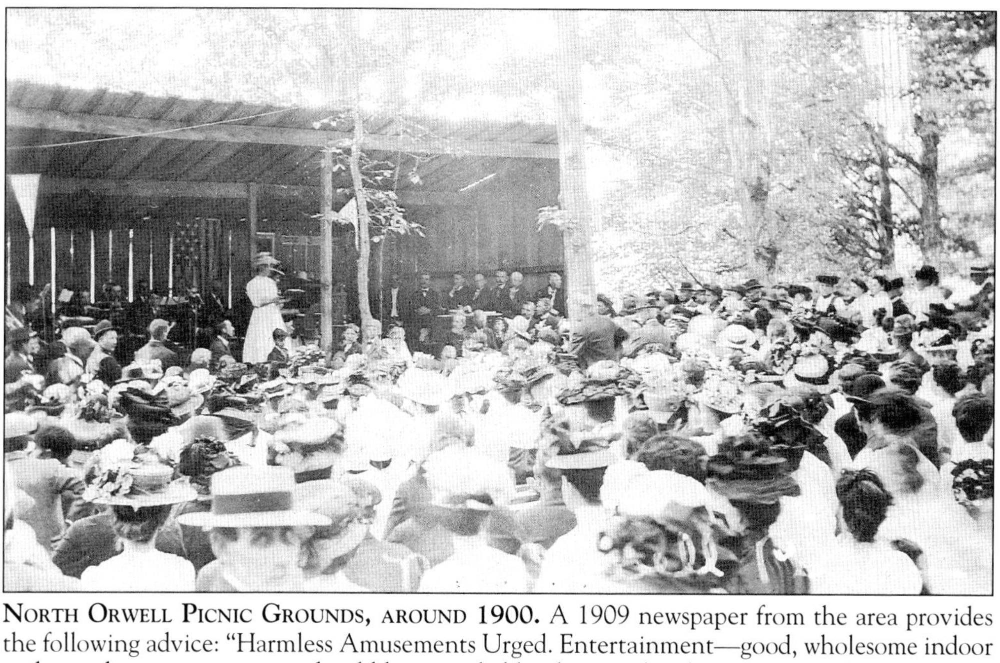

NORTH ORWELL PICNIC GROUNDS, AROUND 1900. A 1909 newspaper from the area provides the following advice: "Harmless Amusements Urged. Entertainment—good, wholesome indoor and outside entertainment—should be provided by the wise heads in every neighborhood and village in our agricultural regions. That is one of the best means known for keeping the boys and girls on the farm and preventing restlessness and a tendency of the young people to flock to the cities and towns. Proper entertainment will also go far toward solving the problem of farm laborers. The hired man will work better on the farm that is part of a 'literary coterie,' or near where he can hear good lectures, good music, can play baseball or football, ride over the hurdles, etc. for 'all work and no play make Jack a dull boy.' " (Postcard courtesy of the Tioga Point Museum.)

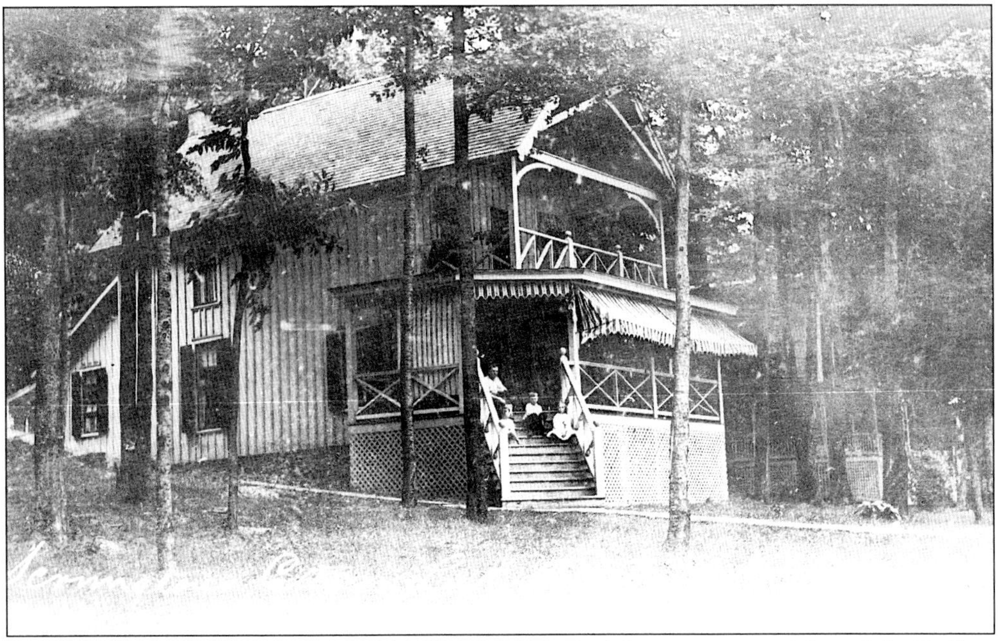

Cottage at Lake Carey, 1914. Lake Carey is typical of the many resort lakes of the Endless Mountains. Accessible by rail in the early 1900s, it offered city dwellers a respite from the summer heat. Summer cottages and hotel resorts, the lake, an amusement park, and picnic grounds afforded comfort and entertainment to the many who traveled here. Lake Carey, like most of the booming tourist lakes of the early part of the century, is now privately owned. The resorts are gone.

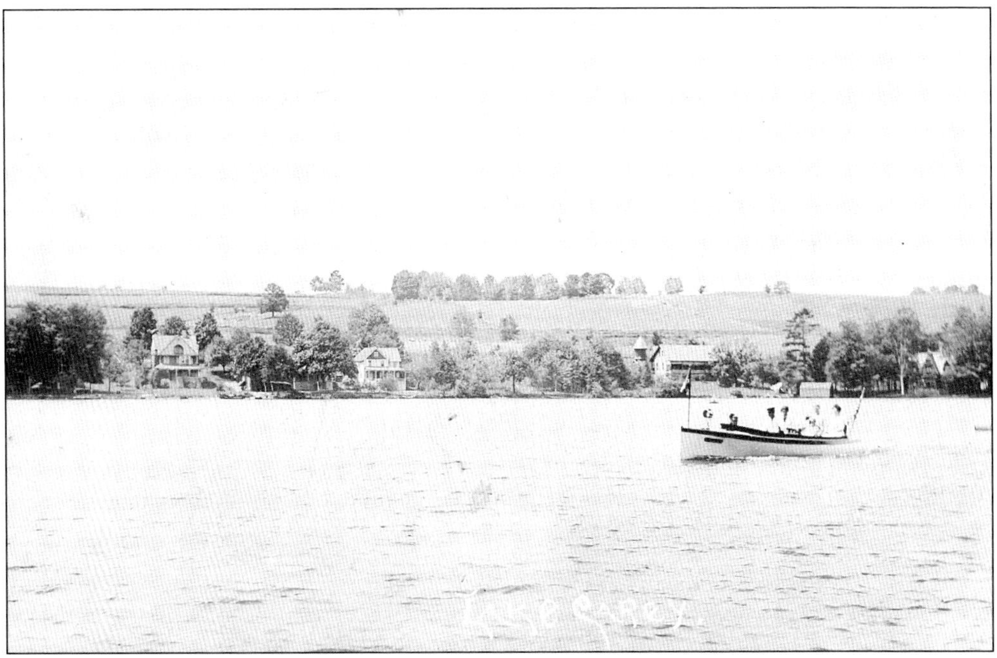

Boating on Lake Carey.

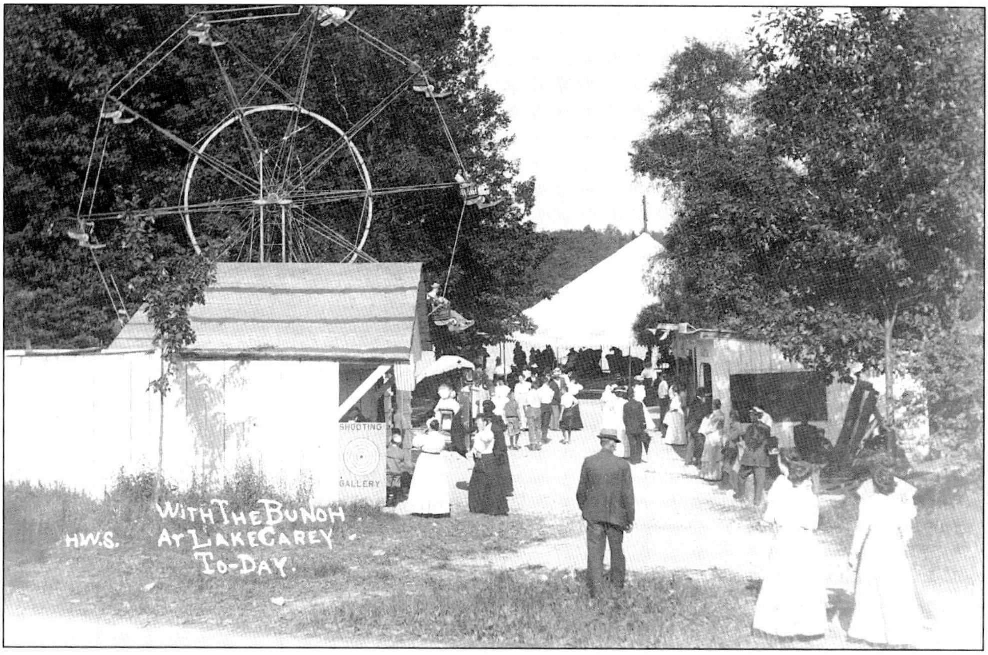

"WITH THE BUNCH AT LAKE CAREY TODAY."

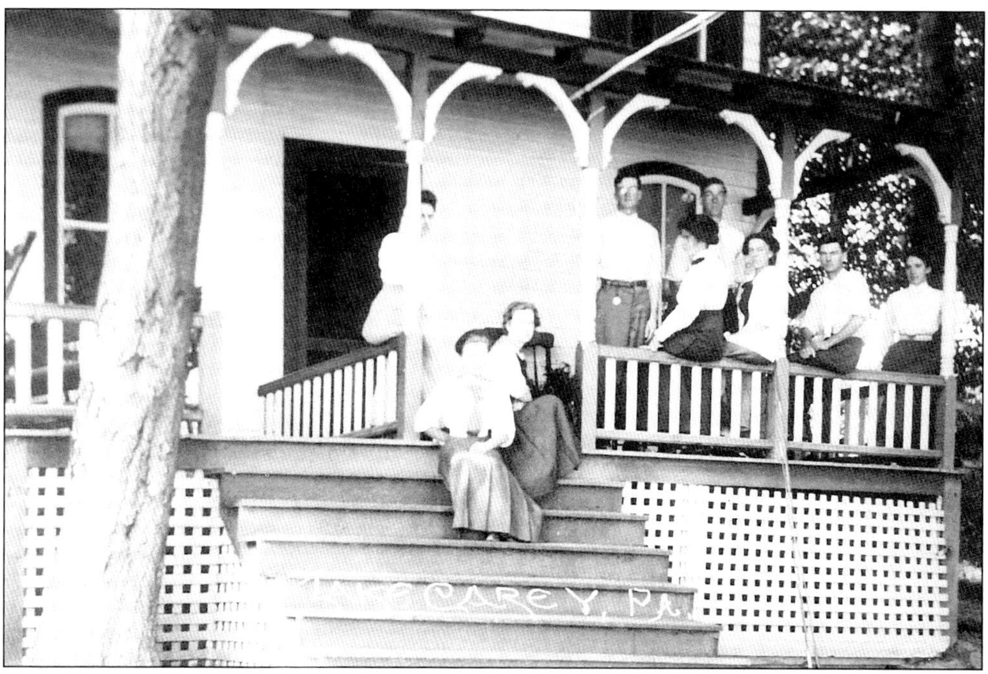

ON A COTTAGE PORCH AT LAKE CAREY.

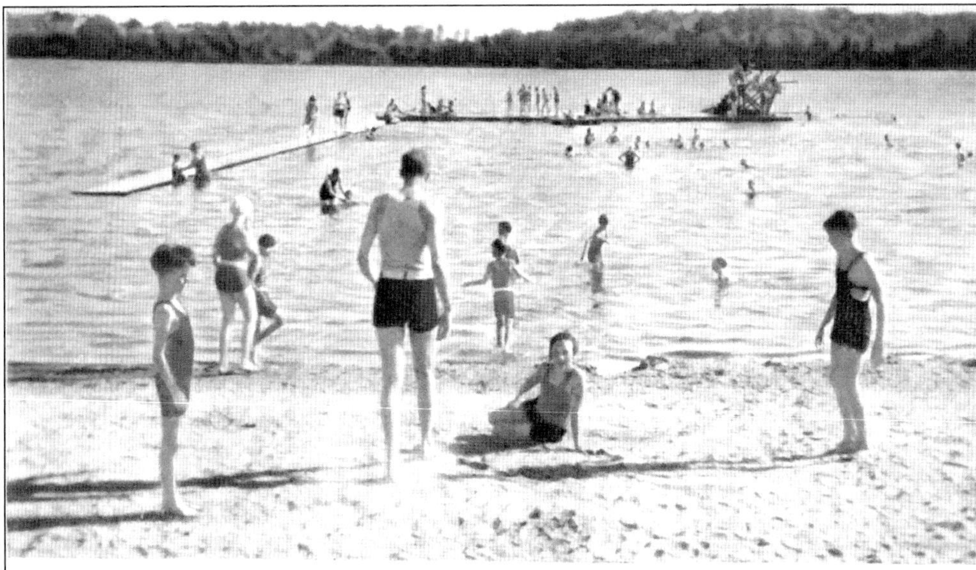

BATHING BEACH AND DIVING PIER EAGLES MERE PENNSYLVANIA

BATHING BEACH AND DIVING PIER, EAGLE'S MERE. "The beach is safe for all bathers, sloping so gradually that it is fully one hundred yards from shore before the water is too deep for an adult to stand in. There are no strong currents in the lake, and winds from the south never cause anything approaching surf . . ." This glowing report of the bathing conditions at Eagle's Mere appears in a 1944 history of the lake. (Postcard courtesy of the Tioga Point Museum.)

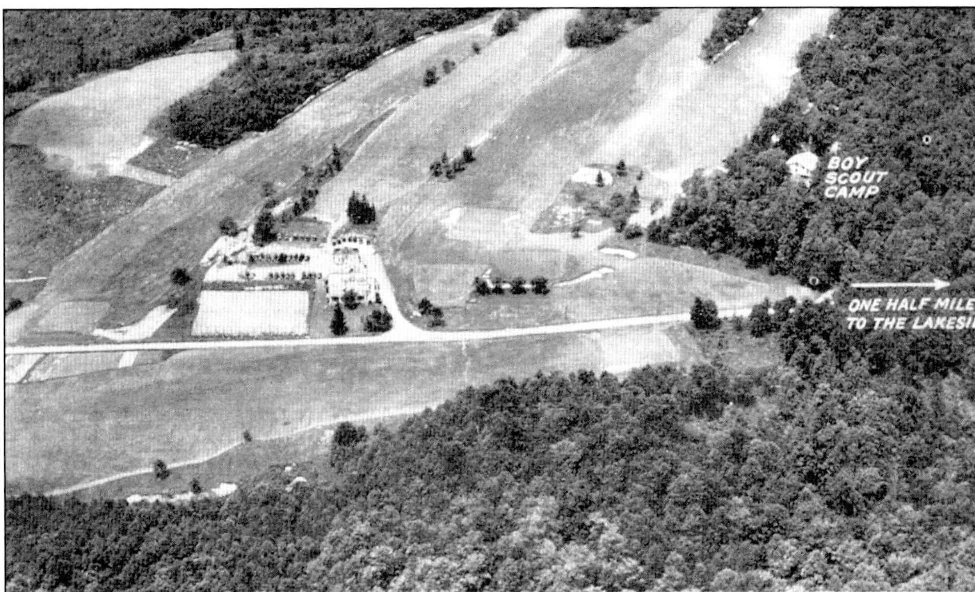

Aerial View of Eagles Mere Golf Course and Club House

AERIAL VIEW OF THE EAGLE'S MERE GOLF HOUSE AND CLUBHOUSE. The golf club was formed in 1911 and the course constructed on the Avery farm, about 3/4 of a mile from the lake. At first it was a nine-hole course, but in 1916 it was expanded to 18 holes. A 1922 hiking map offered nine different trails, one of which was a loop off the golf course. (Postcard courtesy of the Tioga Point Museum.)

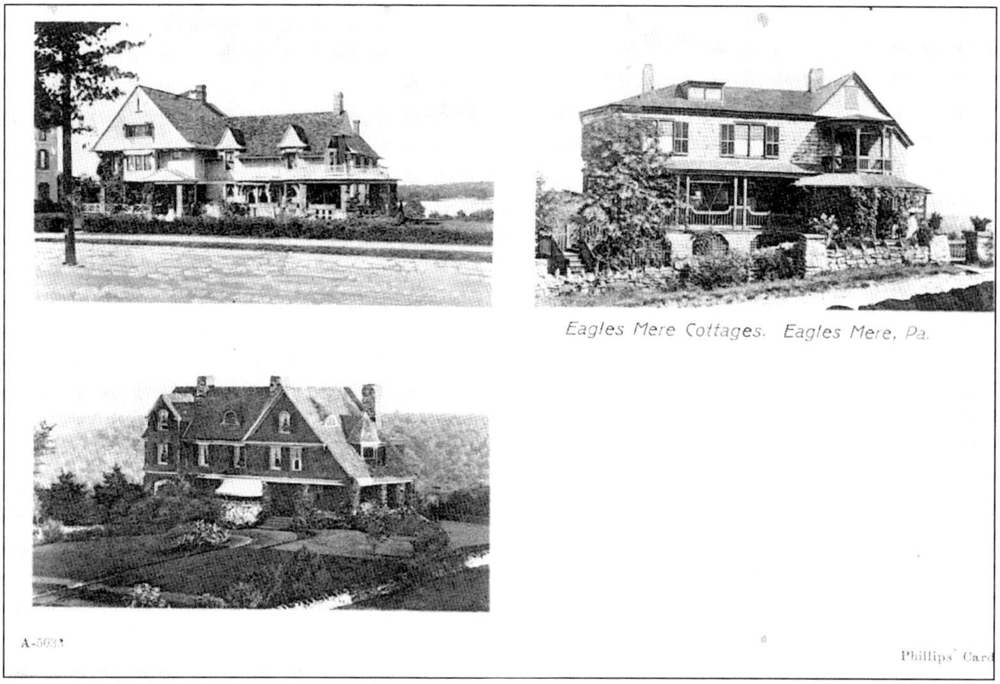

Eagle's Mere Cottages, 1914. The first cottage was constructed in 1880, and by 1892 there were 90. Many of these are still standing, but the grand hotels have been torn down. Early vacationers had to reach the lake by stage from Muncy, but in 1892 a rail connection was built. By the 1940s the area was easily reached by automobile. (Postcard courtesy of the Bradford County Historical Society.)

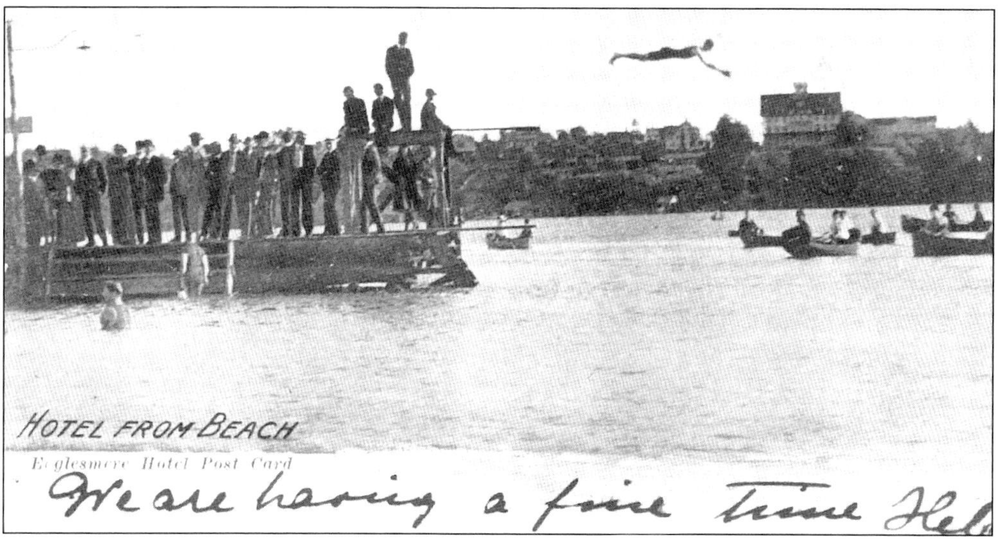

Bathing at Eagle's Mere. "Absent from this region are amusements of the carousel, roller-coaster, and related variety as well as objectionable roadside stands. It is, rather, a vacation region adapted to wholesome recreation." Littering was also frowned on. "The throwing about of candy-boxes, lunch remains and newspapers is a wrong. It is unfair. Please see that all such material is rolled into a small space and tucked under a rock or a stone out of sight from the trail." (Postcard courtesy of the Bradford County Historical Society.)

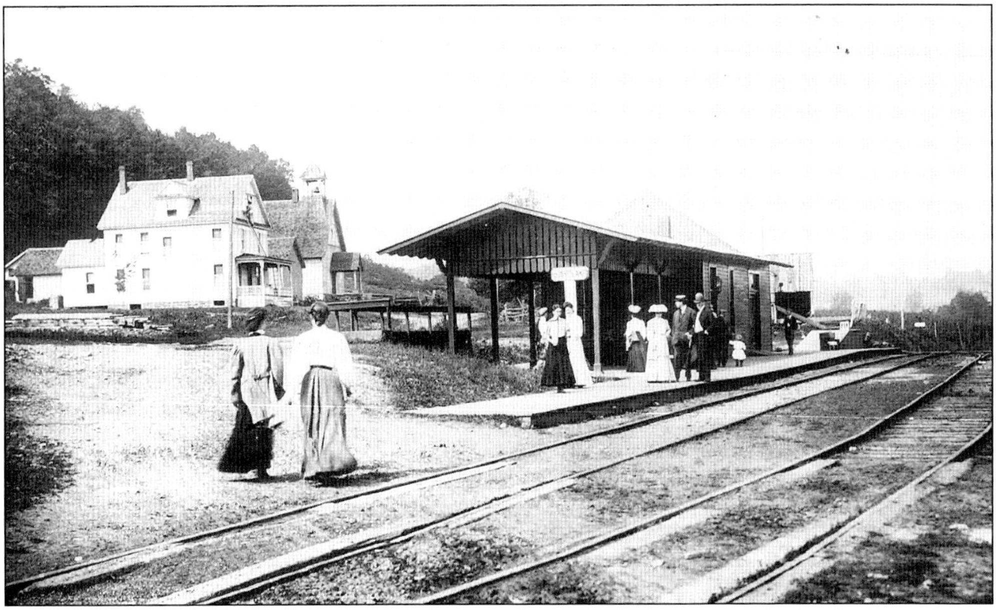

HEART LAKE RAILROAD STATION. The Heart Lake station was a stop on the Lackawanna & Montrose Railroad, which ran from Montrose to Alford, where it connected with the Delaware & Lackawanna line. The lake had many entertainments for the people who made the journey, including picnic grounds, dance halls, a merry-go-round, and a restaurant. (Postcard courtesy of the Susquehanna County Historical Society.)

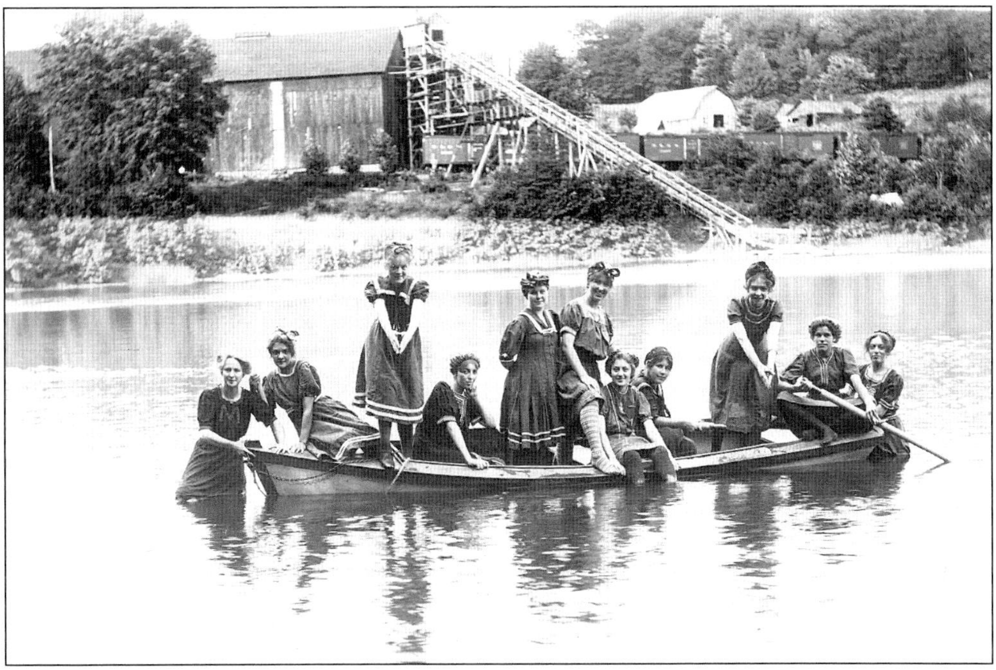

BATHING AND BOATING AT HEART LAKE. These young ladies are enjoying water sports in 1910 while wearing dark-colored bathing costumes, stockings (including flashy striped ones), and kerchiefs over their hair. The railroad and ice house are visible in the background. (Postcard courtesy of Norm Brauer.)

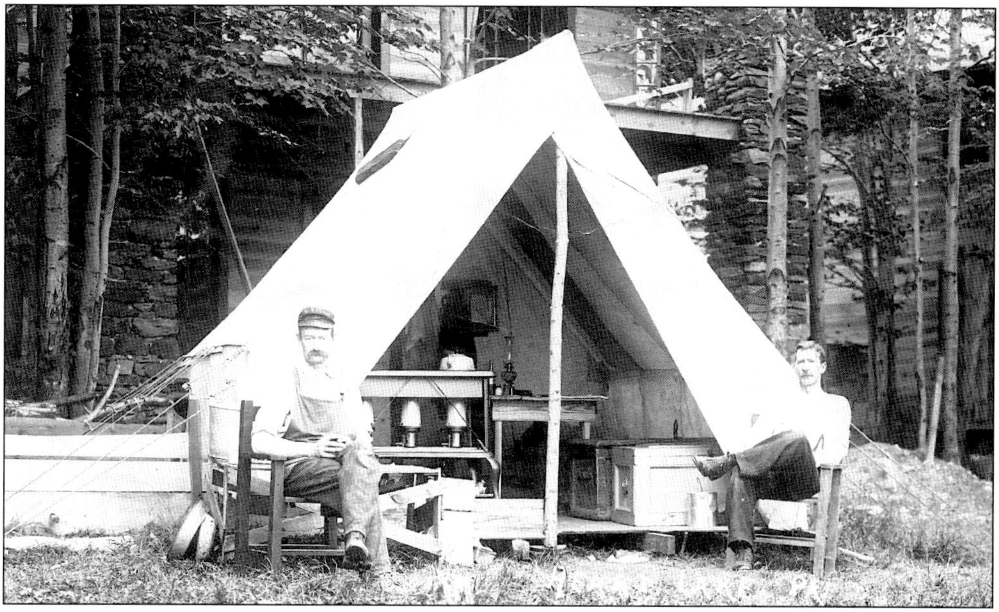

Roughing It at Heart Lake, Summer, 1914. This tent, pitched directly in front of a large cottage, is equipped with a two-burner stove, a dining table, a mirror, two trunks, and a wood floor. (Postcard courtesy of Norm Brauer.)

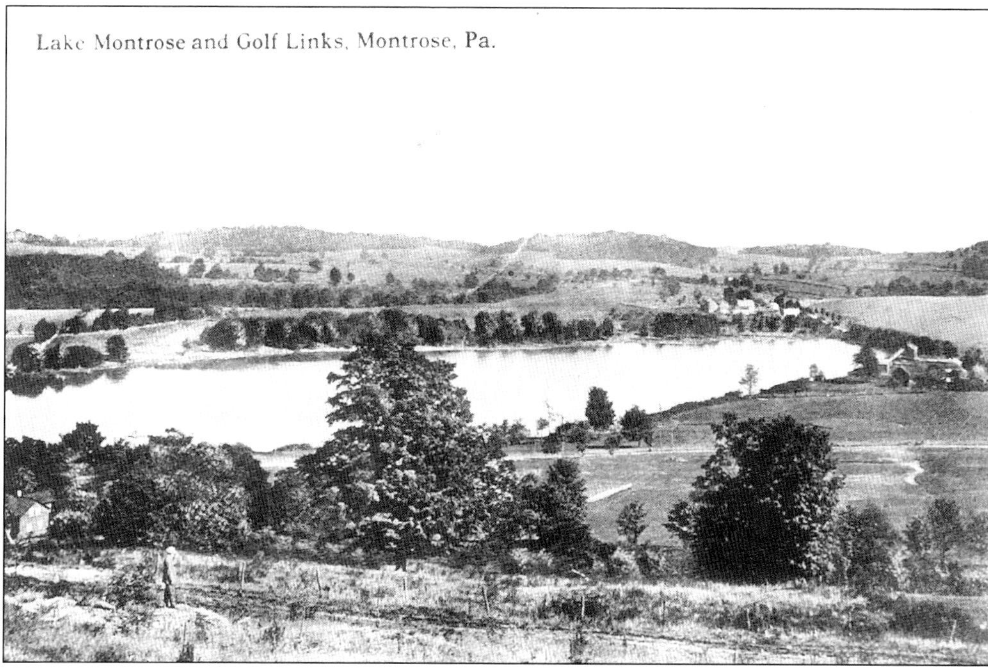

Lake Montrose and Golf Links. The Lakeside Country Club advertised "No humidity; no insects. Bonniest golf links outside of Scotland . . . Superior to Berkshire, Adirondaks or Maine." The country club was founded in 1898 and by 1909 it had 200 members, both permanent and summer residents. Another promotion boasted that "The mercury in well-regulated thermometers rarely ever rises above about 80." (Postcard courtesy of the Susquehanna County Historical Society.)

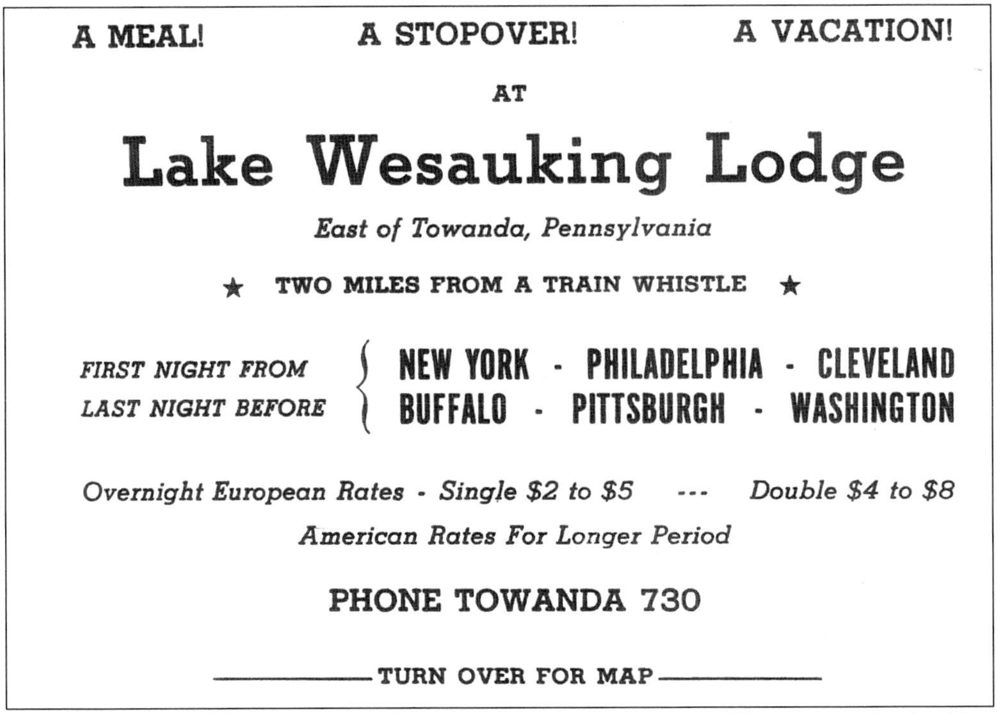
A MEAL! A STOPOVER! A VACATION!

AT

Lake Wesauking Lodge

East of Towanda, Pennsylvania

★ TWO MILES FROM A TRAIN WHISTLE ★

FIRST NIGHT FROM	NEW YORK - PHILADELPHIA - CLEVELAND
LAST NIGHT BEFORE	BUFFALO - PITTSBURGH - WASHINGTON

Overnight European Rates - Single $2 to $5 --- Double $4 to $8

American Rates For Longer Period

PHONE TOWANDA 730

TURN OVER FOR MAP

ADVERTISEMENT FOR LAKE WESAUKING LODGE. Tourists came from all over to enjoy the lake. This advertisement promotes the convenience of getting to the lodge. A Wilkes-Barre woman who visited the lake as a child reminisced, "When we got off the train, the hotel surrey was waiting for us, and some kind of rig for our trunks." The hotel was built in 1895. Early proprietors were a Mr. Harris, Ella Shores, and Edward Overton. (Postcard courtesy of the Bradford County Historical Society.)

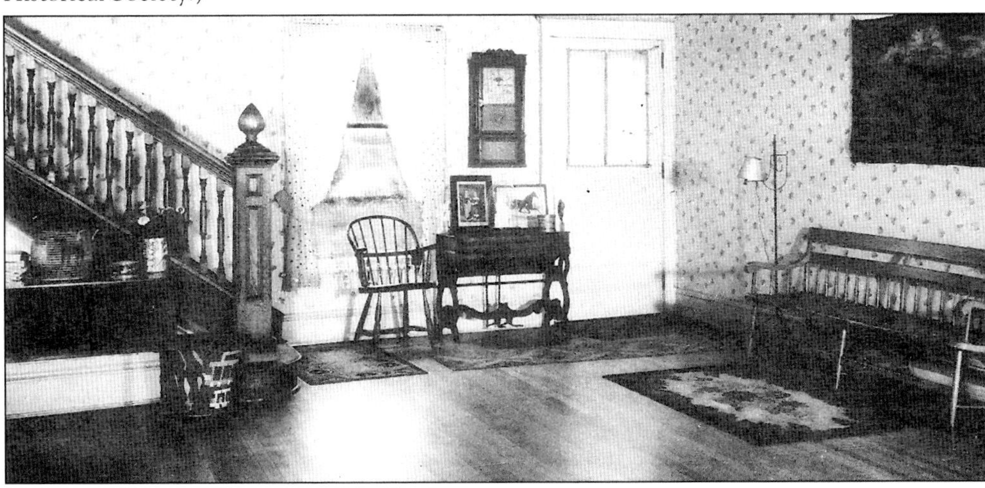

CORNER OF LOBBY, LAKE WESAUKING LODGE, TOWANDA. "The fast crowd from Towanda would drive up on certain afternoons and take over the parlor. All the regular lady boarders sat on the porch in rocking chairs. The young folks had pompadours, very tight corsets, lacy petticoats which showed when they did the two-step, and high heels." The Lake Wesauking Lodge closed shortly after World War II and was demolished in the 1950s. (Postcard courtesy of the Bradford County Historical Society.)

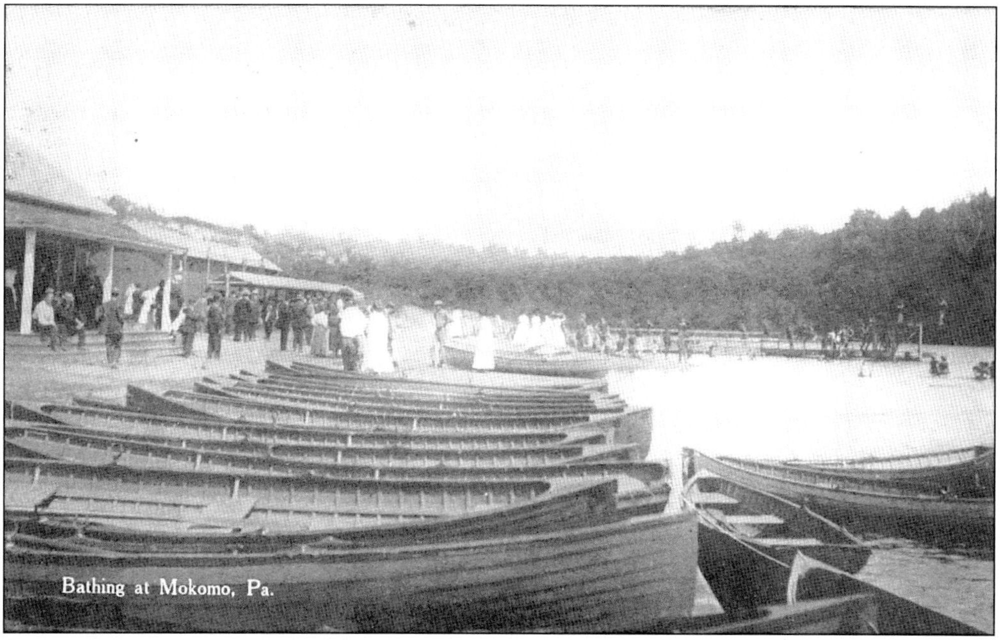

Boats on Lake Mokoma. This lake near Laporte was enlarged in 1889 by damming the mill creek. The Williamsport and North Branch Railroad ran along the west shore and brought summer visitors from Williamsport. (Postcard courtesy of the Bradford County Historical Society.)

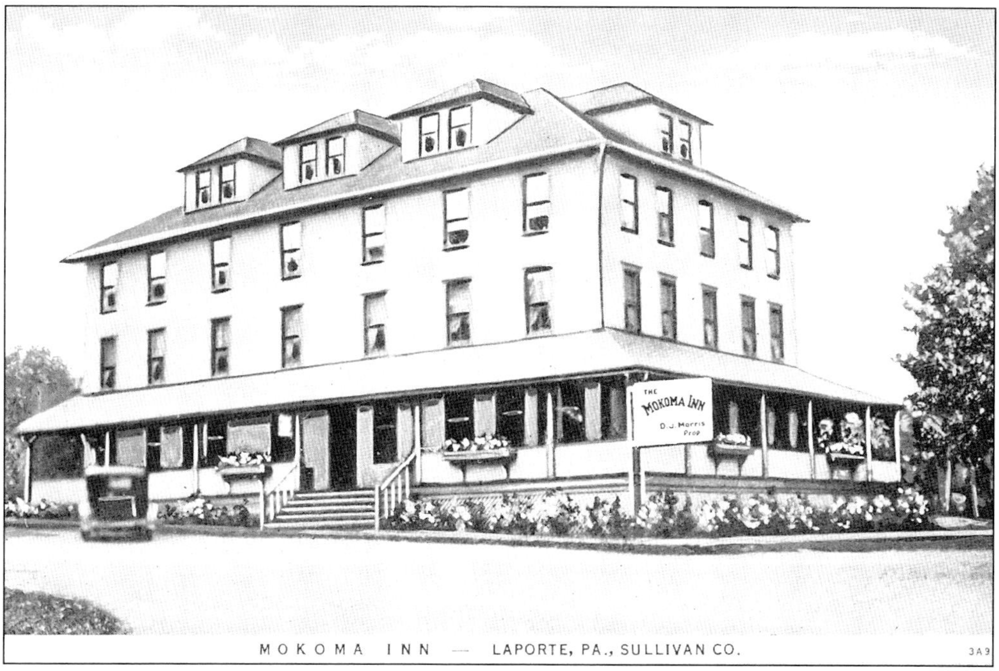

Mokoma Inn, Laporte, 1935. Summer was not the only time tourists visited the Endless Mountains. Hotels such as this one were open year-round and attracted hunters and fishermen. One book states that "Sullivan County may well claim to be the Switzerland of Pennsylvania because of its high relief and its glacial lakes and ponds." (Postcard courtesy of French Azilum.)

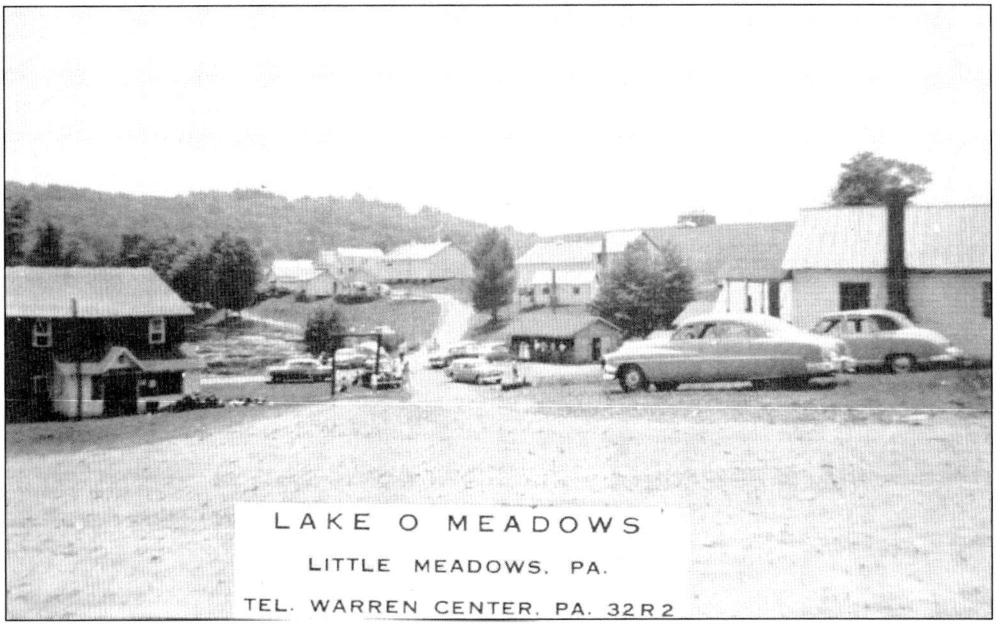

LAKE O MEADOWS, LITTLE MEADOWS. Little Meadows is in the very northwest corner of Susquehanna County, but the lake itself is in both Bradford and Susquehanna Counties. Warren Center is in Bradford County. (Postcard courtesy of the Bradford County Historical Society.)

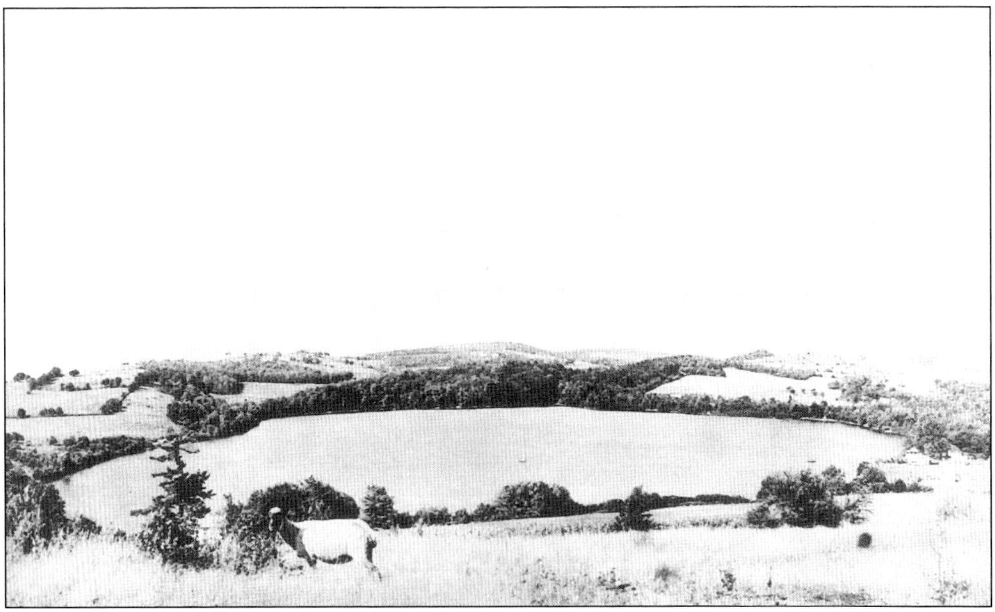

ELK LAKE. In the left foreground of this card is, I believe, an elk. Elk were hunted out of existence in Pennsylvania long ago, but in the early 20th century the game commission reintroduced the animals into various areas of the state. The elk that were reintroduced into Susquehanna County did not ultimately succeed in establishing a herd, but this may be an individual from one of those attempts. Either that or the photographer tethered it there for effect. (Postcard courtesy of the Susquehanna County Historical Society.)

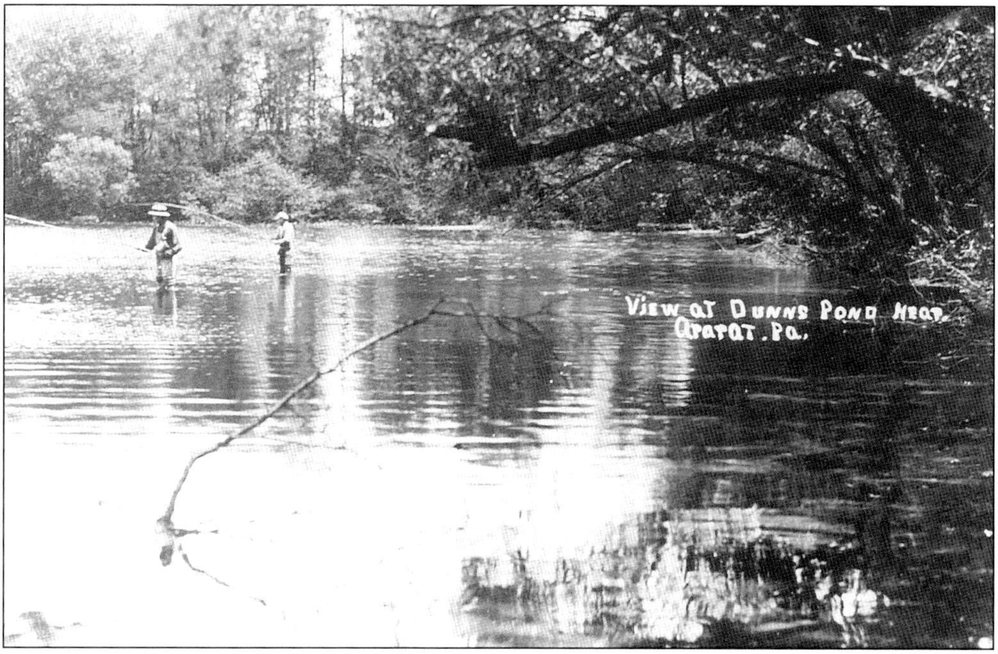

VIEW AT DUNN'S POND, NEAR ARARAT. Dunn's Pond is named for James Dunn, originally from Scotland, who settled here in 1820. J.C. Bushnell writes: "That a man with his talent, education and training should plunge into this dense forest and squat upon the shore of this forest gem from mere fancy or admiration of its primitive loveliness, is not presumable. Though beautiful the seclusion, there was not enough of it for either convenience or profit." (Postcard courtesy of the Susquehanna County Historical Society.)

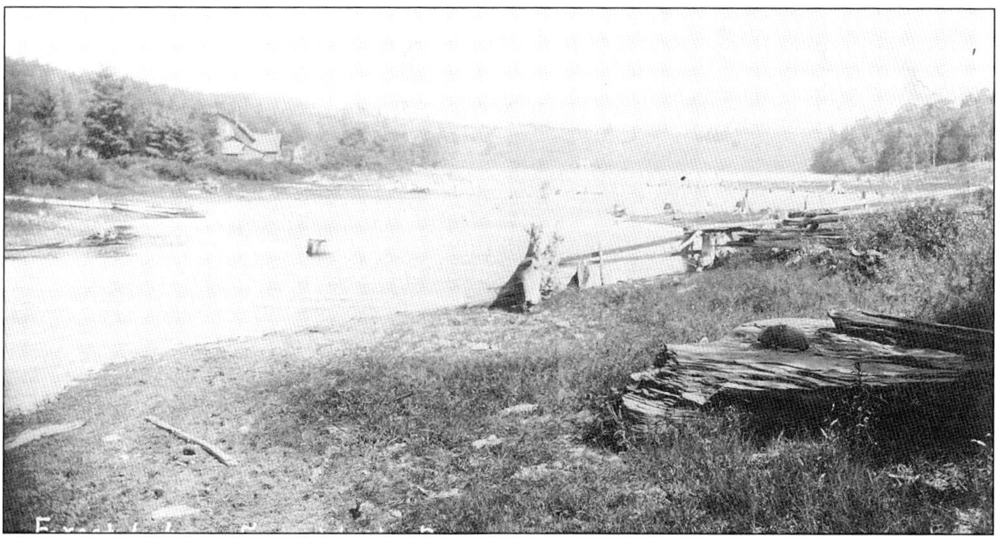

FOREST LAKE, 1907. Located in the Susquehanna County Township of the same name, a 19th-century author calls the lake ". . . a pretty sheet of water, lying low among the surrounding hills, and its outlet flows south through Jessup into the East Branch of the Wyalusing. Its volume is not strong, but it has good mill sites." He goes on to say that the many springs and hilly nature of the country "adapt it well for the principal pursuit of the inhabitants—dairying." (Postcard courtesy of the Susquehanna County Historical Society.)

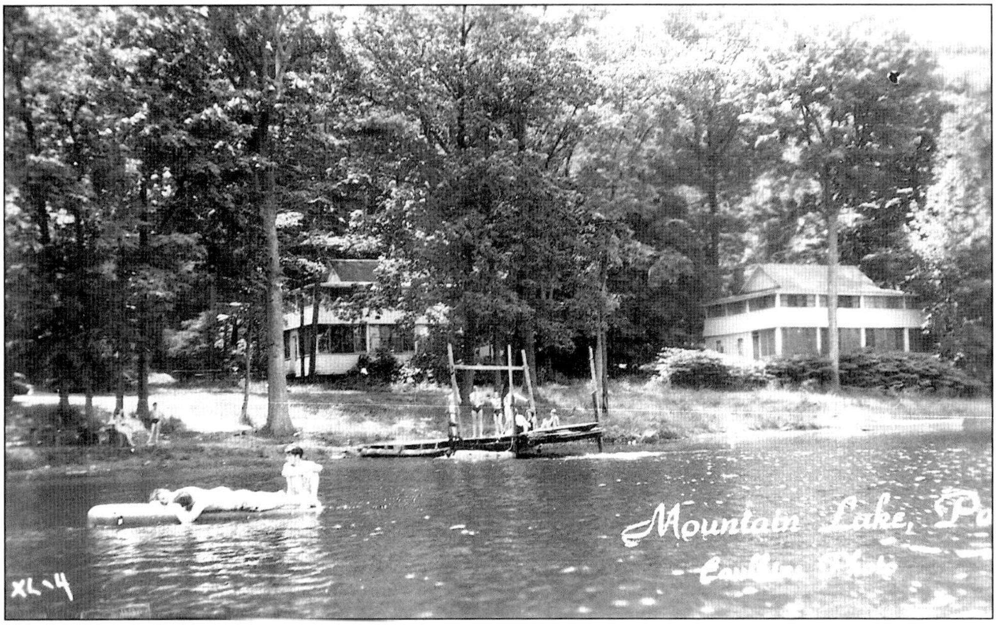

MOUNTAIN LAKE. Like other lakes in the area, this is now private, but it used to be a tourist attraction. It is located just south of Burlington and retains its peaceful character, in part because motorboats are not allowed. (Postcard courtesy of the Bradford County Historical Society.)

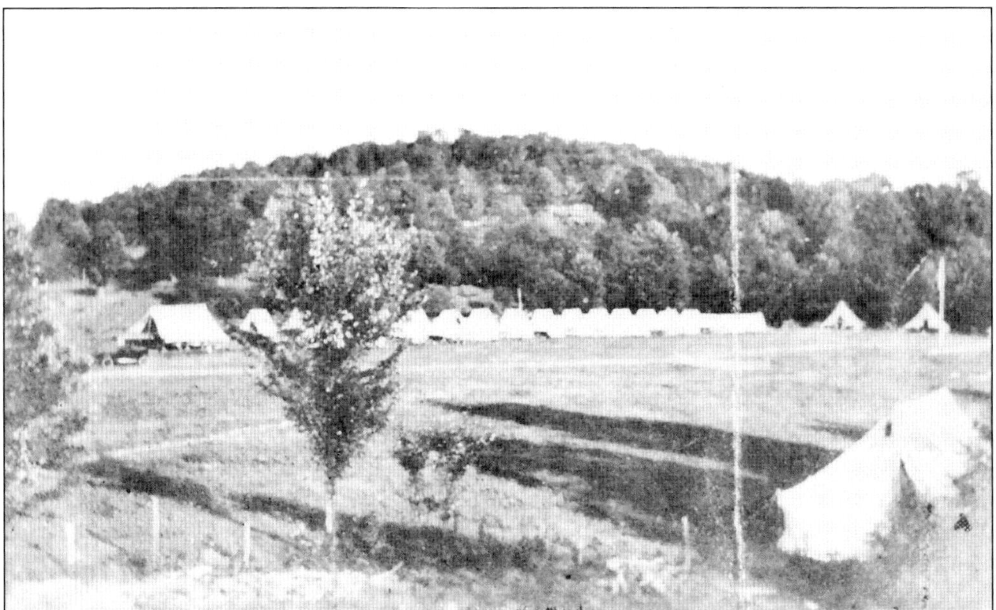

Camp Archbald, Girl Scouts, Lake Ely, Brooklyn, Pa.

CAMP ARCHIBALD, LAKE ELY. The many parks, lakes, and trails make the Endless Mountains perfect for scout camps, and this was one of many. (Postcard courtesy of the Susquehanna County Historical Society.)

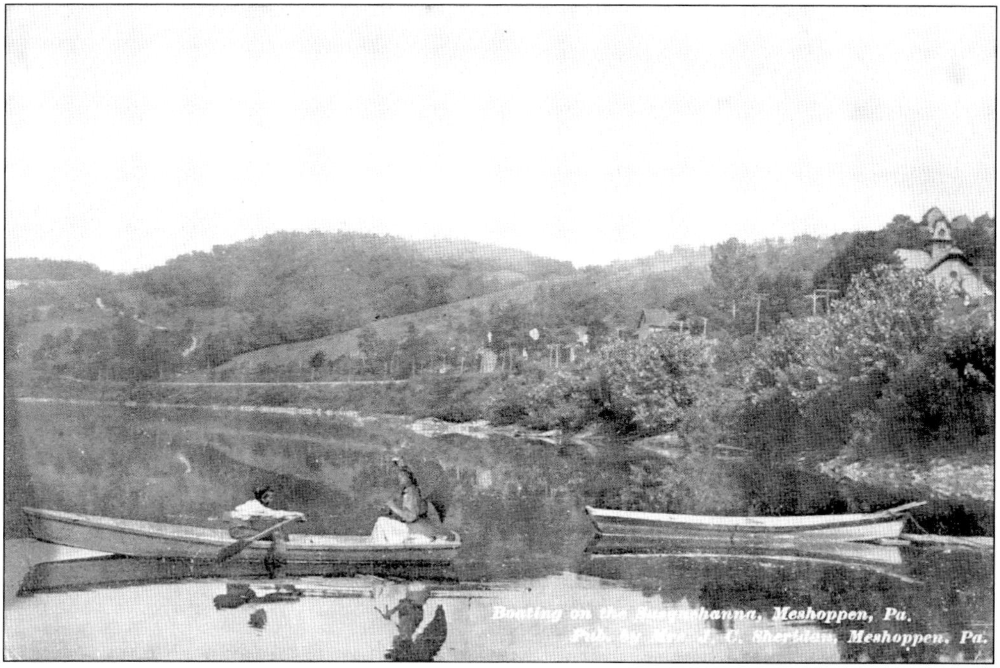

BOATING ON THE SUSQUEHANNA NEAR MESHOPPEN. Unlike many of the resorts, the river was and continues to be used by the people who live along it. It has always been common for owners of river front property to keep a canoe or rowboat pulled up on shore for fishing or just a leisurely paddle. (Postcard courtesy of the Tioga Point Museum.)

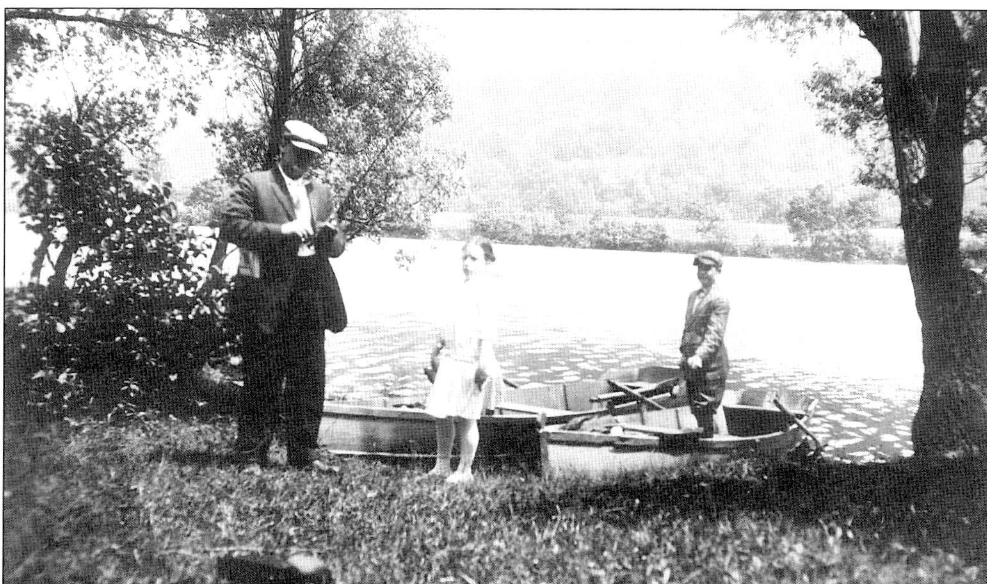

FISHING ON THE SUSQUEHANNA. Bass, muskellunge, walleye, carp, pickerel, and perch are among the fish that sportsmen catch on the river. (Postcard courtesy of the Tioga Point Museum.)

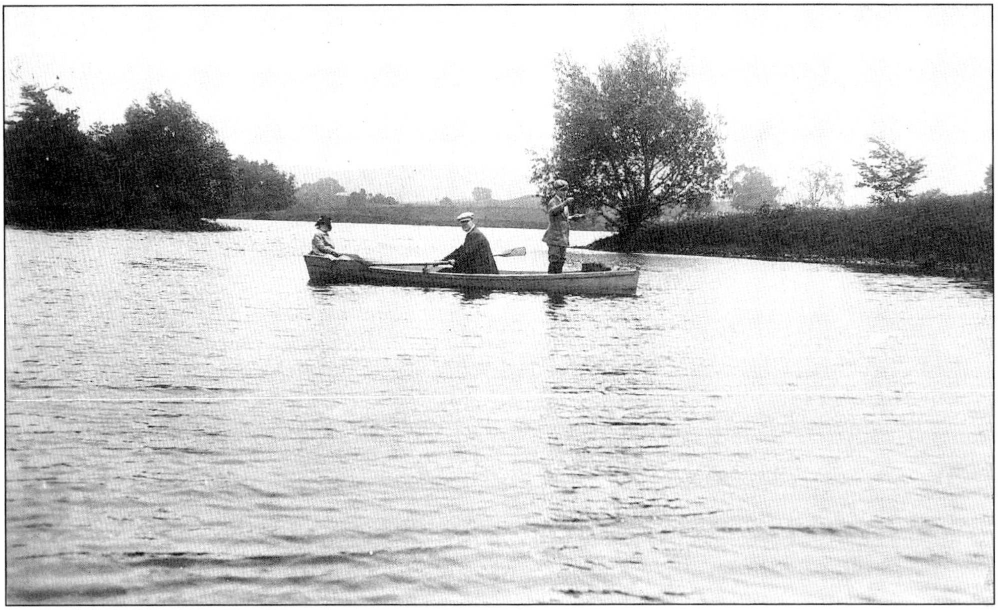

MORE FISHING ON THE SUSQUEHANNA. The non-fishermen (two out of three in this party) also enjoy the beauty and wildlife along the river. Blue herons, osprey, hawks, and occasionally even bald eagles have been spotted. (Postcard courtesy of the Tioga Point Museum.)

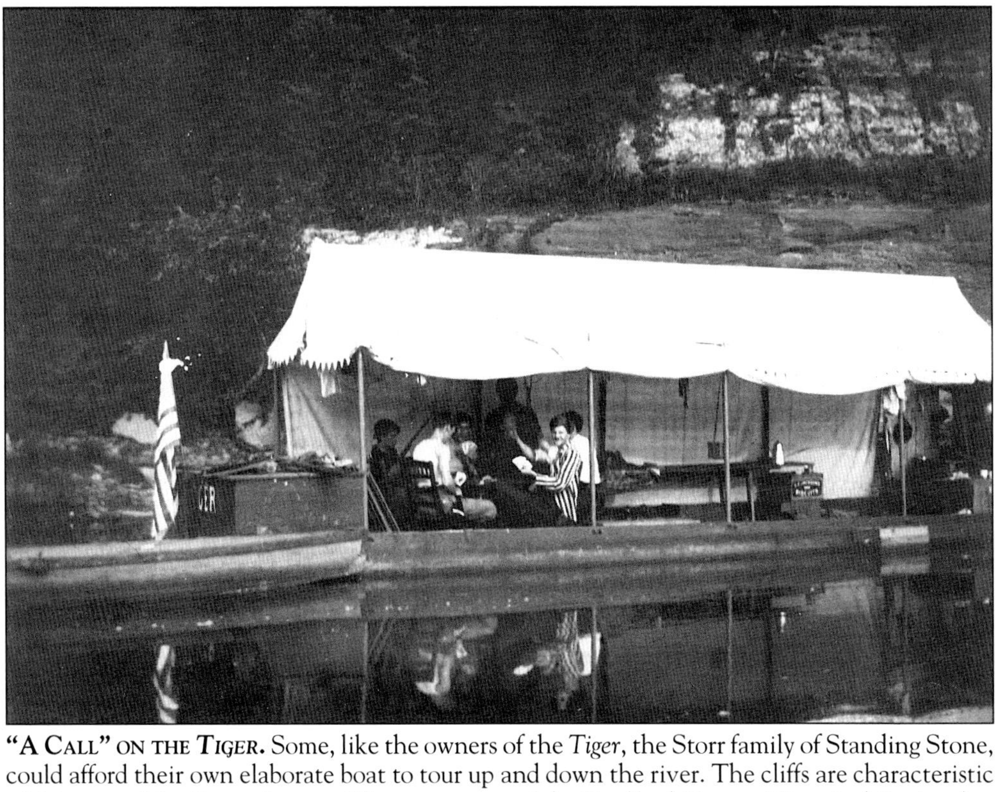

"A CALL" ON THE *TIGER*. Some, like the owners of the *Tiger*, the Storr family of Standing Stone, could afford their own elaborate boat to tour up and down the river. The cliffs are characteristic of this part of the Susquehanna. (Photo courtesy of the Bradford County Historical Society.)

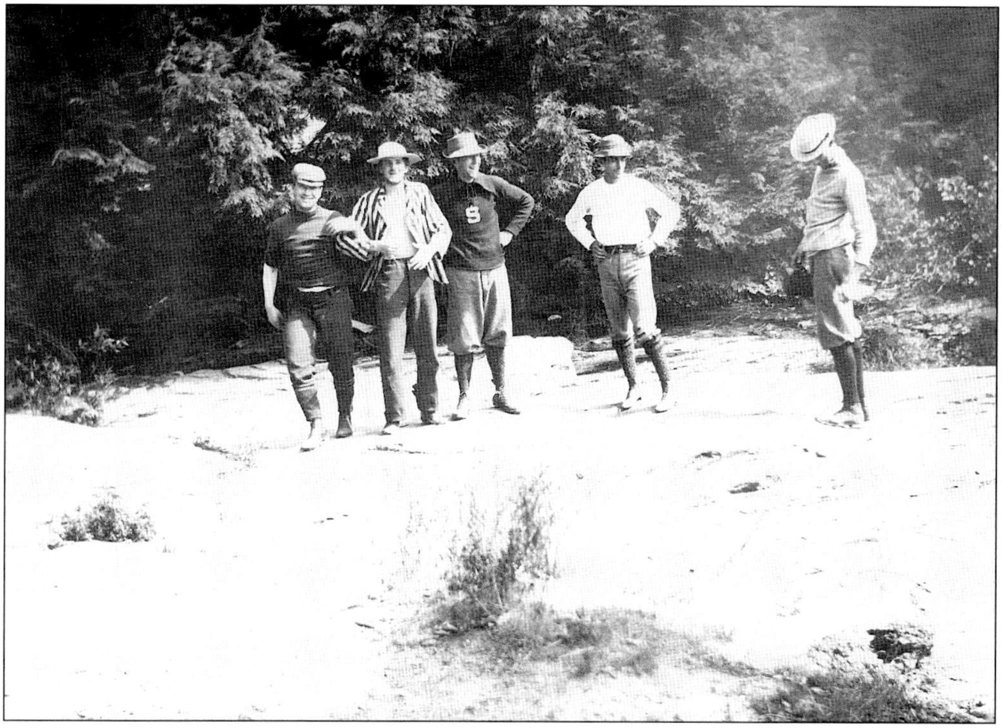

AT FALLING SPRING & QUEEN ESTHER'S PATH. The party from the *Tiger* has left the boat to explore the rocky shore of the river. (Photo courtesy of the Tioga Point Museum.)

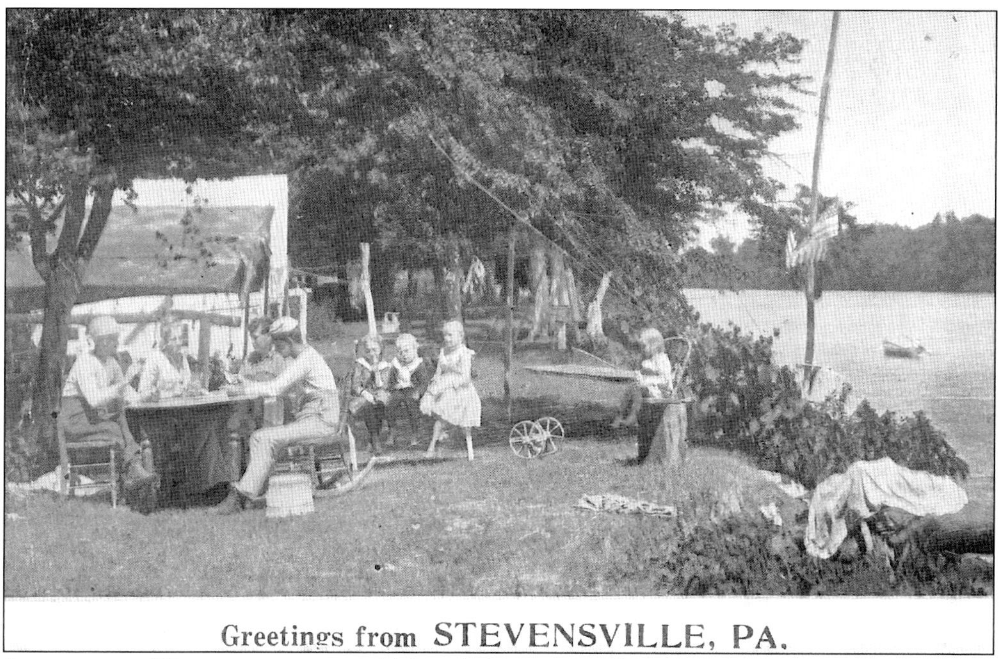

STEVENSVILLE WATERFRONT, 1923. Although the postcard does not identify the site, it is probably along Wyalusing Creek. (Postcard courtesy of the Bradford County Historical Society.)

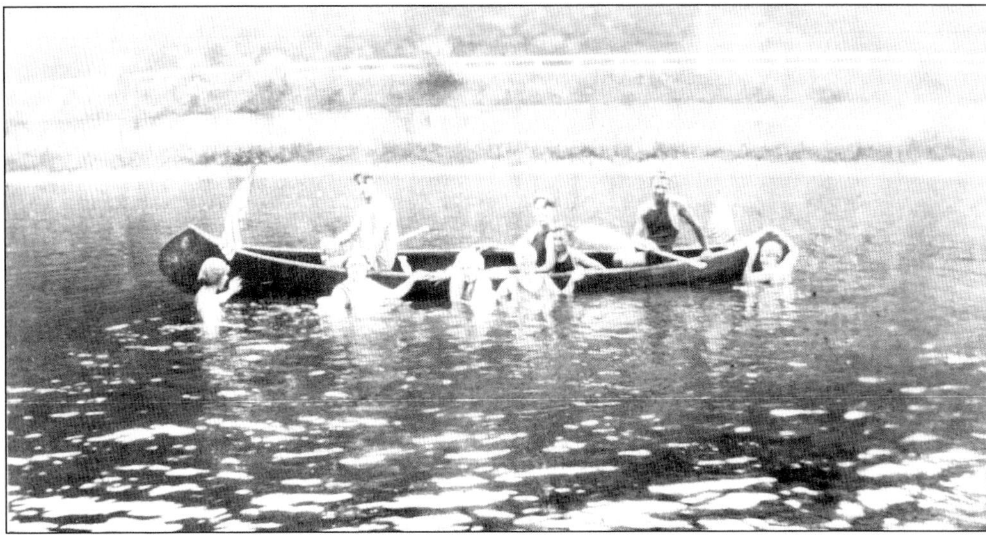

FUN ON THE SUSQUEHANNA RIVER, LANESBORO. Of course swimming in the river was a popular pastime. This is at Lanesboro, on the Great Bend of the Susquehanna. (Postcard courtesy of the Susquehanna County Historical Society.)

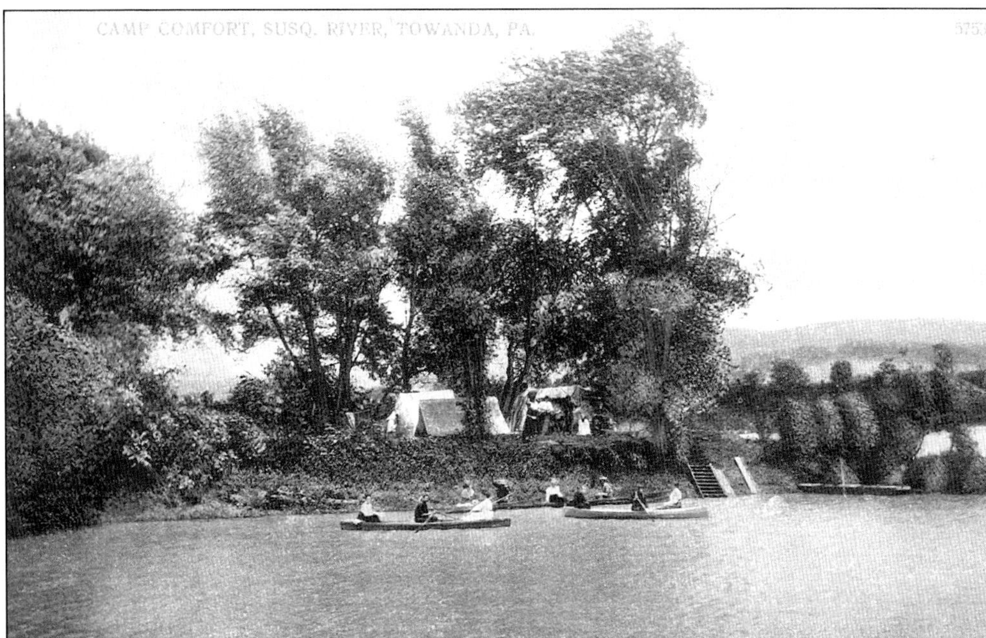

CAMP COMFORT, NEAR TOWANDA. Camping along the river is a recreational activity of long standing. A 1938 article notes that "Each town . . . had one cabin camp and several middle class hotels." (Postcard collection of the author.)

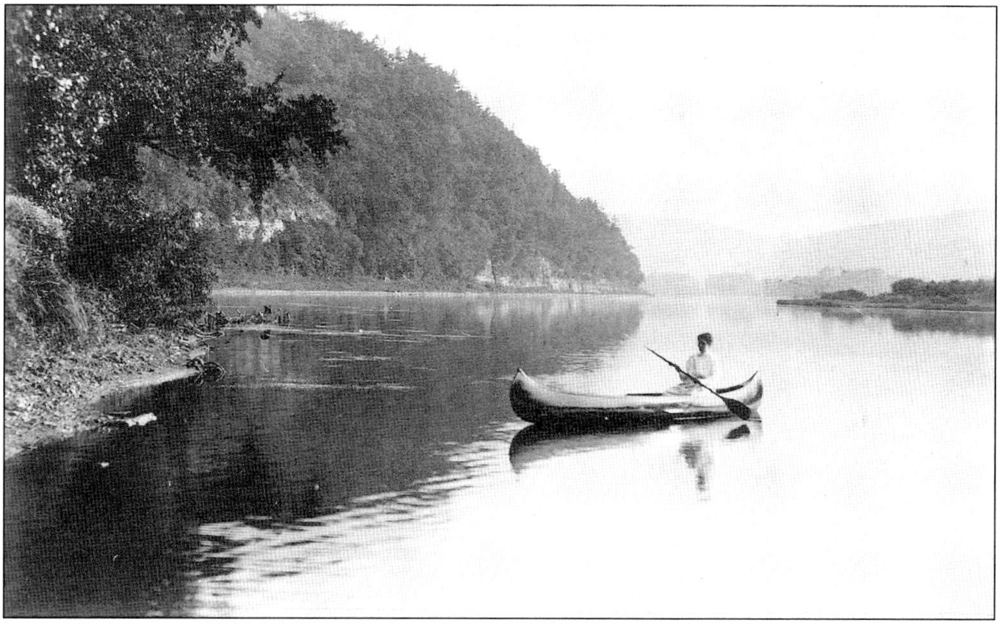

TIOGA POINT AT THE TURN 'O ROCKS. The young lady paddling the canoe is probably Louise E. Murray. She lived in a house on the Susquehanna at Athens, and her family kept a canoe to use on the river. After leaving Athens, Miss Murray became a missionary and moved to Minnesota, where she spent the rest of her life. (Postcard courtesy of the Tioga Point Museum.)

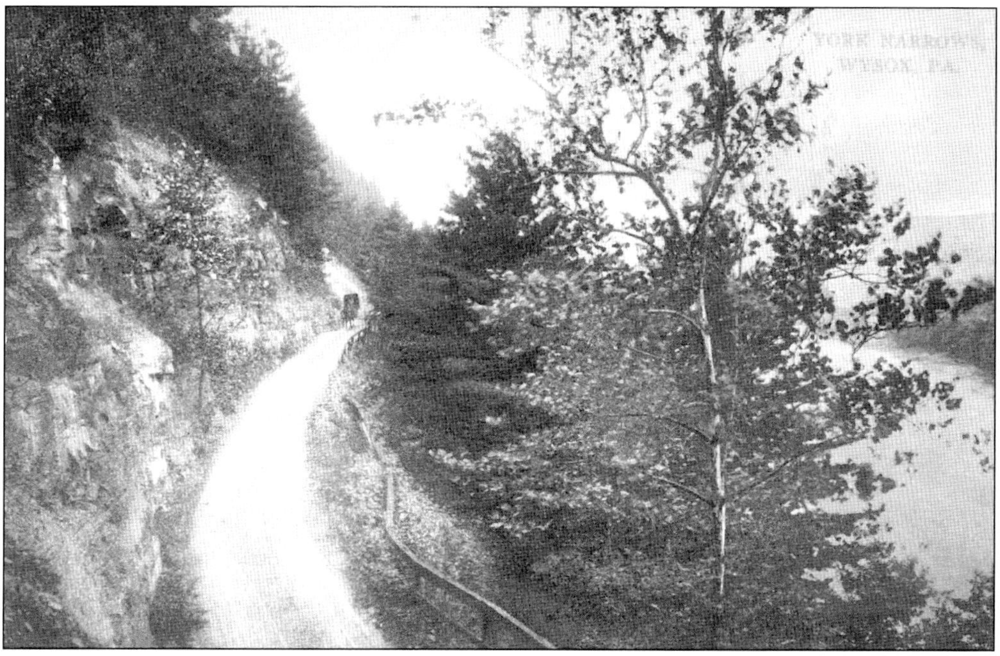

YORK NARROWS, WYSOX. The narrow road where the horse-drawn buggy travels in this card was a difficult passage. The mountain has been blasted back over the years, most recently in 1997, causing some to refer to this stretch as "the wides." (Postcard courtesy of the Tioga Point Museum.)

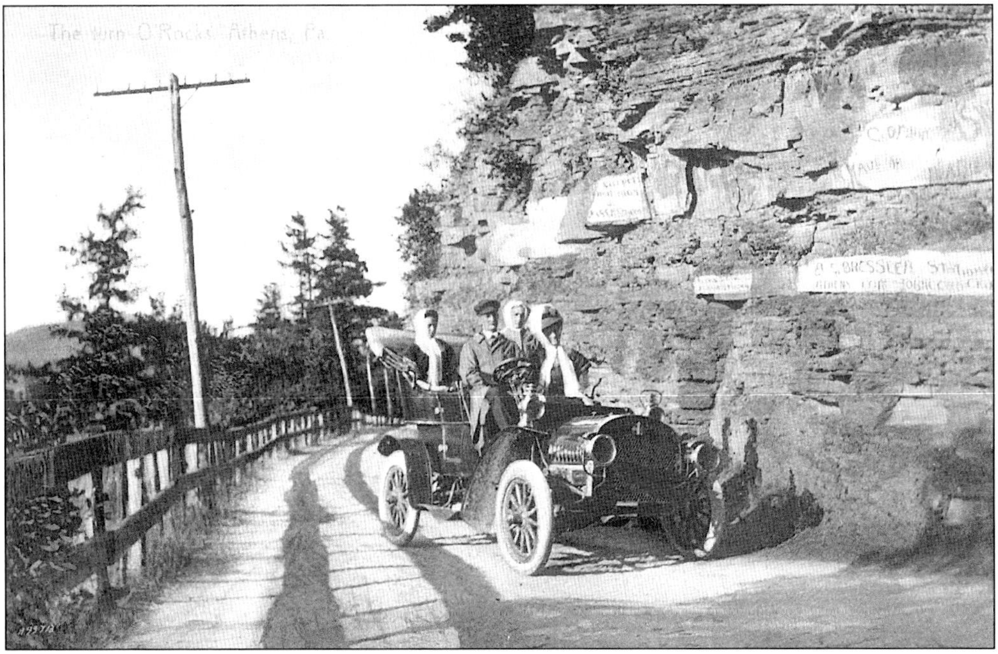

TURN 'O ROCKS, ATHENS, 1911. Motor touring became popular with the advent of the automobile. The cliff here has been painted with advertisements for local businesses, including A.E. Bressler, Stationer and Carpets, and mattings at Kiff & Stacey. (Postcard courtesy of the Tioga Point Museum.)

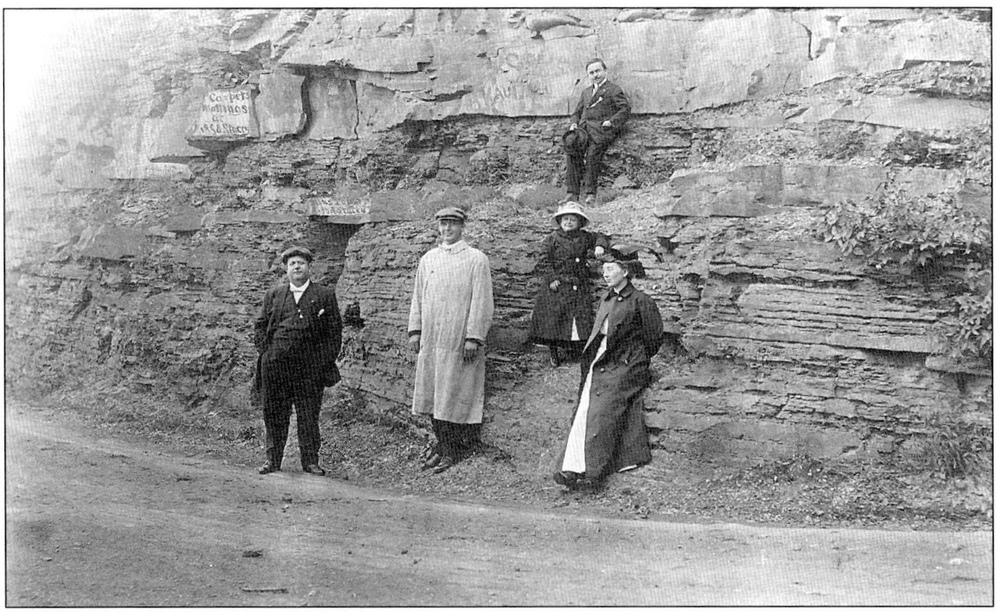

POSING AT THE CLIFF. These tourists have left their auto to have their picture taken. Since so few roads were paved, the "duster" was an important item of clothing. These long, lightweight coats protected travelers' clothing from the ever-present dirt and dust. (Photo courtesy of the Tioga Point Museum.)

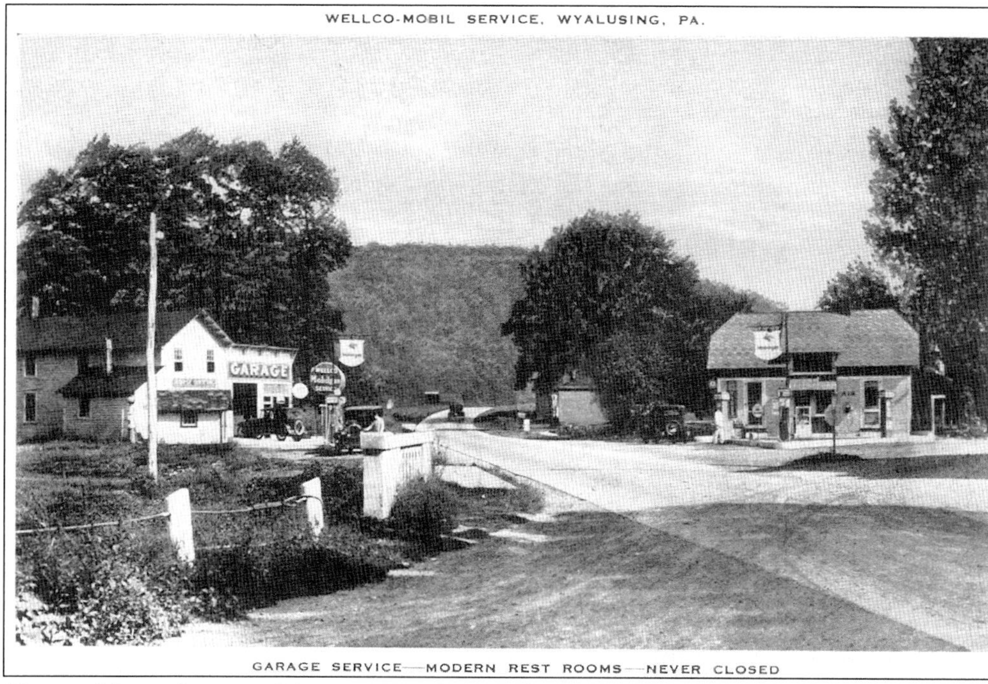

WELLCO-MOBIL SERVICE, WYALUSING. Along with the automobile came the need for service stations. Cars needed fuel, and they broke down a lot. This station had pumps on both sides of the roads, and "modern restrooms." (Postcard courtesy of Norm Brauer.)

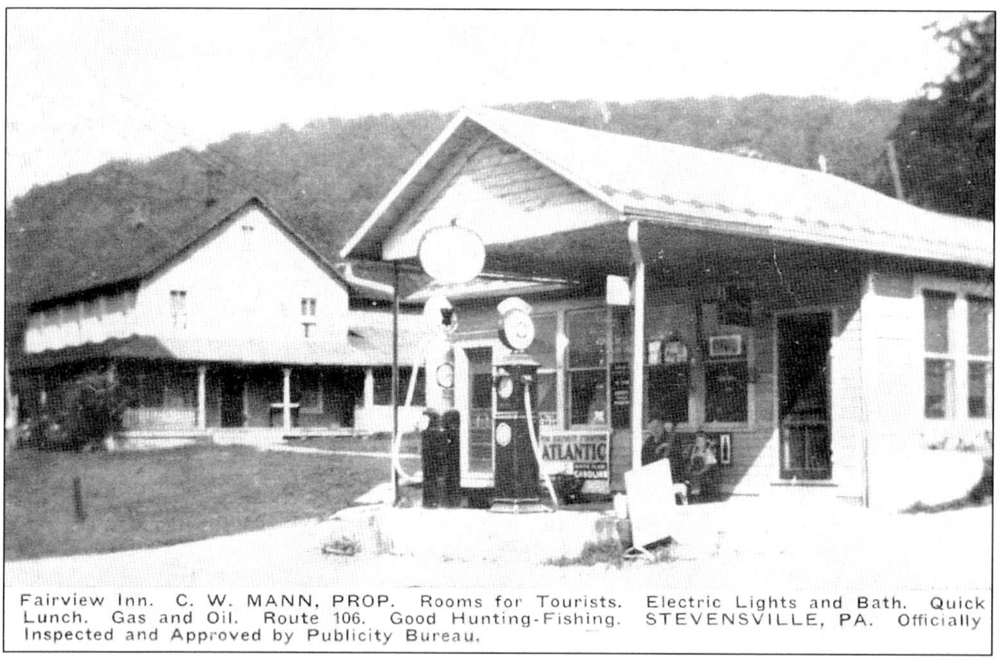

FAIRVIEW INN, STEVENSVILLE. Each town offered travelers accommodation, sometimes in the form of guesthouses or rooms to let, sometimes as inns or hotels. (Photo courtesy of the Tioga Point Museum.)

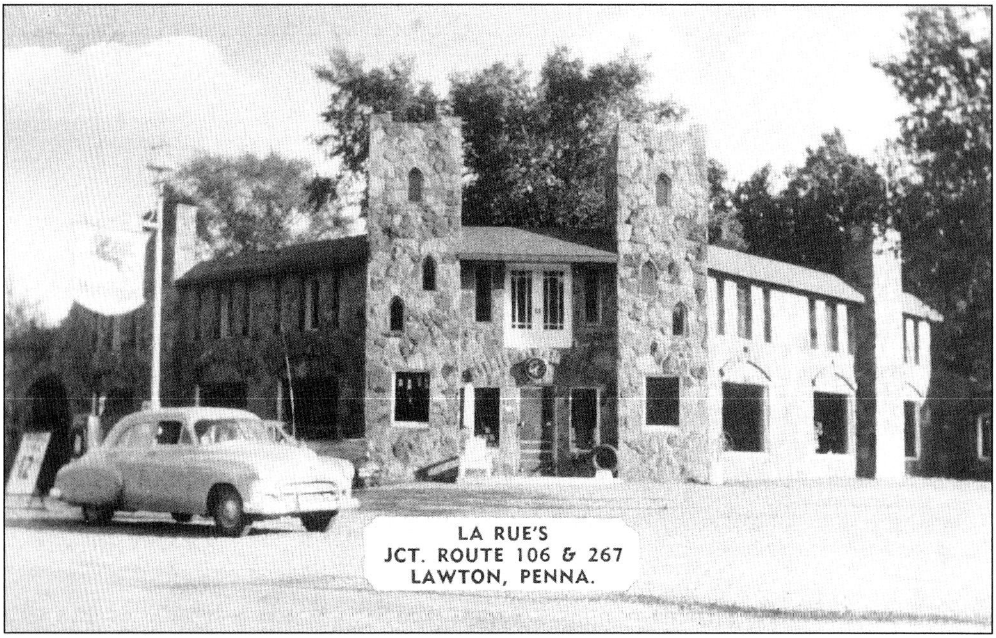

LA RUE'S, LAWTON. Roadside architecture was sometimes fanciful, as in the case of this unusual gas station and gift shop. The castle style was continued in a motel next door. This building is still in use. The car in the picture places the date in the late 1930s or early '40s. (Postcard courtesy of the Tioga Point Museum.)

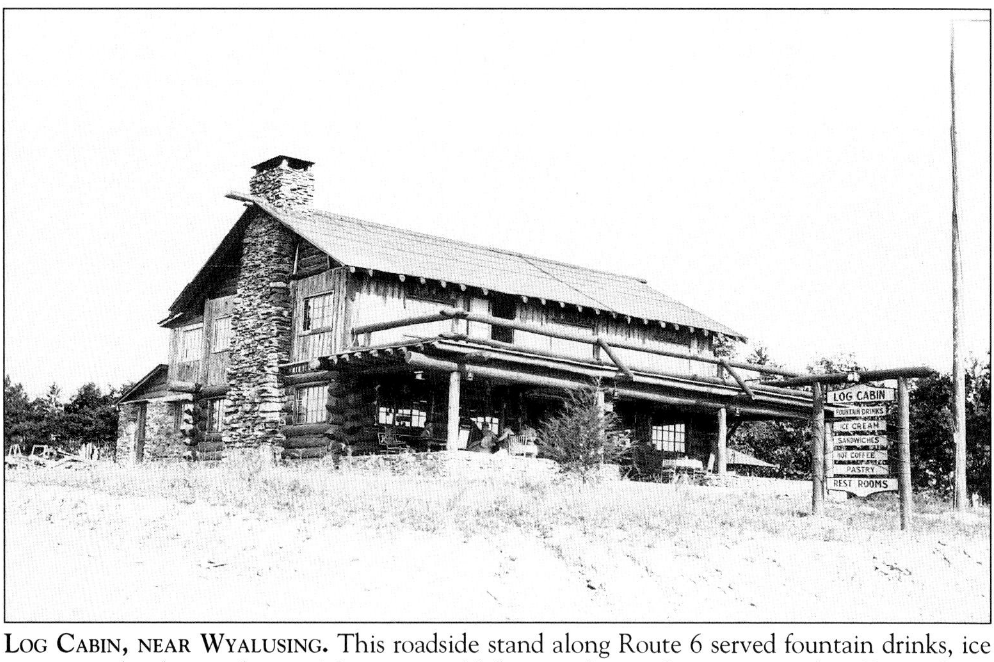

LOG CABIN, NEAR WYALUSING. This roadside stand along Route 6 served fountain drinks, ice cream, sandwiches, and more. Motorists could dine on the porch in nice weather. Route 6 was known as the Roosevelt Highway (after Teddy, not FDR). One of the projects to enlarge the nearby narrows required the demolition of the building. (Postcard courtesy of Norm Brauer.)

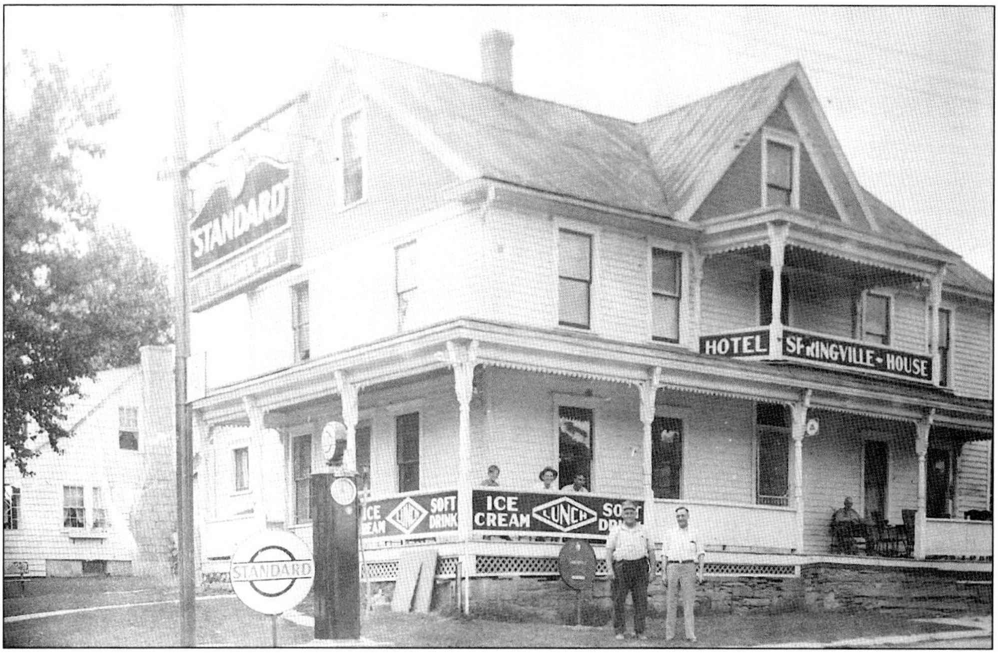

SPRINGVILLE HOUSE. A lone pump stands in front of this house turned hotel-gas station. (Postcard courtesy of the Susquehanna County Historical Society.)

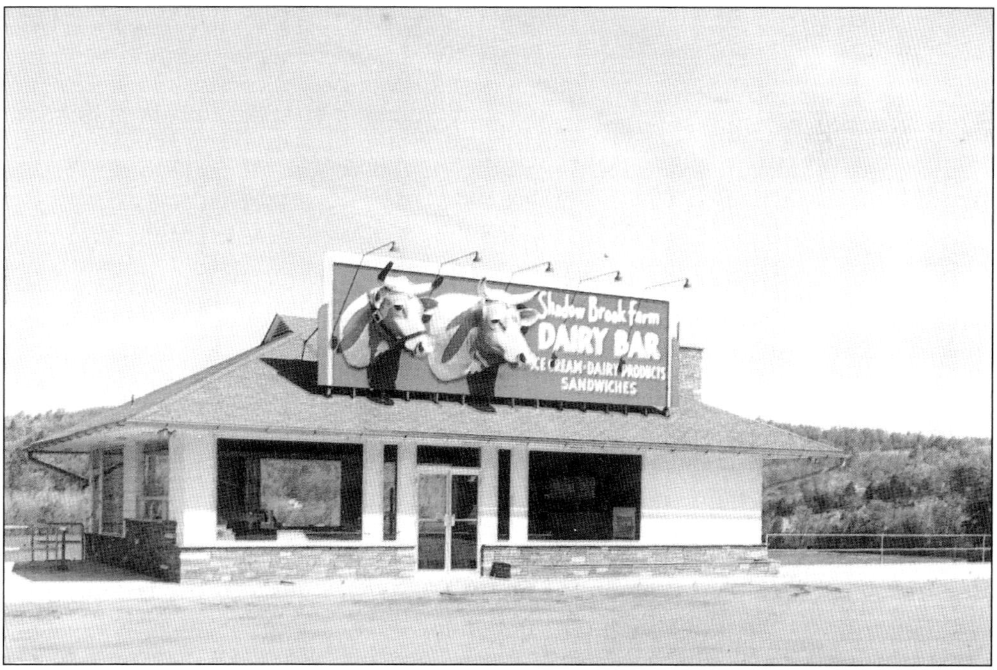

SHADOWBROOK, TUNKHANNOCK. A Route 6 landmark, Shadowbrook has grown considerably since this postcard was published. At that time it boasted a dairy bar, bowling lanes, an 18-hole regulation golf course, a miniature golf course, a swimming pool, and a cocktail lounge. (Postcard courtesy of Norm Brauer.)

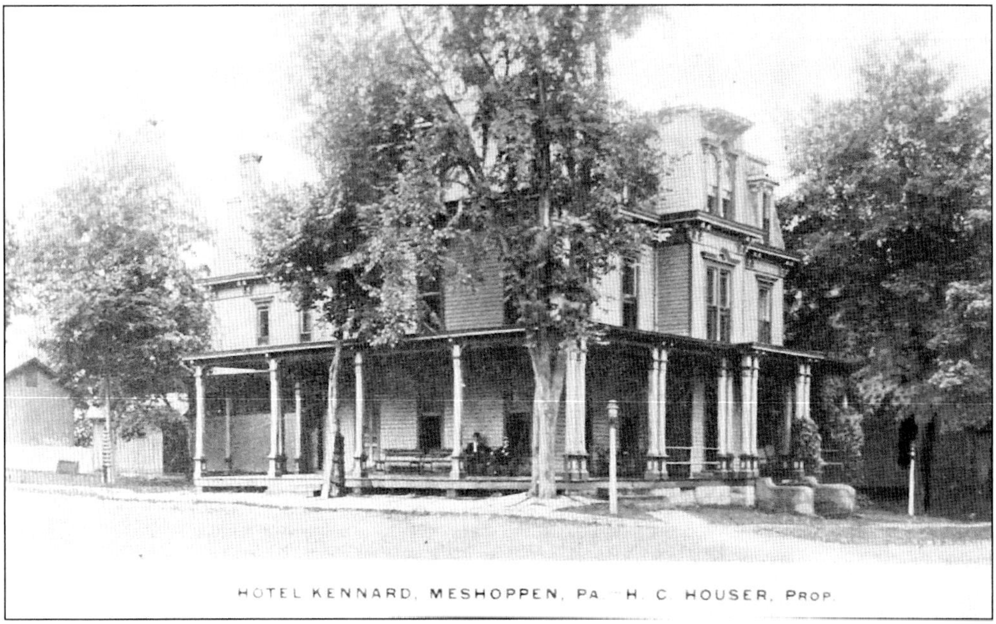

HOTEL KENNARD, MESHOPPEN. (Postcard courtesy of the Susquehanna County Historical Society.)

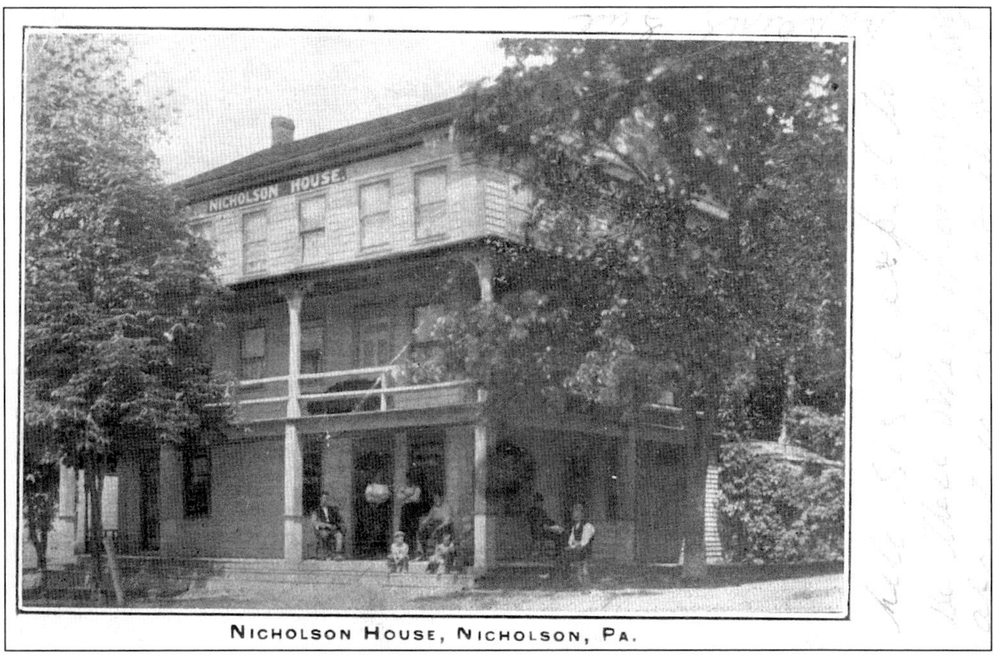

NICHOLSON HOUSE. (Postcard courtesy of the Tioga Point Museum.)

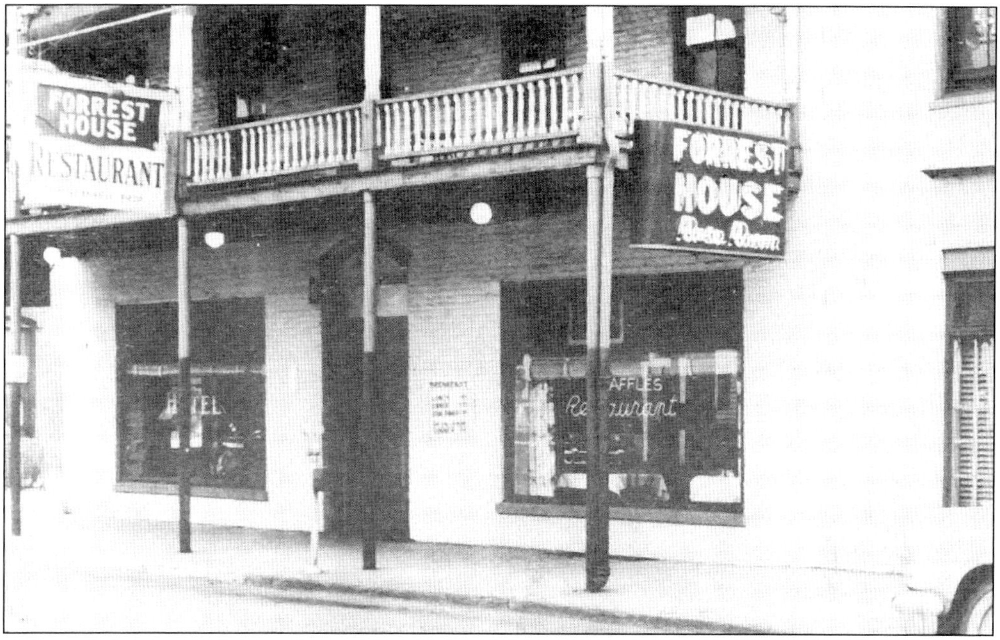

FORREST HOUSE, ATHENS. Michael Scannell ran this well-loved Main Street hotel in the early 20th century. The building was torn down after it was severely damaged in the 1972 flood. (Postcard courtesy of the Tioga Point Museum.)

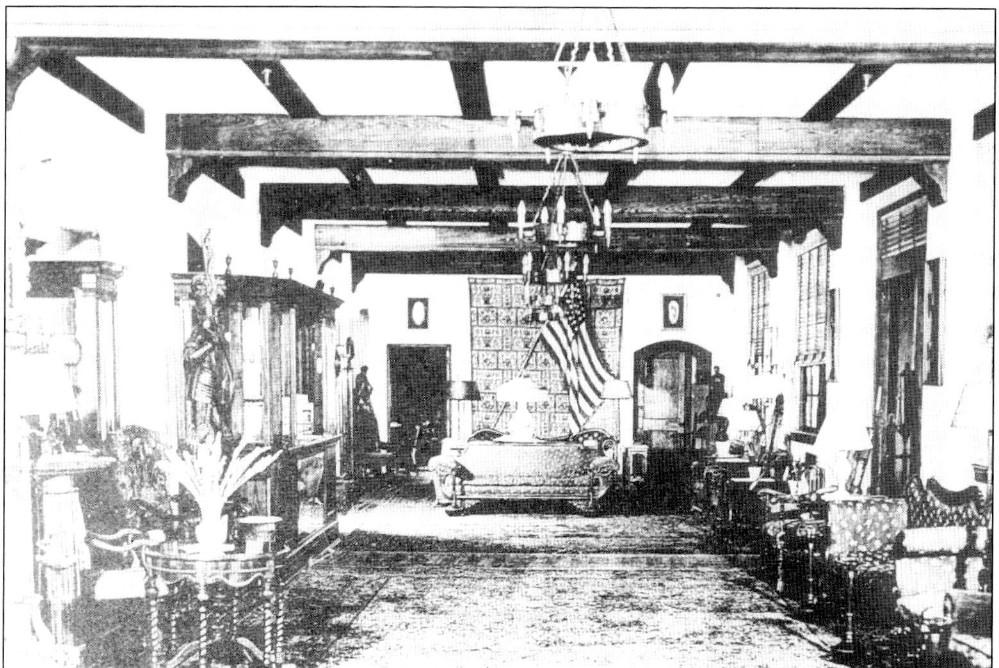

INTERIOR OF THE MONTROSE INN. The timbers in the sitting room echo the Tudor-style exterior of this inn. The building still stands, but it is now a bank. (Postcard courtesy of the Tioga Point Museum.)

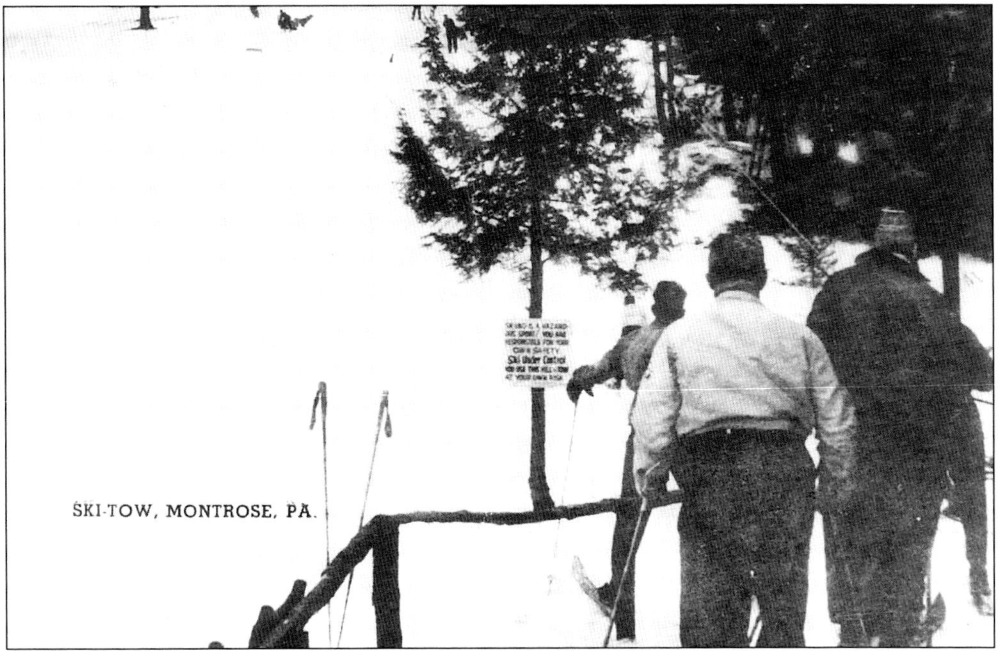

Ski Tow, Montrose. Cross-country skiing is more common than downhill in the Endless Mountains but, as this card shows, there were ski sites in the area, most quite small. An exception is Elk Mountain in Susquehanna County, a large skiing facility that is still in operation. Other winter sports traditionally enjoyed are sledding, tobogganing, and ice skating. (Postcard courtesy of the Susquehanna County Historical Society.)

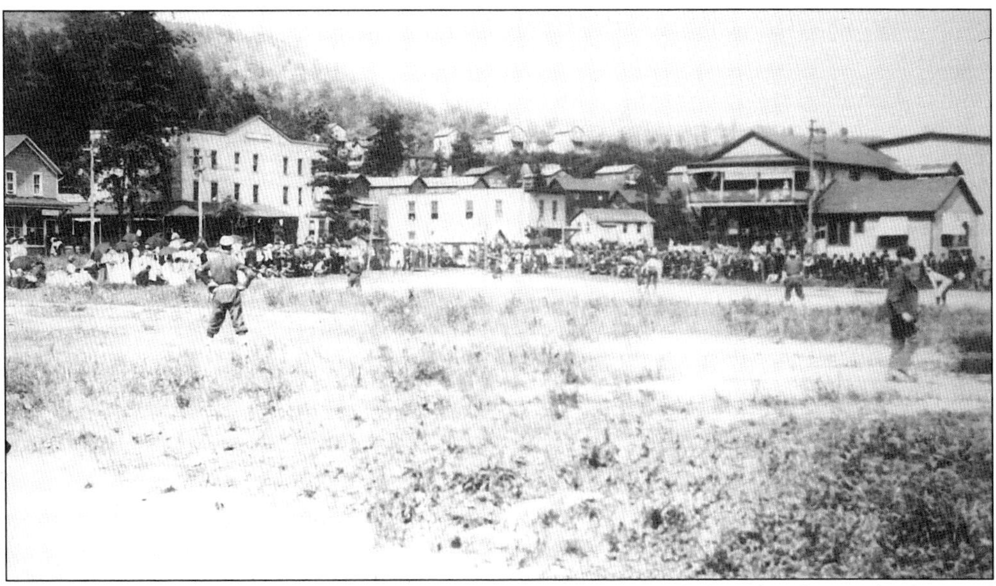

Baseball at Laquin. The people of Laquin loved baseball, and their local team had a good reputation in Bradford County. Some team members (not necessarily shown on this card) were Herb Henry, Carl Beers (Lefty), Carl Beers (Righty), Syd Barclay, Fred Dale, and Stub Smith. (Photo courtesy of the Bradford County Historical Society.)

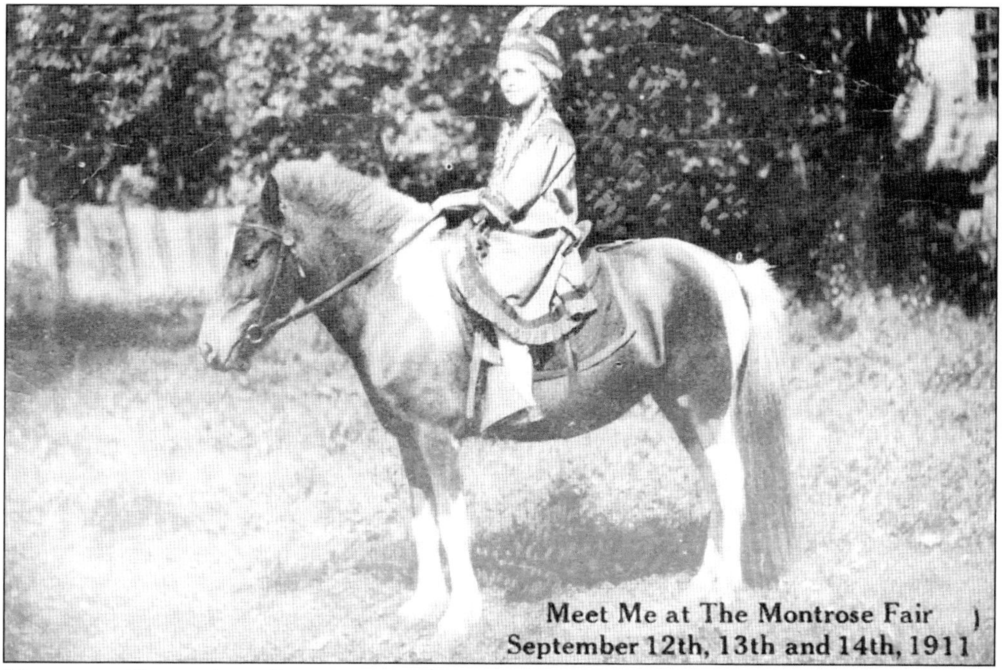

MONTROSE FAIR, 1911. Fairs were, and continue to be, popular in the communities of the Endless Mountains. Besides attending to the serious business of exchanging farm products and livestock, the people who came to the fair were able to socialize and enjoy many exciting activities and tasty foods. (Postcard courtesy of the Susquehanna County Historical Society.)

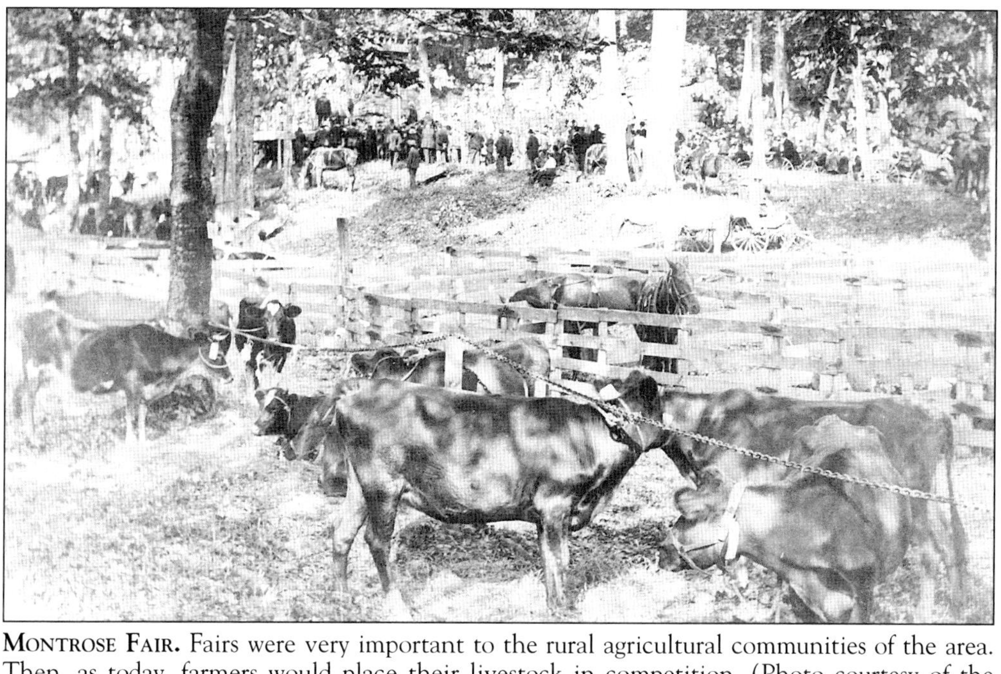

MONTROSE FAIR. Fairs were very important to the rural agricultural communities of the area. Then, as today, farmers would place their livestock in competition. (Photo courtesy of the Susquehanna County Historical Society.)

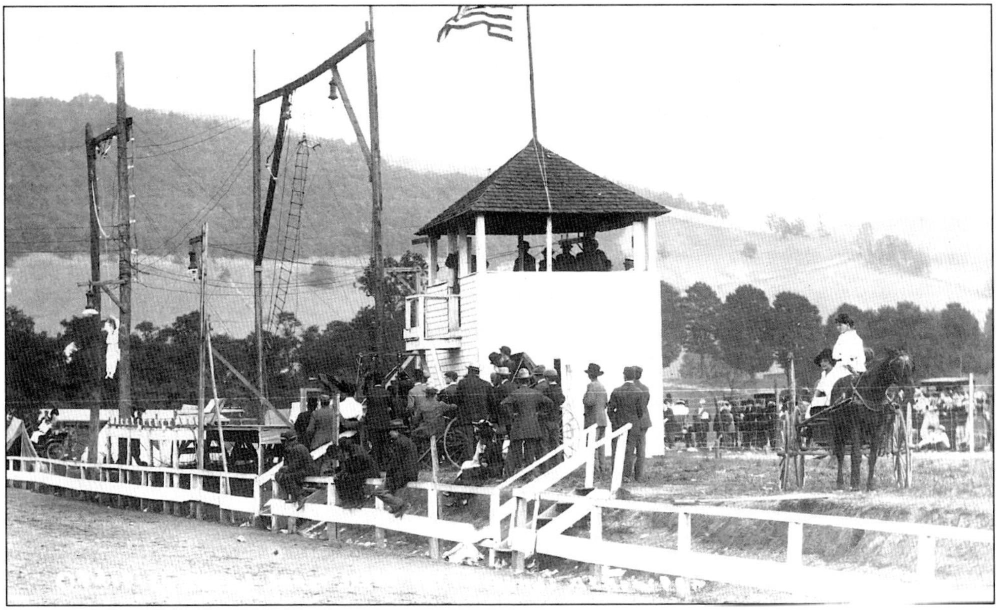

Official Stand, Interstate Fair Grounds, Athens. There were rides, horse racing and horse pulling contests, and other entertainments to lure visitors to this fair in East Athens. Automobiles were new and were considered attractions at the fairs; in the second decade of the century airplane shows became popular. The apparatus on the left in the card was used for acrobat shows. (Postcard courtesy of the Tioga Point Museum.)

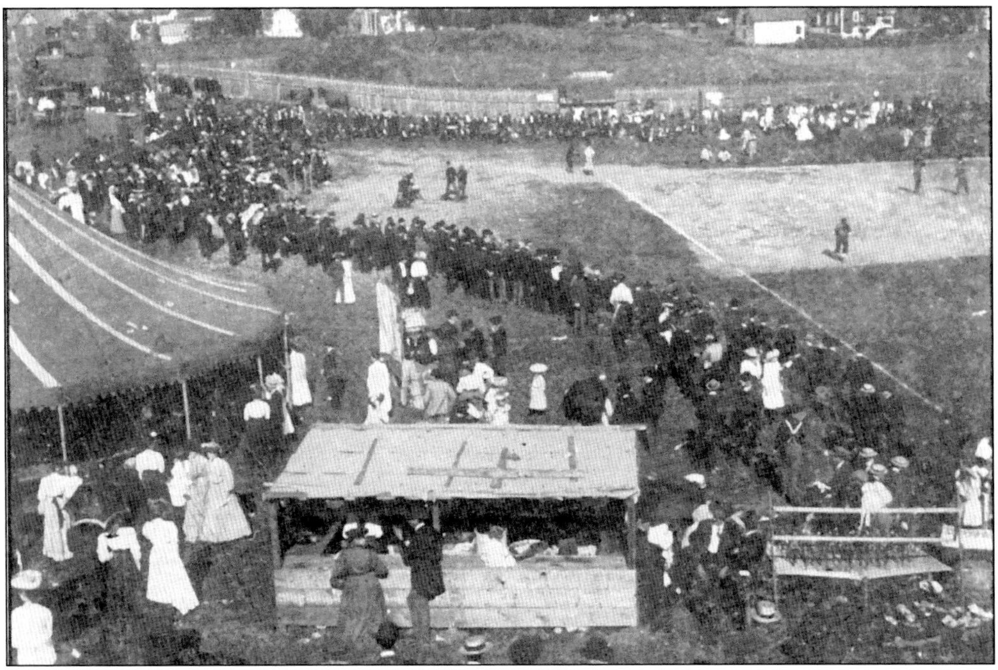

Wyalusing Fair. This fair has been held since 1903. The card is not dated or mailed, but judging from the clothing of the fair-goers, it is from one of the first Wyalusing fairs. There is a baseball game going on, and the crowds indicate much interest in the sport. (Postcard courtesy of Norm Brauer.)

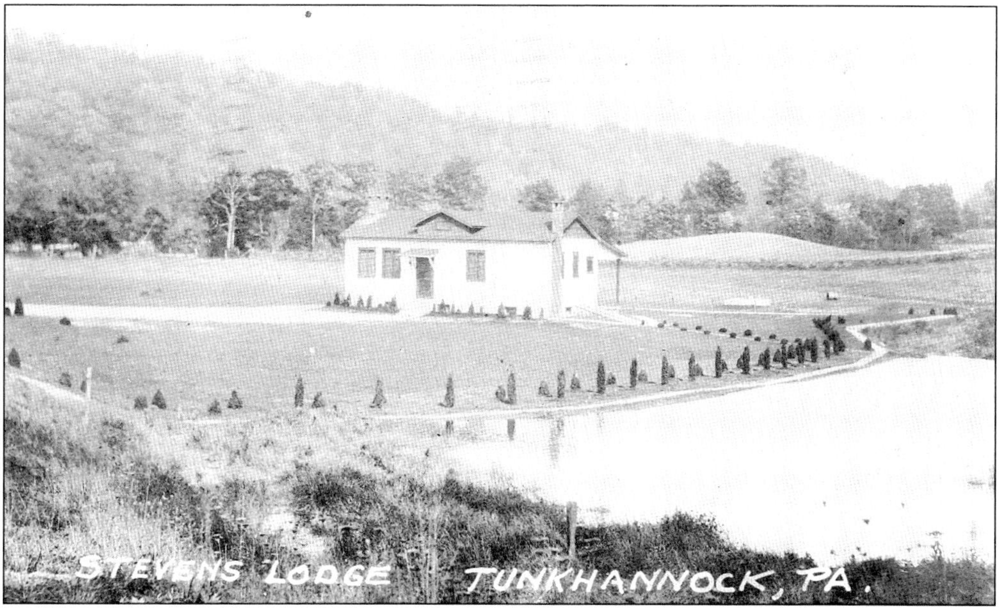

STEVENS LODGE, TUNKHANNOCK, 1932. The back of this card announces a trapshooting meet here at Stevens Lodge. The meet ran from 10 a.m. to 9 p.m., and participants were invited to "Stay during the evening and shoot with flood lights." Prizes were "Cash and Poultry, etc." (Postcard courtesy of the Tioga Point Museum.)

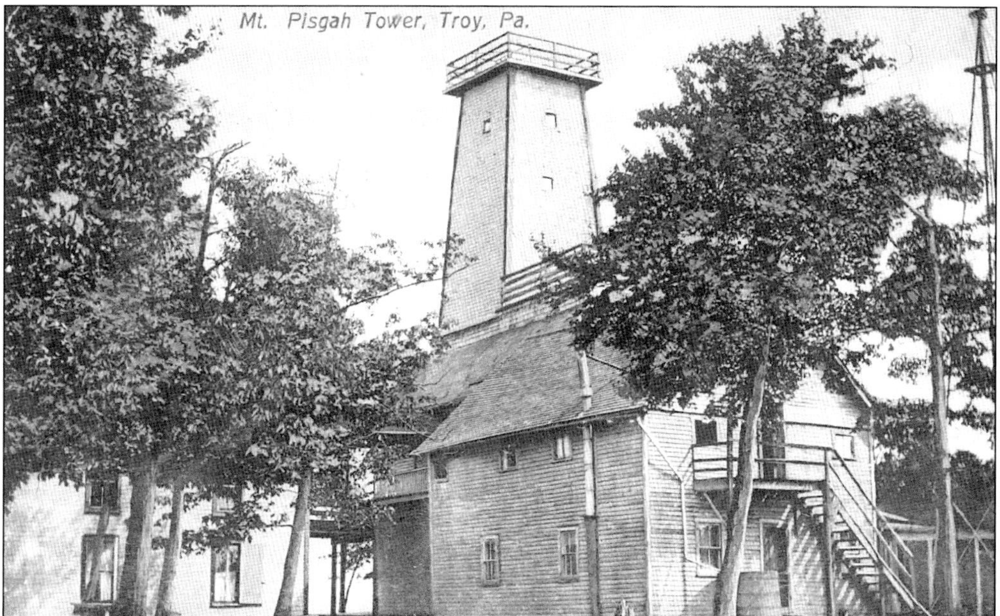

MOUNT PISGAH TOWER, TROY, 1911. This observation tower was built before 1880 by photographer Moses Gustin of Troy, whose wife, Mary Galusha, was descended from the farmer who cleared the land in 1831. The land belongs to the Mount Pisgah State Park. In 1977, Steven Foster Lake was created by damming Mill Creek. Boating, fishing, swimming, skiing, and sledding can be done at the park. (Postcard courtesy of the Tioga Point Museum.)

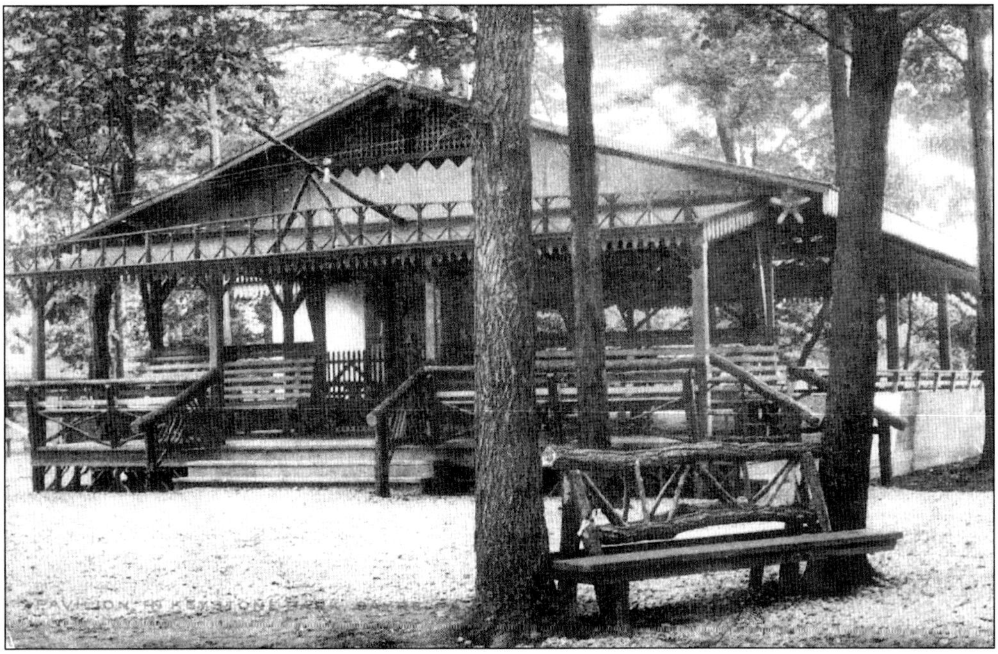

PAVILION AT KEYSTONE PARK, SAYRE. The Waverly, Sayre and Athens Traction Company owned this amusement park and used it to increase ridership on its line. The architecture was rustic and the structures were nestled among the trees. The opening day 1909 promotional flier calls the park "A cool, delightful spot to bring the mothers and babies." (Postcard courtesy of the Tioga Point Museum.)

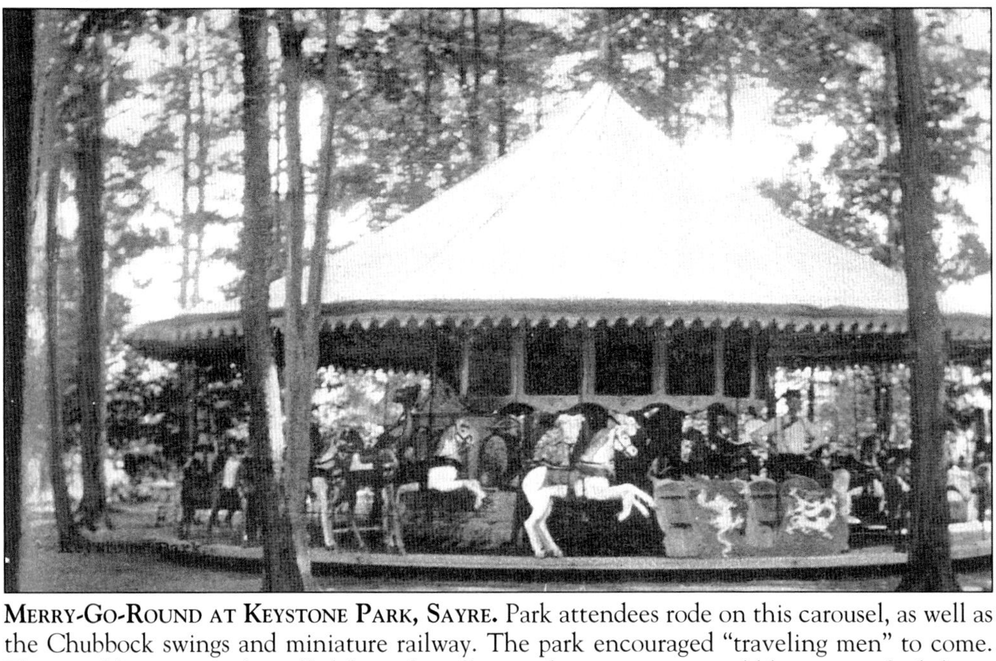

MERRY-GO-ROUND AT KEYSTONE PARK, SAYRE. Park attendees rode on this carousel, as well as the Chubbock swings and miniature railway. The park encouraged "traveling men" to come. They could arrange to be called from the office, and a messenger would be sent to find them, "thus enabling one to attend to business and enjoy their leisure moments at the park." (Postcard courtesy of the Tioga Point Museum.)

Four

A Tour of the Endless Mountains

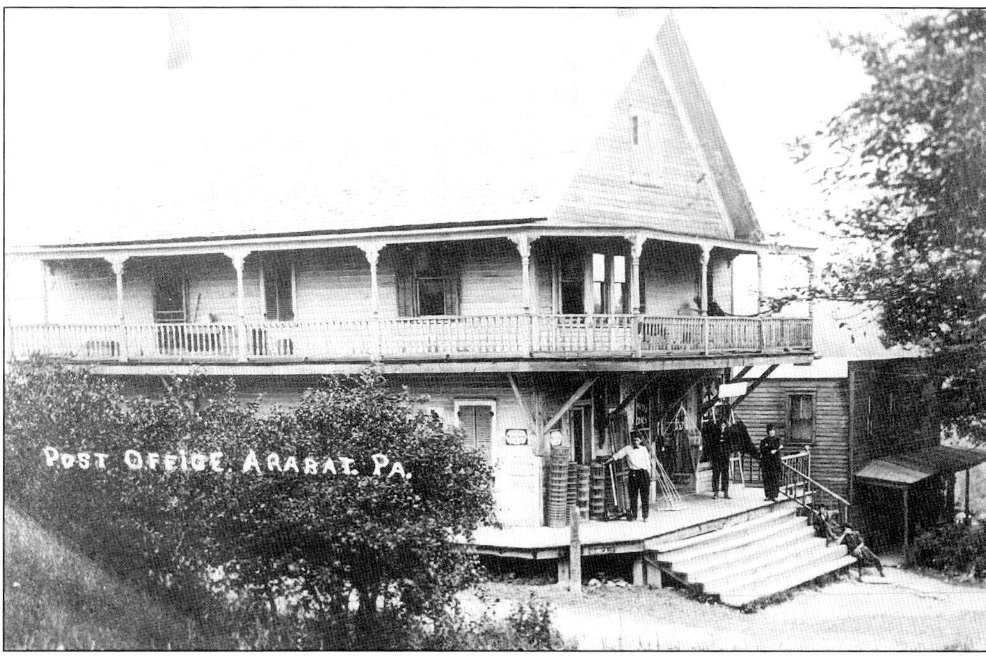

Ararat. Post offices were often located in stores, and sometimes even in the home of the postmaster. The history of the Ararat Post Office is typical of many towns. Stocker, the author of the *Centennial History of Susquehanna County*, describes it as follows: "Ararat post-office was established June 14, 1852, with Albert Bushnell as first postmaster. He had his office at his house, on the corner near the church. His successors have been Gurry O. Baldwin, 1856; James E. Payne, who had the post-office at his store, and was succeeded by his wife, Mary C. Payne, in 1872. Josiah Barton was appointed in 1886, and moved the office to N.A. Walker's store at the railroad station." (Postcard courtesy of the Susquehanna County Historical Society.)

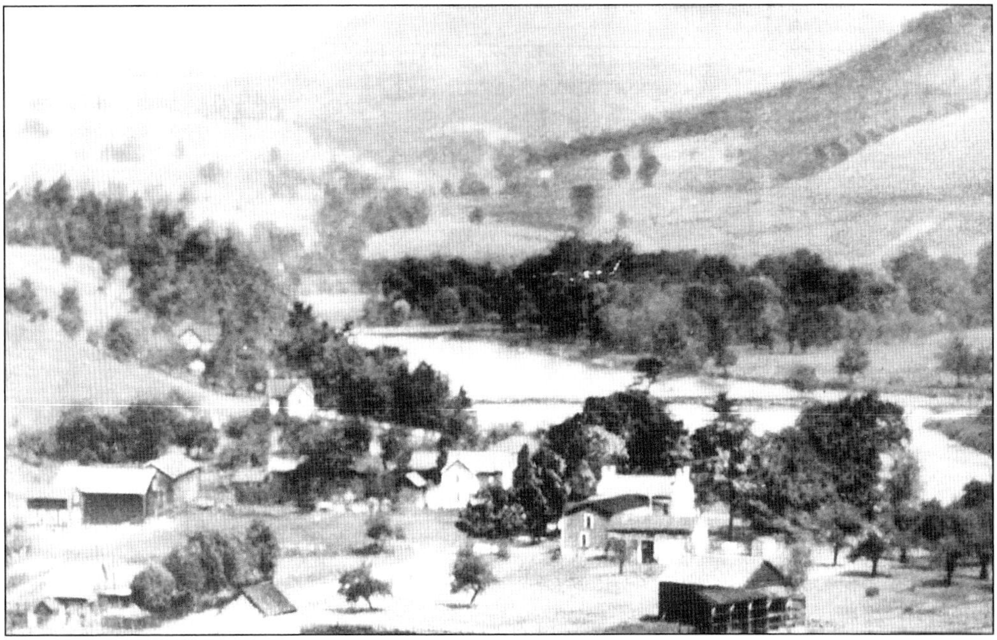

SUSQUEHANNA. This is a bird's-eye view of the Beach Sanitarium in Susquehanna along the Great Bend of the river, in the northern part of the county. Susquehanna benefited from the introduction of the railroad line to Binghamton in 1848. Not only did many new businesses and hotels start up, but the New York, Erie & Western Railroad established its shops there. (Postcard courtesy of the Susquehanna County Historical Society.)

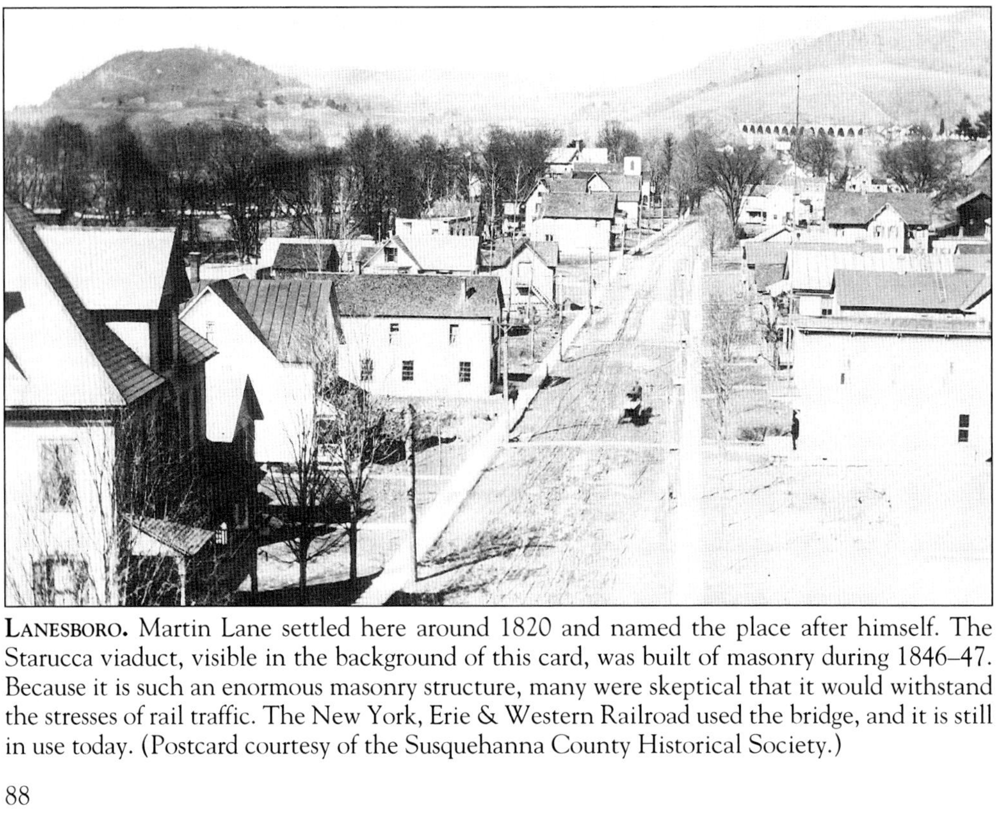

LANESBORO. Martin Lane settled here around 1820 and named the place after himself. The Starucca viaduct, visible in the background of this card, was built of masonry during 1846–47. Because it is such an enormous masonry structure, many were skeptical that it would withstand the stresses of rail traffic. The New York, Erie & Western Railroad used the bridge, and it is still in use today. (Postcard courtesy of the Susquehanna County Historical Society.)

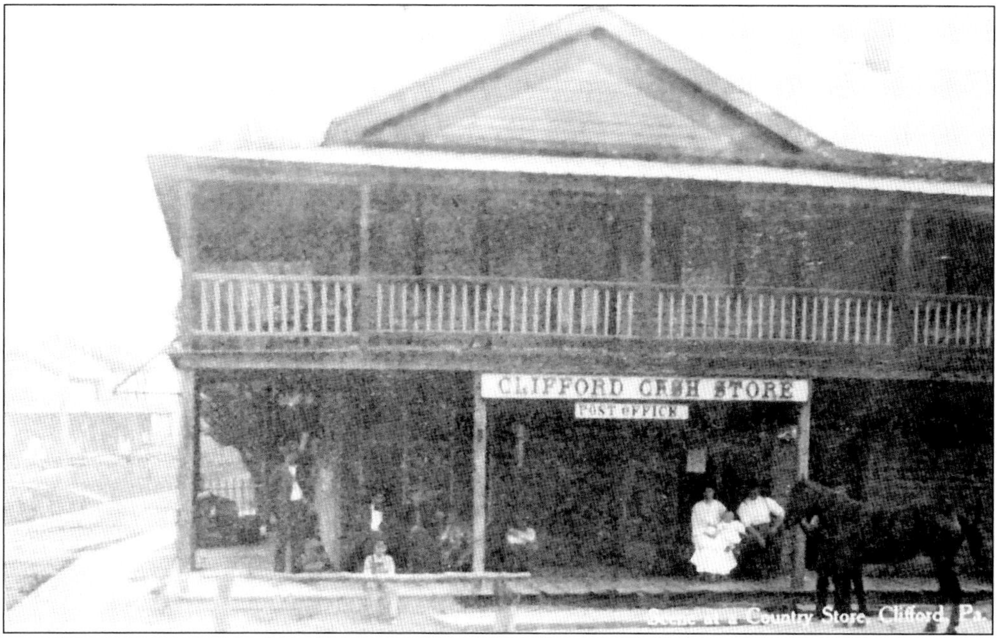

CLIFFORD. The town was founded in 1847 when the Clifford and Carbondale Turnpike was built. This building could be the one described in the 1887 county history as having been put up by the Patrons of Husbandry, with the upper hall used for their meetings and the ground floor a store and post office run by J.M. Robinson. (Postcard courtesy of the Susquehanna County Historical Society.)

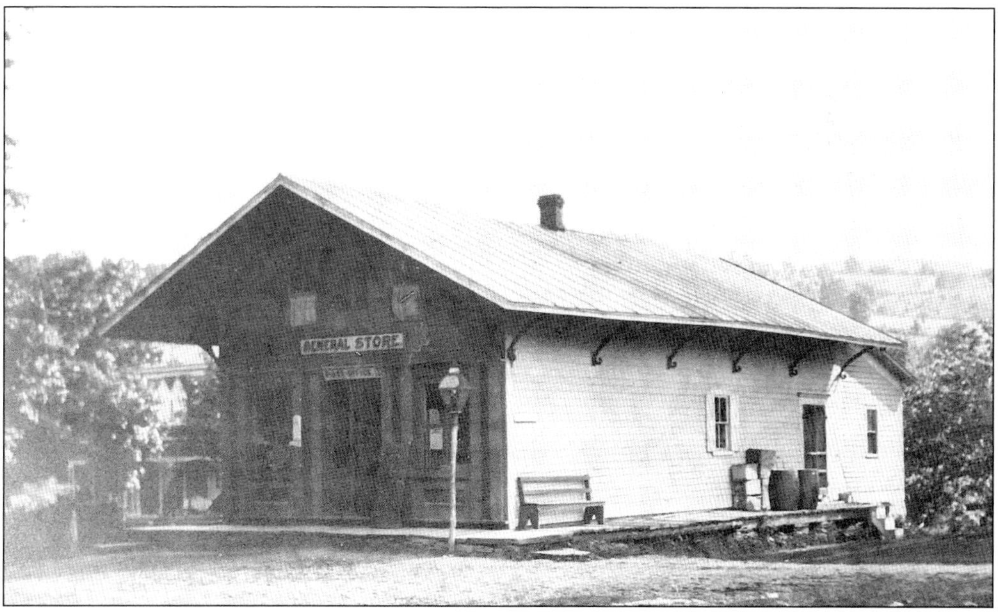

ROYAL. When it came time to establish a post office, and a name for the community had to be chosen, resident Walker Felts ignored tradition. He did not choose a name like "Feltsville" or "Feltston," instead he suggested "Royal," after the Royal Baking Powder Company, which, by the way, is not located here. The president of the company was pleased, and he sent a flag for the post office. (Postcard courtesy of the Susquehanna County Historical Society.)

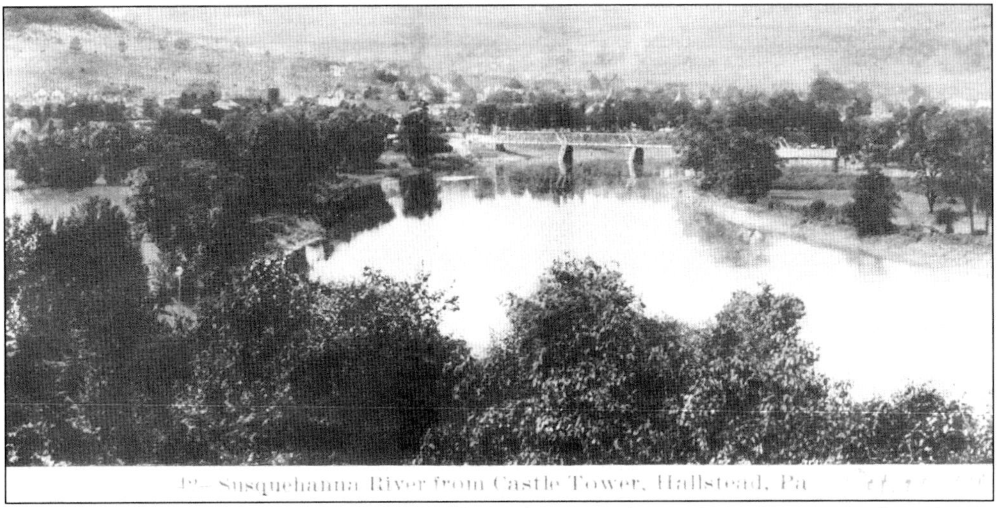

HALLSTEAD, 1907. Formerly Great Bend Village, the town changed its name to avoid confusion with Great Bend, immediately to its north on the other side of the river. In 1887 the borough contained "one hotel, a number of stores, a graded school and two churches—Presbyterian and Baptist." In 1909 its handsome residences, paved streets, shade trees and other attractions made it one of the "towns beautiful" in northeastern Pennsylvania. (Postcard courtesy of the Susquehanna Historical Society.)

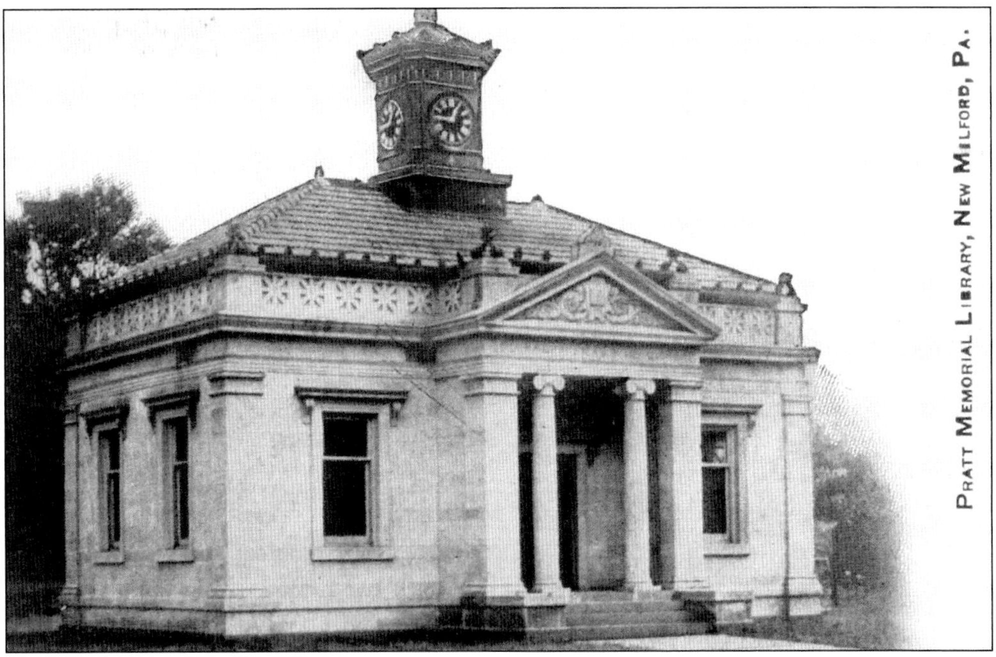

NEW MILFORD. This town, "neatly laid out, and surrounded by all the natural advantages that an enterprising place could desire," was only sparsely settled in the early part of the 19th century, but in 1851 the Delaware, Lackawanna & Western Railroad established a depot there, and by 1859 it was large enough to incorporate into a borough. The lovely Pratt Memorial Library stands on Route 11, right downtown. The Old Mill Village Museum, just south of town, offers a look at the way people lived in the past. (Postcard courtesy of Norm Brauer.)

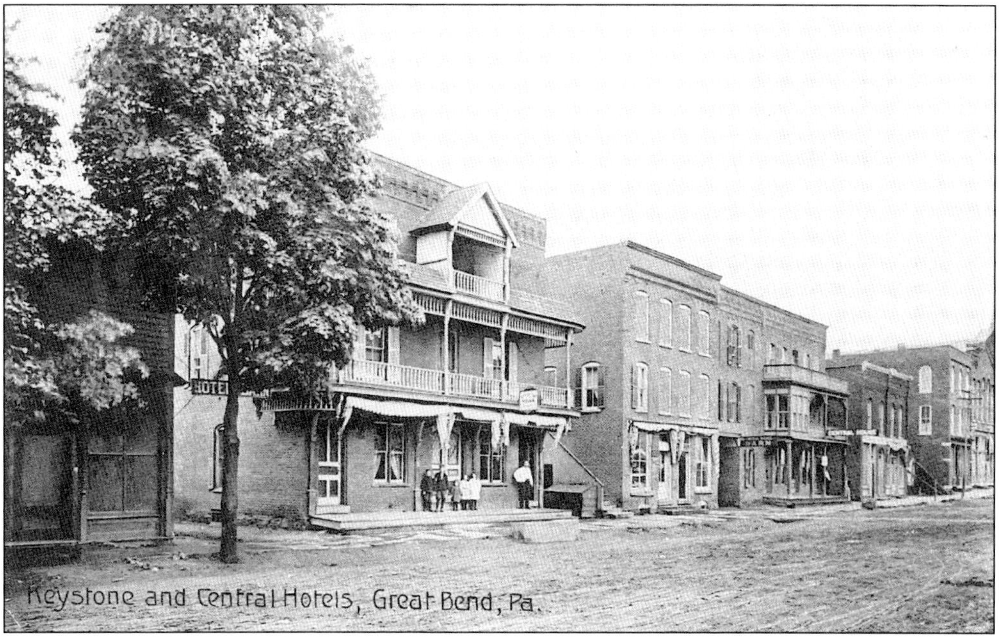

GREAT BEND, 1915. An early history brags that Great Bend had better sidewalks than any other town in the county. The sidewalks in this card lead to the Keystone and Central Hotels. The Central Hotel was built in 1876 after a fire destroyed the building that had stood in its spot. It slept about 40. The Keystone had the "Best table of any hotel in this region. Steam heat. Electric call bells." In 1909 the room rate was $1.50 per day. (Postcard courtesy of Betty Smith.)

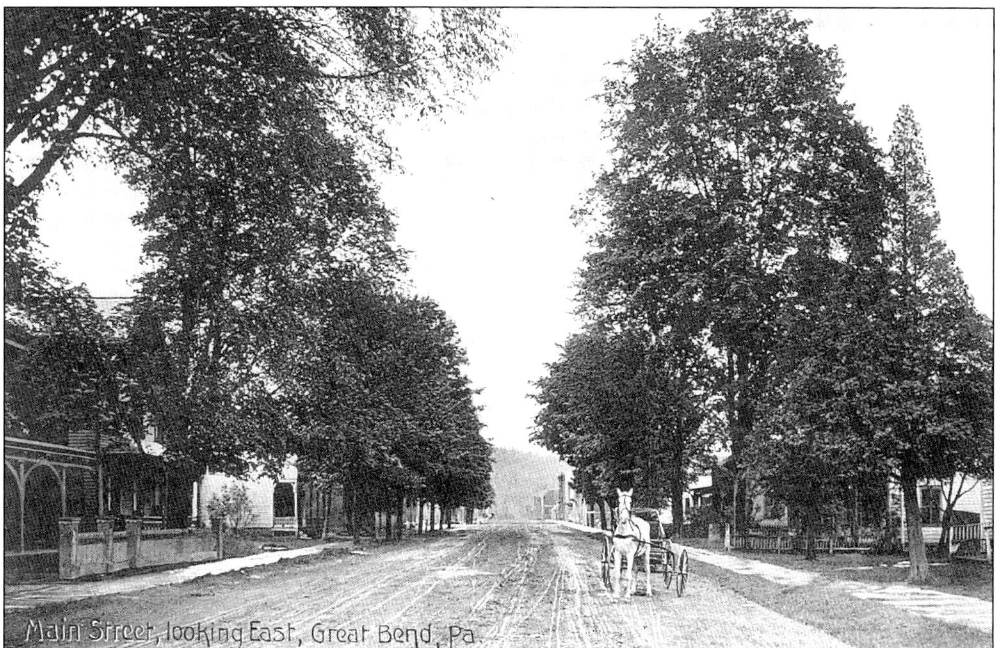

GREAT BEND, 1915. The borough was incorporated in 1861. This view shows Main Street looking east through a residential neighborhood. The downtown can be seen in the distance. Very nice sidewalks are visible to the left and right. (Postcard courtesy of Betty Smith.)

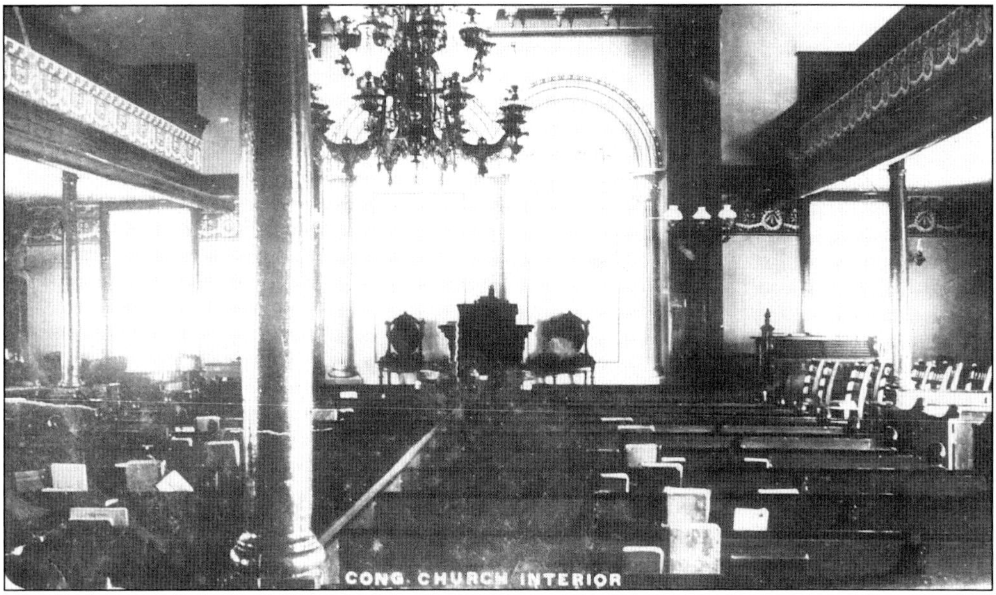

HARFORD. The 1887 Susquehanna County History credits the small village of Harford with the best agricultural fair in Susquehanna County; the same fair is still held every year. Another fine feature of the town is its Congregational church, constructed after 1922 and augmented over the years. Its architecture reflects the New England origins of its founders. (Postcard courtesy of the Susquehanna County Historical Society.)

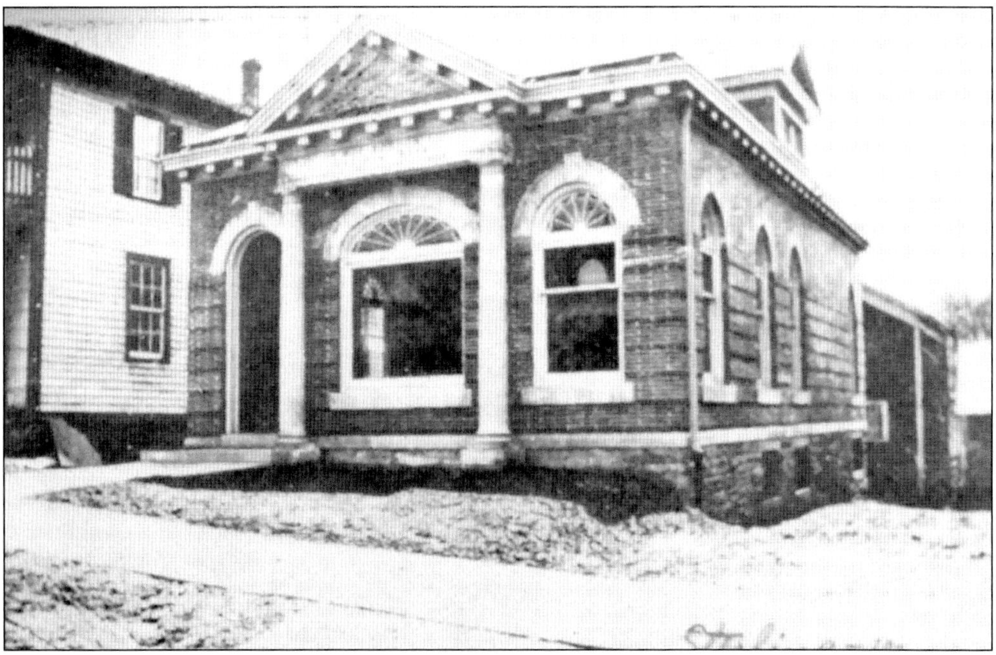

HOP BOTTOM, 1912. Named for the hops that grew along the creek, this town owed its early existence to the Delaware, Lackawanna & Western Railroad. The Hop Bottom National Bank card shown here has the bank's report of condition on the reverse. It shows an $8,752.43 increase in deposits between December 1911 and February 1912. "Our steady growth tells its own story." (Postcard courtesy of the Susquehanna County Historical Society.)

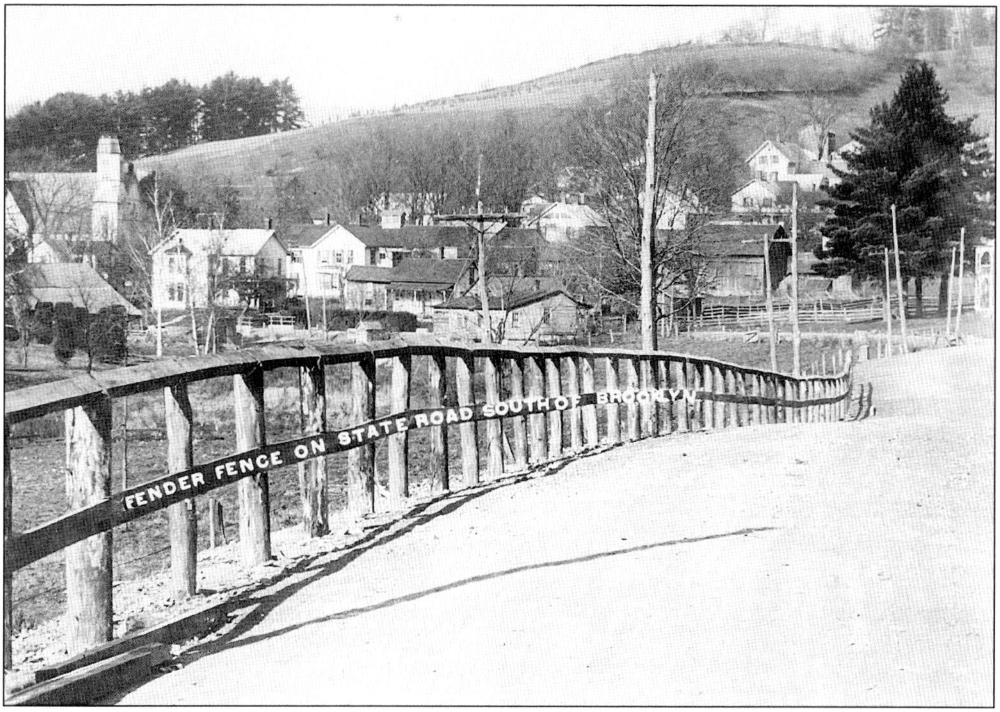

BROOKLYN. This road takes you into Brooklyn. George Catlin, the famous painter of Native Americans, taught school here as a young man. He left town to study law in accordance with his father's wishes, and he was admitted to the Susquehanna County Bar, but he soon abandoned that profession in favor of art. (Postcard courtesy of the Susquehanna County Historical Society.)

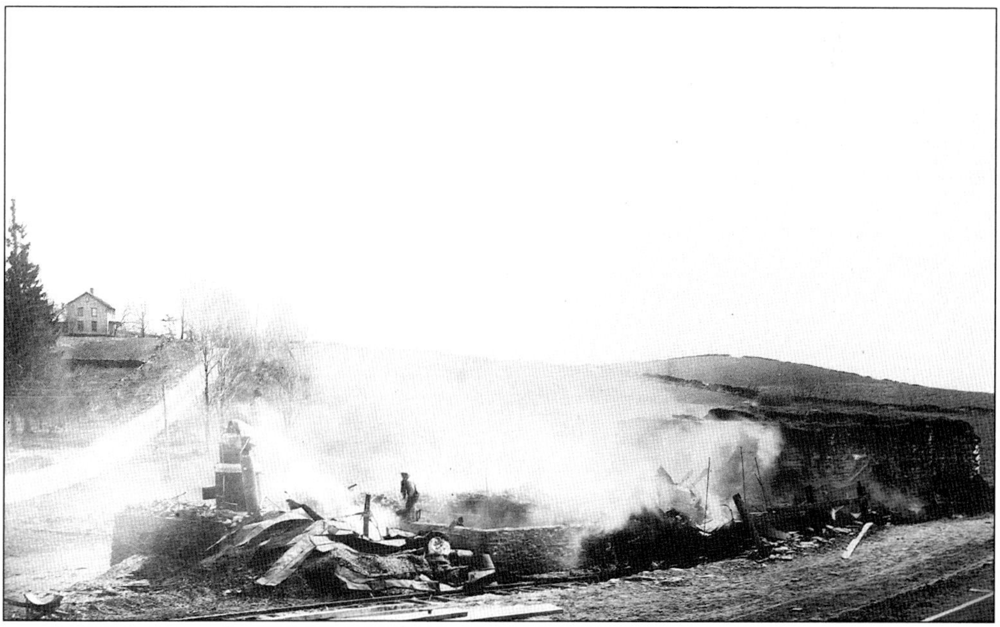

TIFFANY CORNERS. There are quite a few cards that show this fire, which completely destroyed a creamery. (Postcard courtesy of the Susquehanna County Historical Society.)

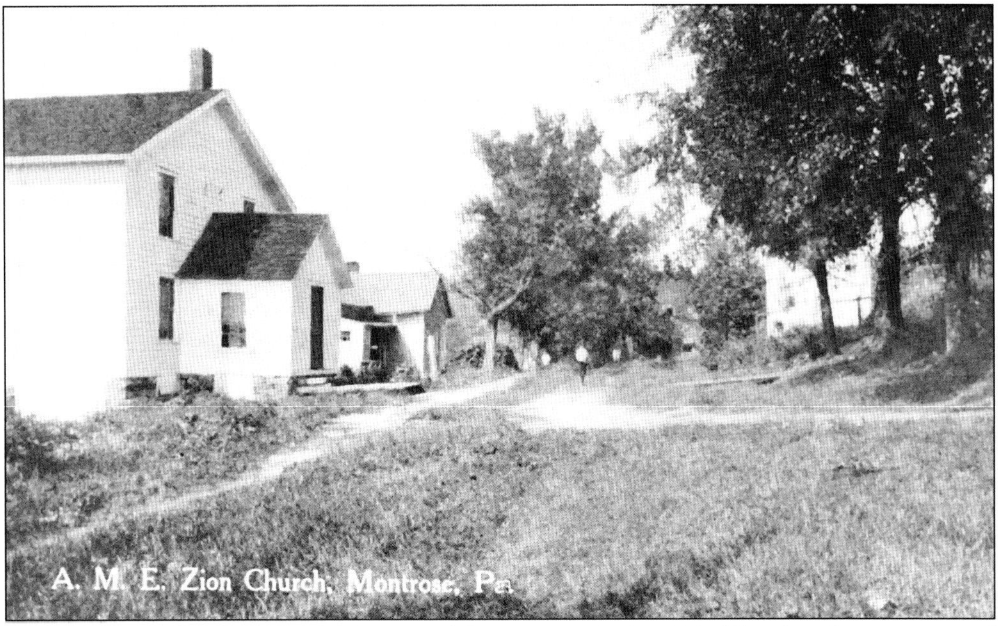

AFRICAN METHODIST EPISCOPAL CHURCH, MONTROSE, 1906–1907. The church was organized about 1844, and the building was constructed in 1869 on Berry Street. The trustees of the church were former slaves who escaped from Maryland through the Underground Railroad. The Endless Mountains had many Underground Railroad "stations," homes of people who defied the law to help escaped slaves gain their freedom. (Postcard courtesy of the Susquehanna County Historical Society.)

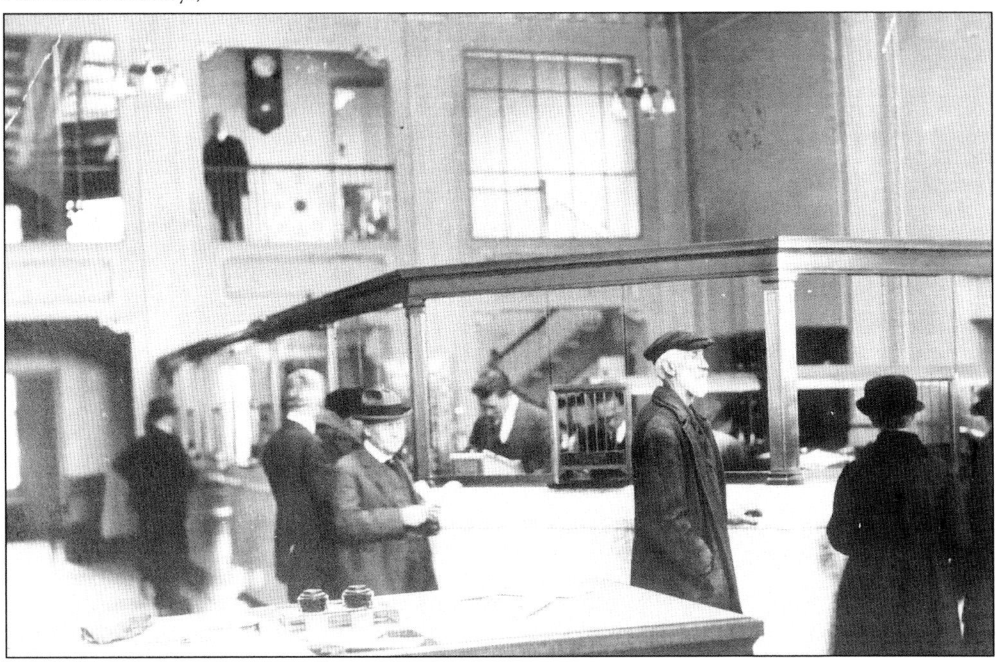

MONTROSE. This card gives a rare interior view of the First & Farmers Bank. It is unusual not only because it was taken inside, but also because it is a "candid." (Postcard courtesy of the Susquehanna County Historical Society.)

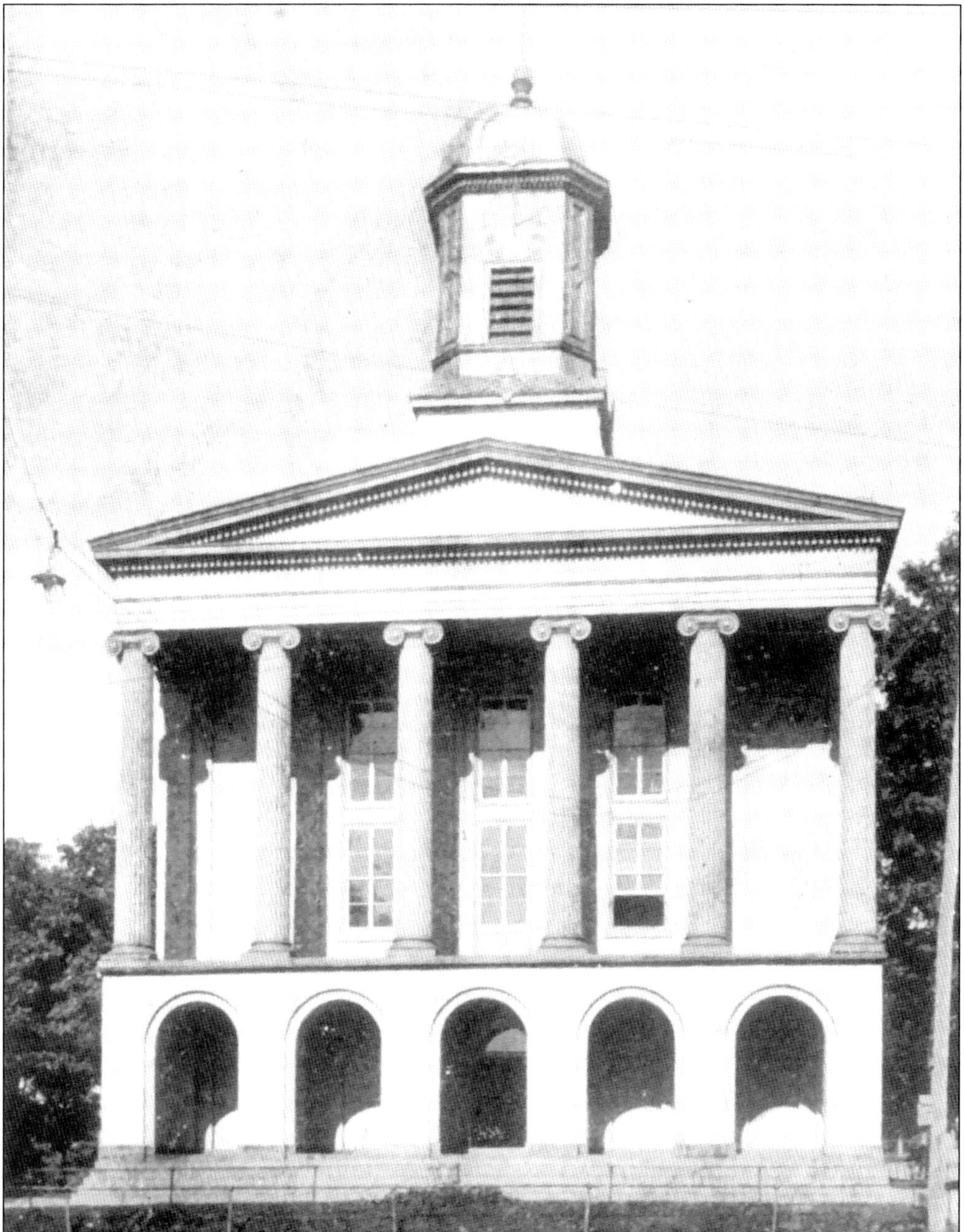

MONTROSE, 1906. Montrose is the Susquehanna County Seat. Isaac Chapman and Isaac Post laid out the village plot in 1812, and the borough was incorporated in 1824. The county courthouse stands at the top of Public Avenue and alongside Monument Square. It was constructed in 1854–55 and has witnessed much of the history of the town and the county. The citizens of Montrose purchased the town clock in the cupola of the courthouse. The civic buildings are not the only architectural pleasures that Montrose has to offer. Many of its 19th-century houses remain to reward a walking or driving excursion. (Postcard courtesy of the Susquehanna County Historical Society.)

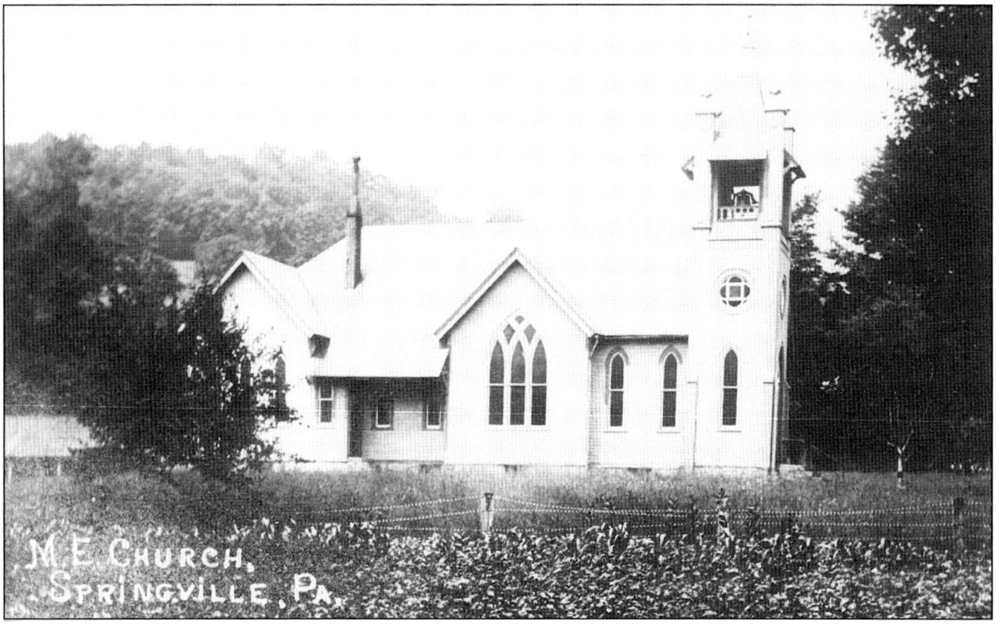

SPRINGVILLE. The town of Springville is located on the old Wilkes-Barre Turnpike, now Route 29. This church was built in 1892, and it still stands. The town was a major shipping point in the area during the era of the railroad, with a carload of butter leaving weekly and, in the fall, large shipments of apples from the orchards of the township. (Postcard courtesy of the Susquehanna County Historical Society.)

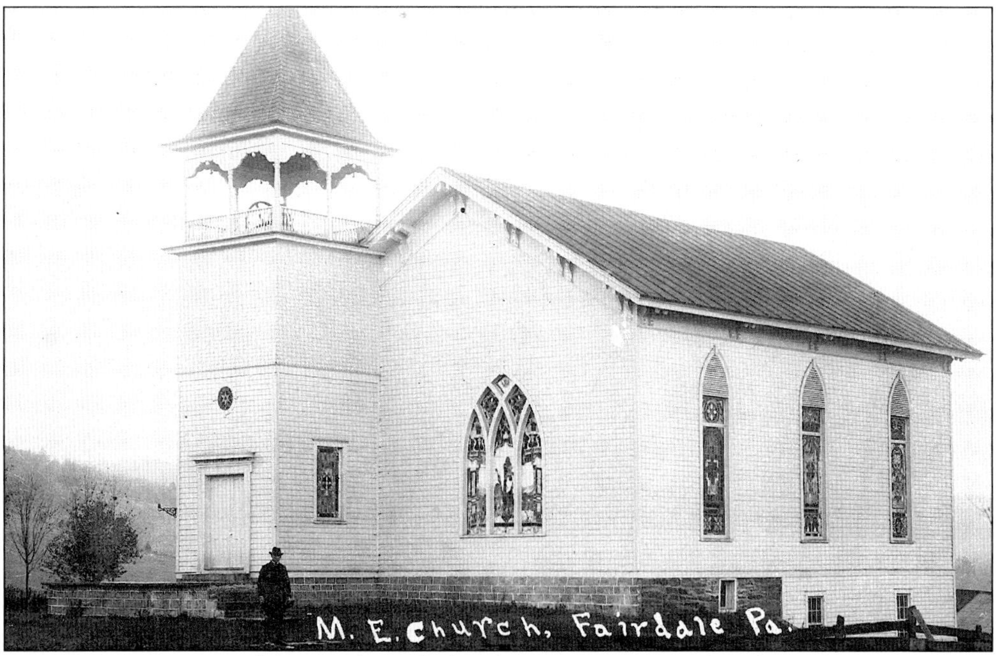

FAIRDALE. In 1880 Fairdale was the only hamlet in Jessup Township (now there is another, Snows Mill), with a population of 75. They were served by this Methodist Episcopal church, which was erected in 1868. Fairdale is on the Wyalusing Creek, west of Montrose. (Postcard courtesy of Norm Brauer.)

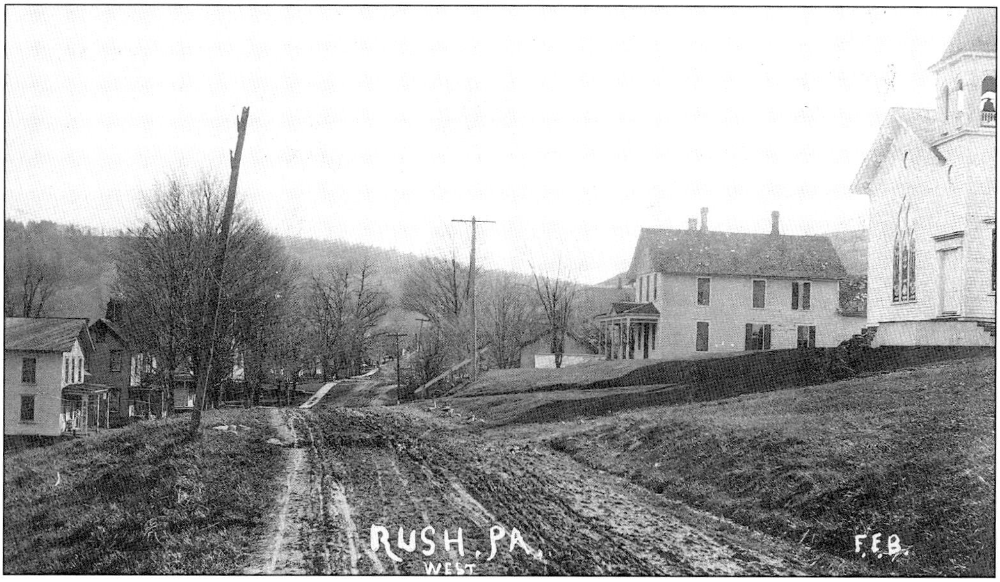

RUSH, 1909. The name "Rush" is sprinkled throughout this part of Susquehanna County, with Rushville, Rushboro, East Rush, and just plain Rush existing within a few miles of one another. There is also a Rush Four Corners that is not on current maps. Compare the church on the right-hand side of this postcard with the two previous pictures, and note the similar building styles. The summer home of Arctic explorer Sir Hubert Wilkins was located near Rush. (Postcard courtesy of Norm Brauer.)

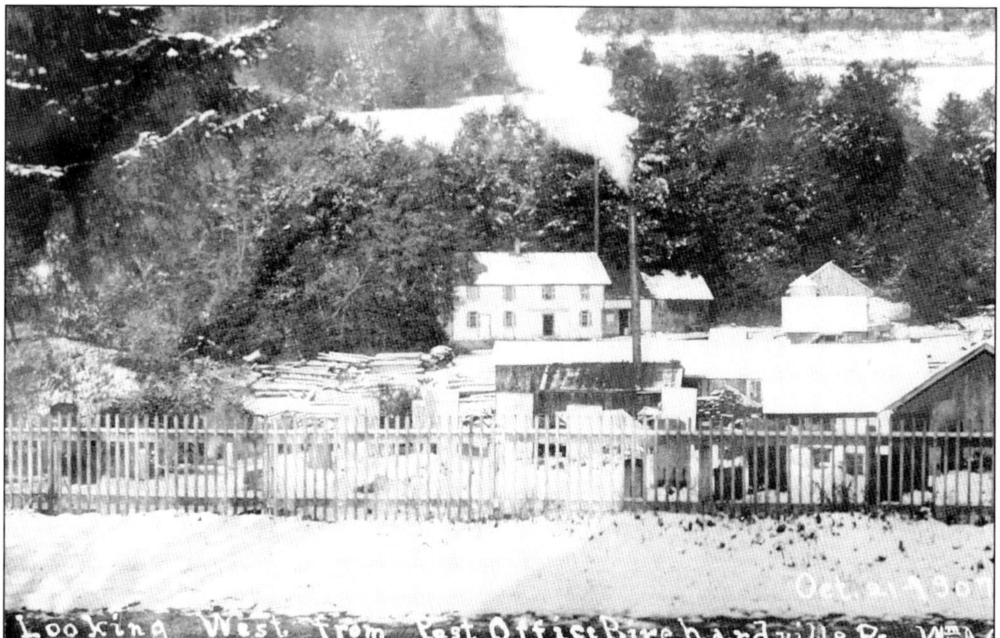

BIRCHARDVILLE, 1907. Settled by the Birchard family in the early 1800s, this town contains the D. Fred Birchard and Sons Store and a preserved one-room schoolhouse. (Postcard courtesy of the Susquehanna County Historical Society.)

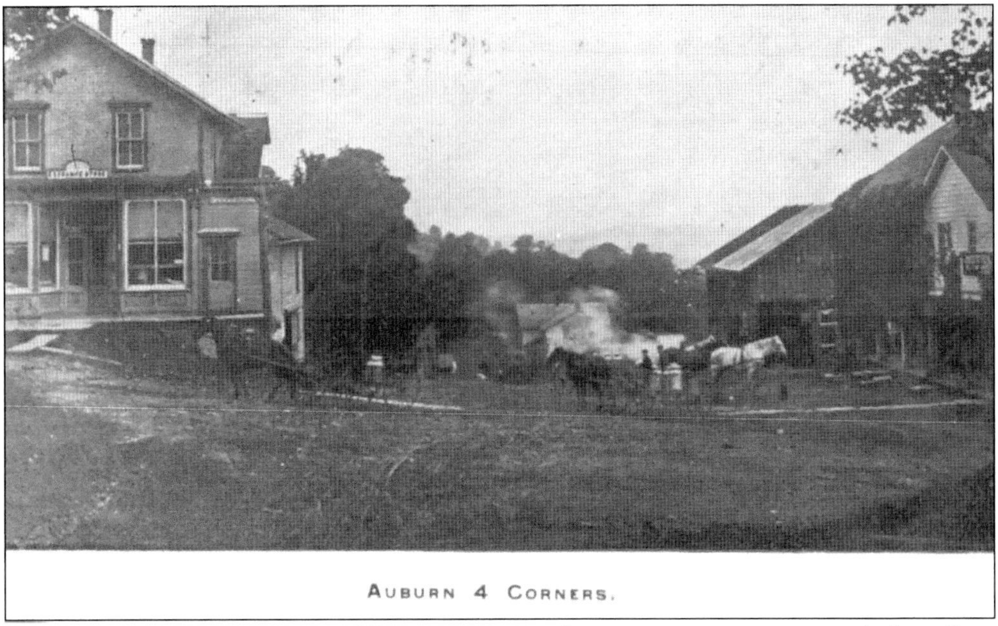

AUBURN FOUR CORNERS, 1909. F.F. Pepper managed a cooperative creamery in Auburn Four Corners, and it was one of the largest in the area, producing 1,500 pounds of print butter daily. "Strictly fancy-print and ready for sale in Philadelphia." A "print" is a pat of butter molded into a shape. (Postcard courtesy of Norm Brauer.)

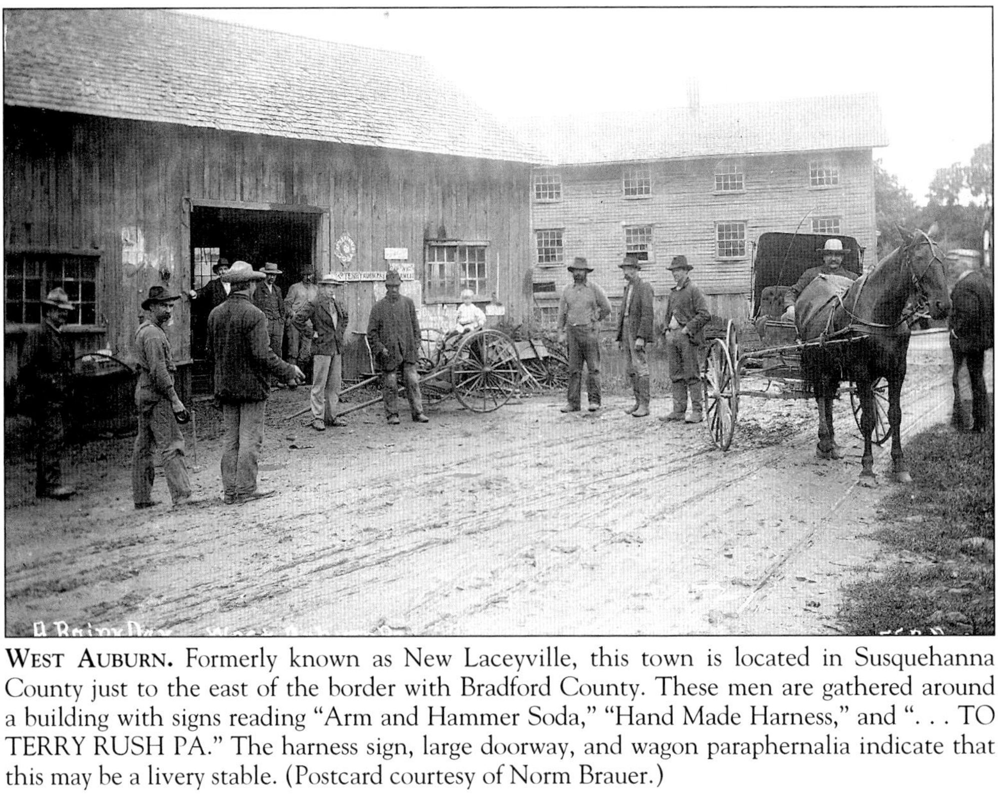

WEST AUBURN. Formerly known as New Laceyville, this town is located in Susquehanna County just to the east of the border with Bradford County. These men are gathered around a building with signs reading "Arm and Hammer Soda," "Hand Made Harness," and ". . . TO TERRY RUSH PA." The harness sign, large doorway, and wagon paraphernalia indicate that this may be a livery stable. (Postcard courtesy of Norm Brauer.)

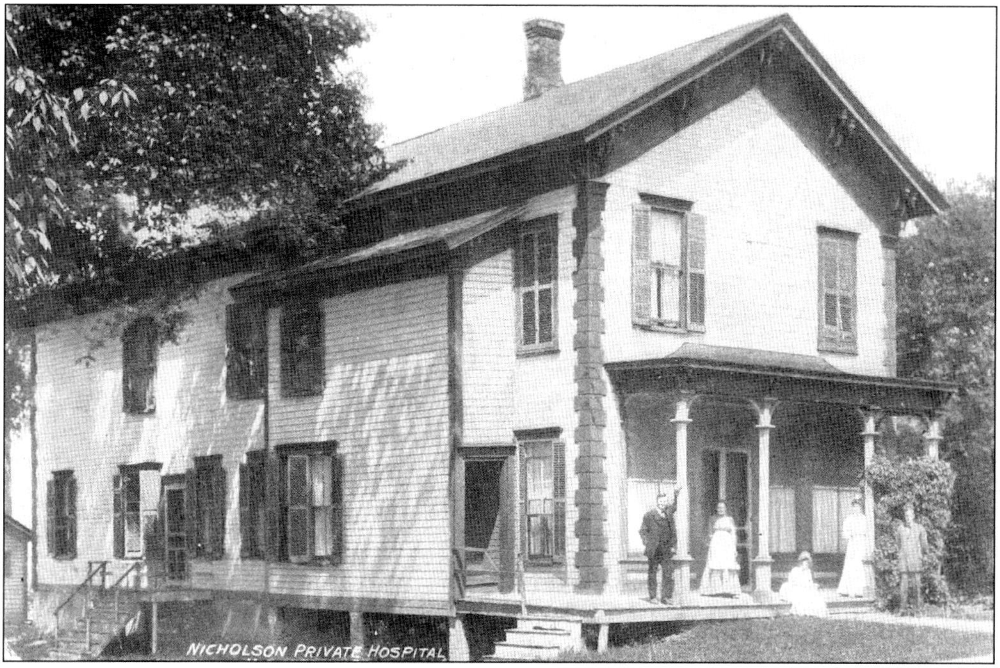

NICHOLSON, 1908. There is more than a fabulous bridge in Nicholson, Wyoming County. It is not clear whether the people on the porch of the Nicholson Private Hospital are staff or patients. (Postcard courtesy of the Tioga Point Museum.)

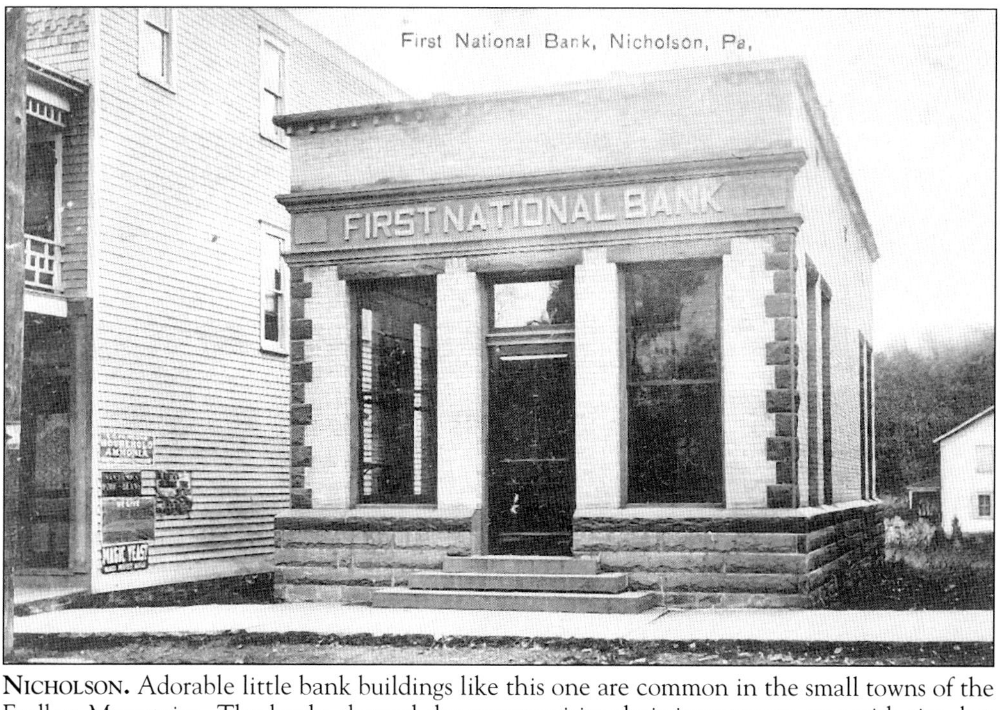

NICHOLSON. Adorable little bank buildings like this one are common in the small towns of the Endless Mountains. The banks showed the communities their importance, not with size, but with detail. (Postcard courtesy of the Tioga Point Museum.)

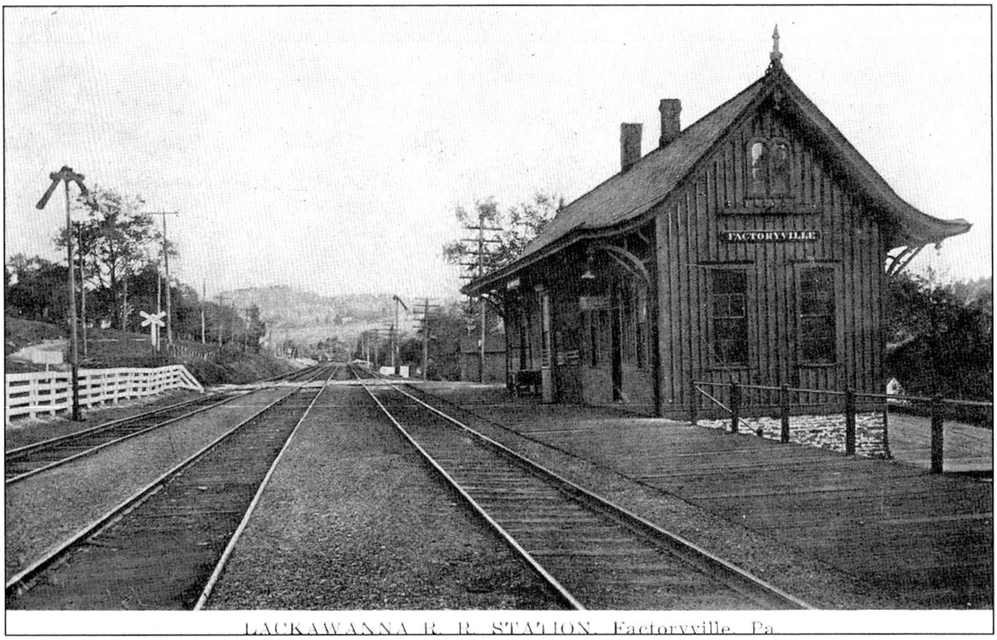

FACTORYVILLE. Railroads often built charming stations, and many of these remain, although they are no longer used in their original function. The Lackawanna Railroad station is typical of the fanciful styles often constructed. The name of this town comes from a cotton factory that once operated here. Factoryville is now the home of Keystone Community College. (Postcard courtesy of Norm Brauer.)

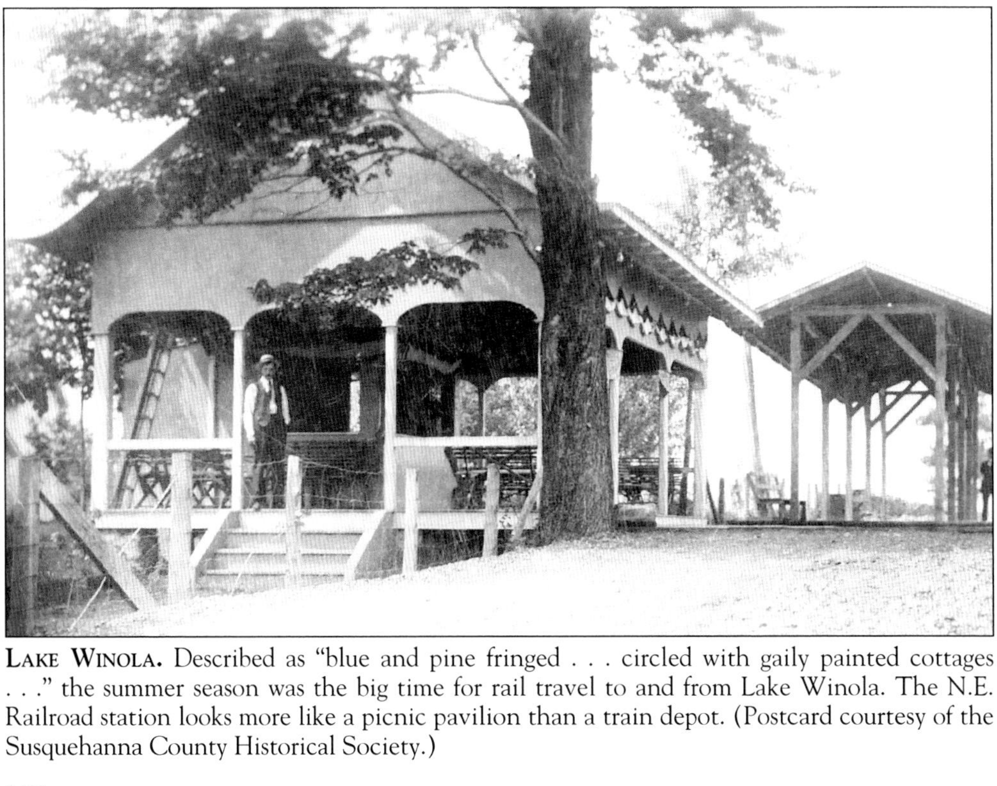

LAKE WINOLA. Described as "blue and pine fringed . . . circled with gaily painted cottages . . ." the summer season was the big time for rail travel to and from Lake Winola. The N.E. Railroad station looks more like a picnic pavilion than a train depot. (Postcard courtesy of the Susquehanna County Historical Society.)

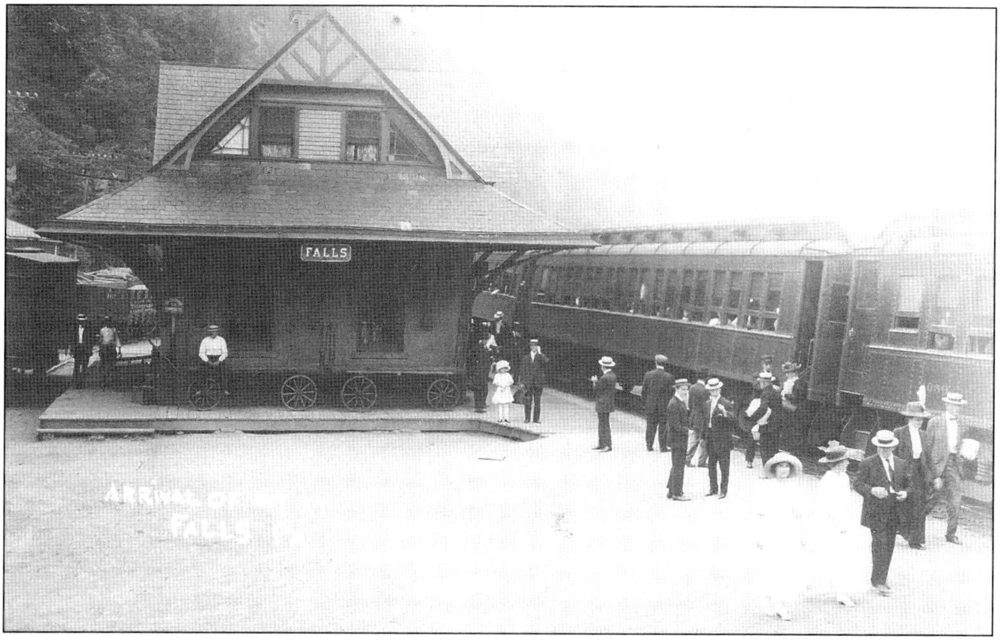

FALLS, 1912. The town is on both sides of the Susquehanna River in southeastern Wyoming County. A 1940 guidebook states that "Although chiefly dependent on fruit raising, the inhabitants derive some income from a summer bungalow community." (Postcard courtesy of Norm Brauer.)

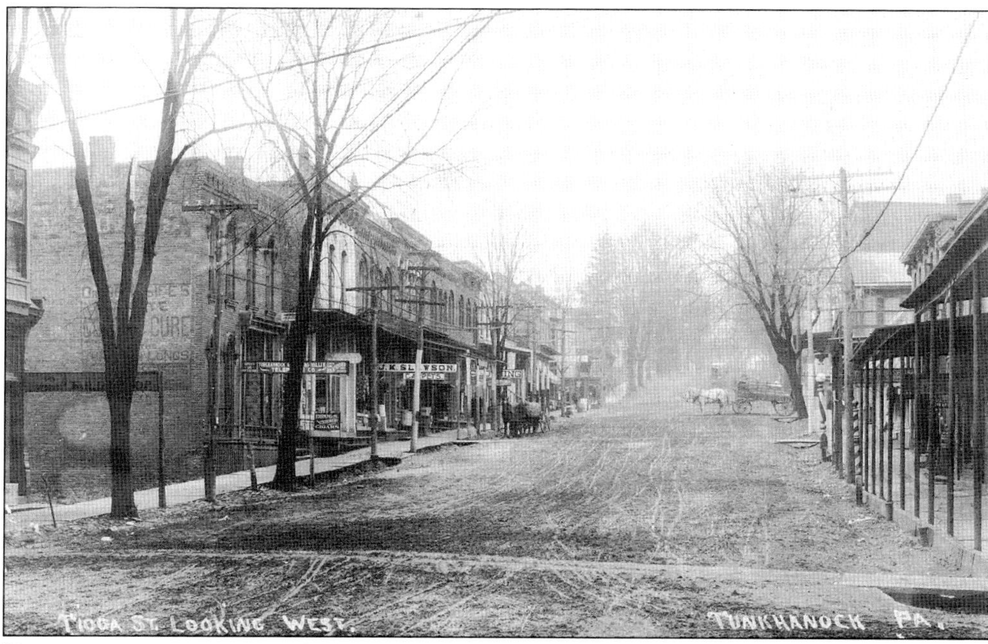

TUNKHANNOCK, 1907. In 1775 Jeremy Osterhout, a Dutch man, built a cabin here to take advantage of trading possibilities along the well-traveled Great Warriors path, a Native-American trail that followed the Susquehanna. The town is the largest in the county, and it is the Wyoming County Seat. (Postcard courtesy of Norm Brauer.)

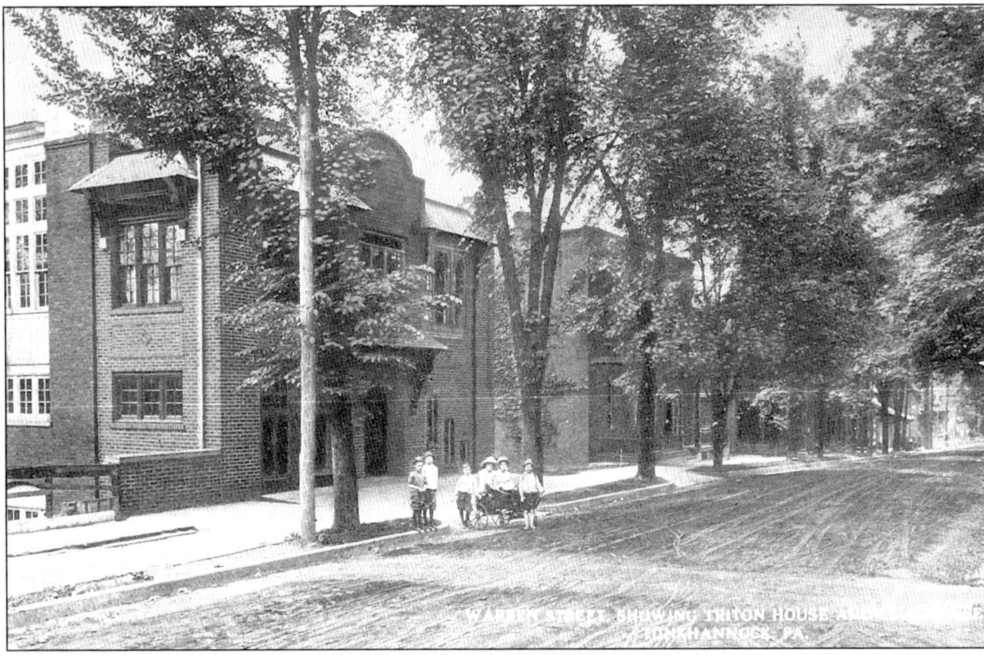

TUNKHANNOCK, 1914. Because so many people from Wyoming County had to travel to Tunkhannock to do business at the courthouse, other businesses, such as stores, sprang up to serve them. The bustling town still retains much of its beautiful 19th-century architecture. (Postcard courtesy of the Tioga Point Museum.)

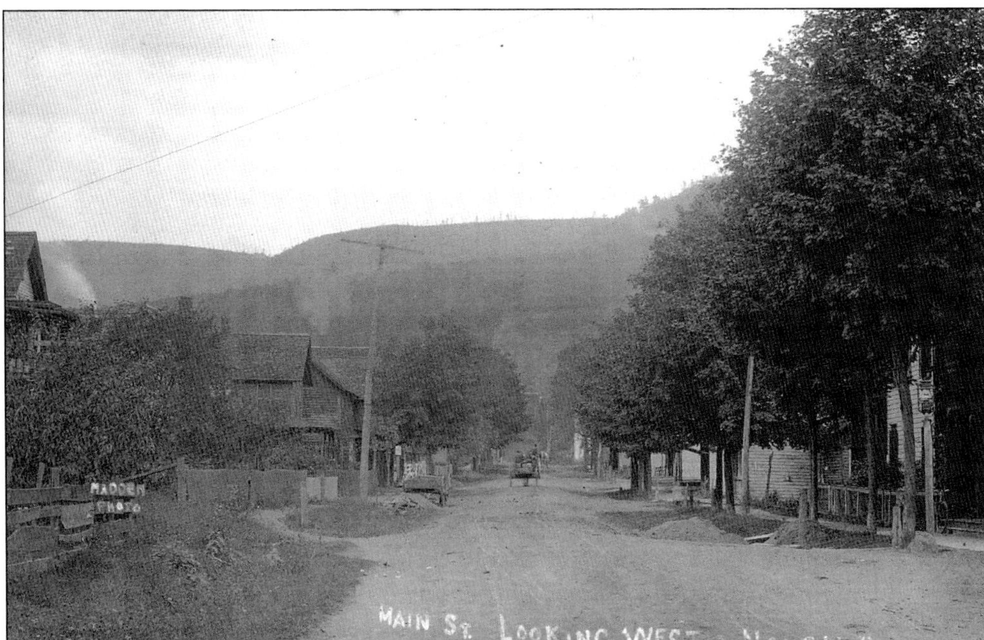

NOXEN. The lumber company of Trexler & Turrell built a sawmill here in 1895. The mill received logs via slides down the mountains. (Postcard courtesy of Norm Brauer.)

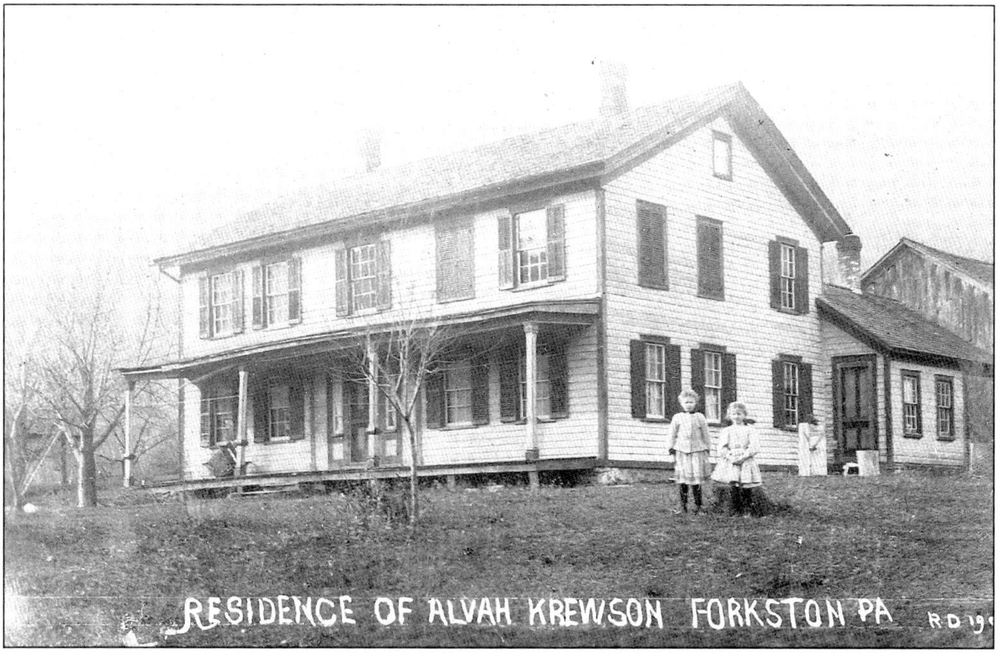

FORKSTON, 1909. The reverse of this card is inscribed "Dear Marry, be a good girl and help your ma and I will send you some nice post cards. I think you will like this because for it was Aunt Anna's home. These little girls is Mary and Francis Krewson. Good bye lovingly yours Ellen F B." (Postcard courtesy of Norm Brauer.)

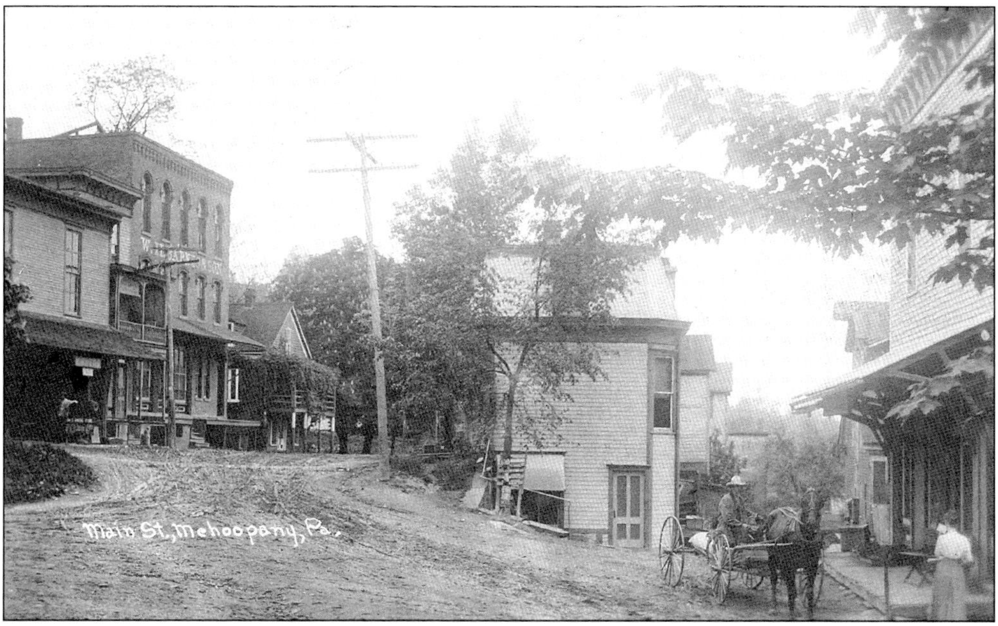

MEHOOPANY. The name comes from an unidentified Native-American language and means "where there are wild potatoes." Amos York settled near here in 1775, then moved to Wyalusing. Soon Elija Phelps settled here, moving into York's house without his permission. The town is now home to a large Procter and Gamble plant. (Postcard courtesy of Norm Brauer.)

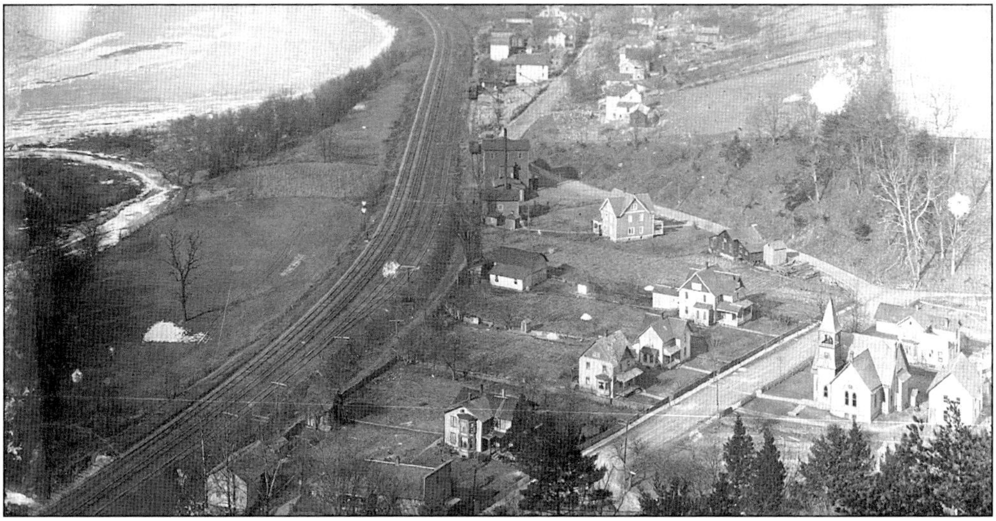

SKINNERS EDDY, 1911. The eddy for which this spot was named made this a convenient stop for boatmen operating the rafts (or arks) that transported logs down the river. Because the Susquehanna is so shallow, this was the only type of commercial boat that could be used, and it could only be used at times of high water. Ebenezer Skinner opened a tavern here in 1792. (Postcard courtesy of the Tioga Point Museum.)

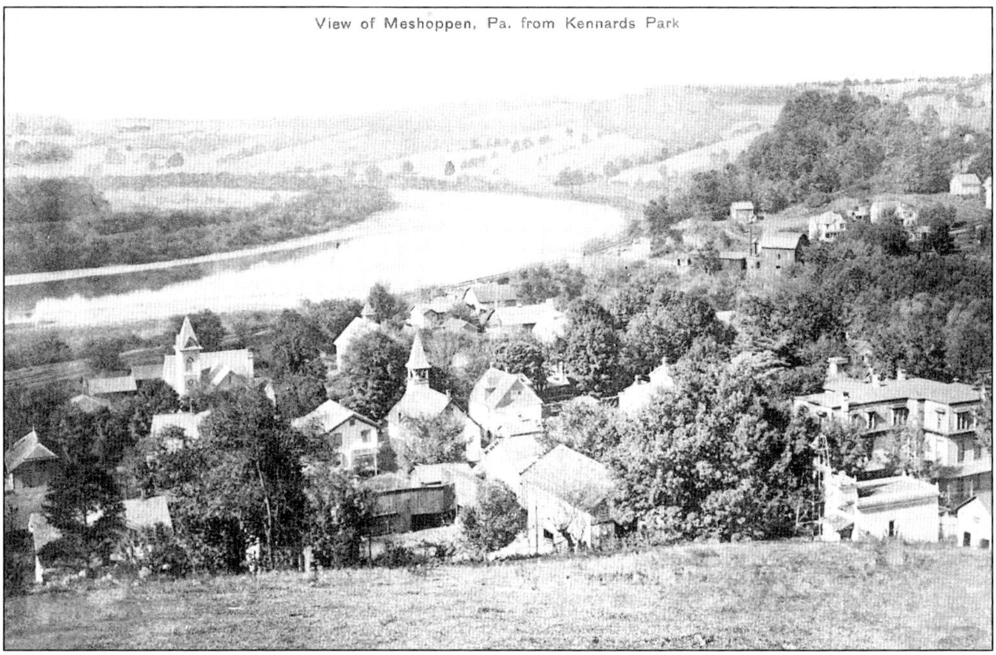

MESHOPPEN, 1912. The town was a stagecoach stop until the arrival of the railroad in 1870. A 1940 guide book says the main industries were agriculture and quarrying. (Postcard courtesy of the Bradford County Historical Society.)

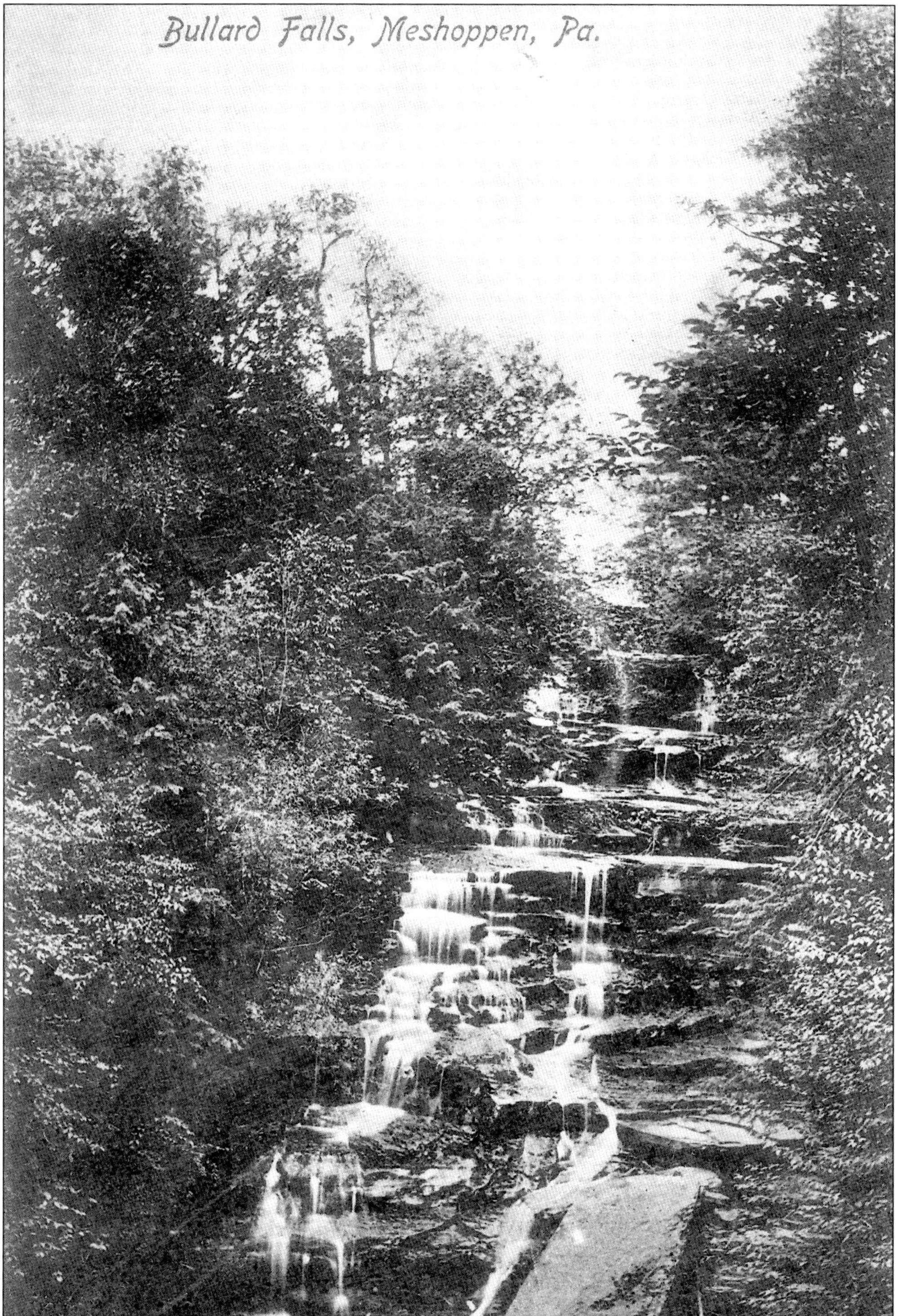

MESHOPPEN. The word means "corals" or "beads." The mountainous terrain makes scenes like this one delightfully common in the area. (Postcard courtesy of the Tioga Point Museum.)

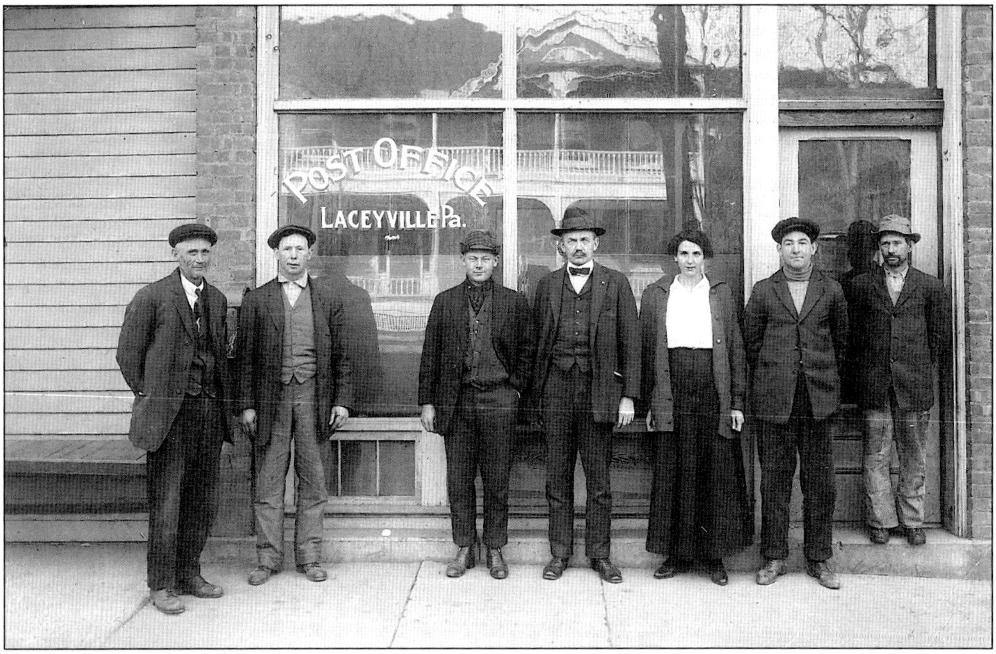

LACEYVILLE, ABOUT 1911–20. Laceyville is located in the very northwest corner of Wyoming County on the Susquehanna. The people standing outside the post office in this card are, from left to right, Fred Pickett, Sam Harrison, Cliff Pickett (substitute), "Mac" Ward (postmaster), Florence Palmer, Art Heller, and John Ferris. The house across the street can be seen reflected in the sparkling clean window glass. (Postcard courtesy of Norm Brauer.)

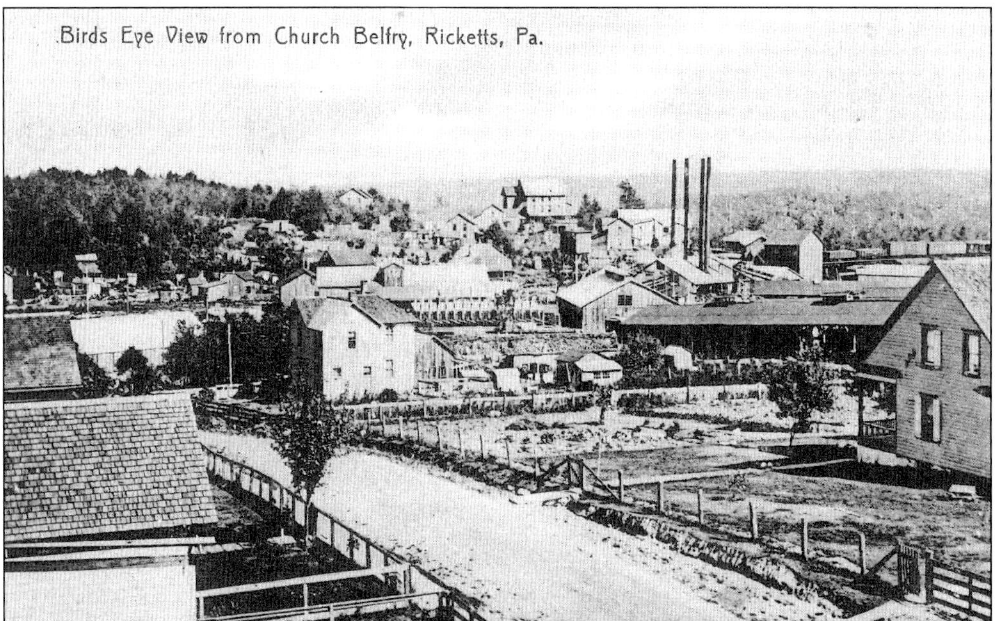

RICKETTS. The lumber village of Ricketts was divided by the Sullivan/Wyoming County line with the railroad, hotel, store, and stave mill in Wyoming County, and houses and sawmill in Sullivan County. (Postcard courtesy of Norm Brauer.)

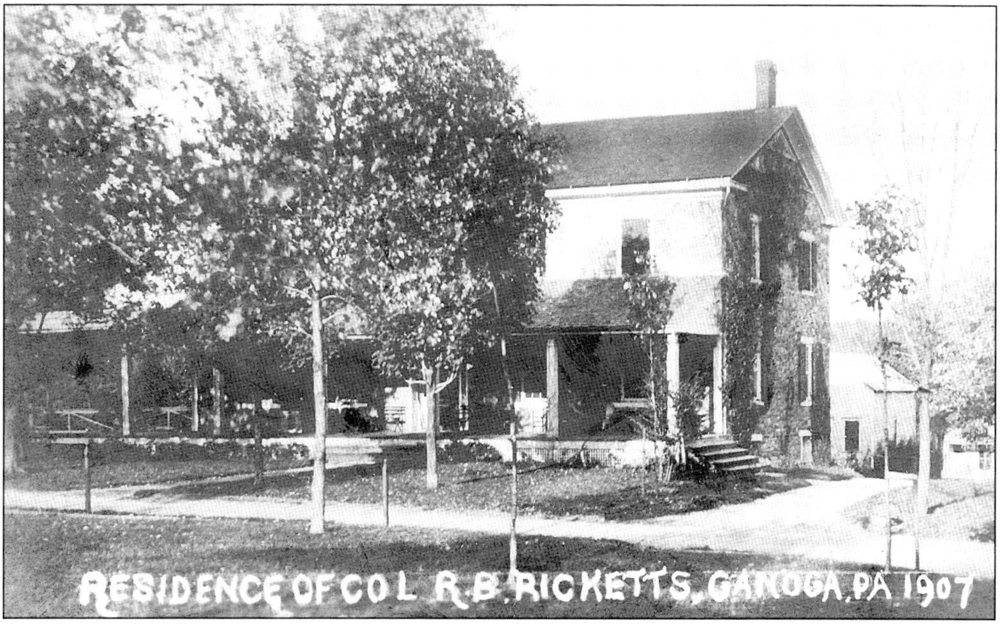

GANOGA, 1907. This was the home of Colonel Robert Bruce Ricketts, the owner of the vast timberlands cut by Trexler & Turrell in 1893. He and his wife are buried under a giant hemlock on the estate. A Lehigh Valley Railroad passenger train opened from Wilkes-Barre to Ganoga so picnickers could come in from the city. (Postcard courtesy of the Bradford County Historical Society.)

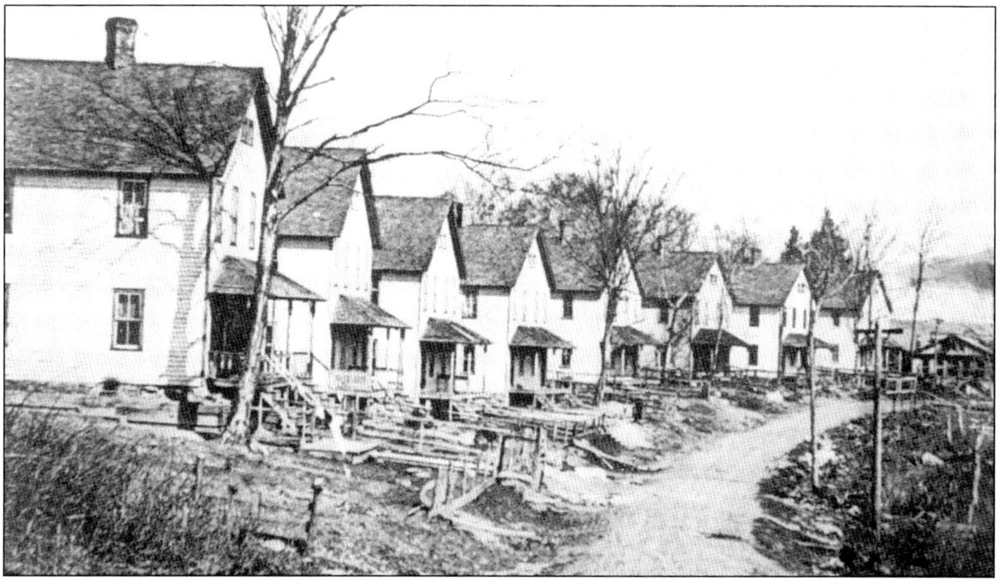

BERNICE, 1917. This scene has the look of a company town, which is what it was. These houses were temporary, because the company only needed to house its workers in a particular town for the time that the logging or mining was going on, usually less than a generation, sometimes only a few years. (Postcard courtesy of the Bradford County Historical Society.)

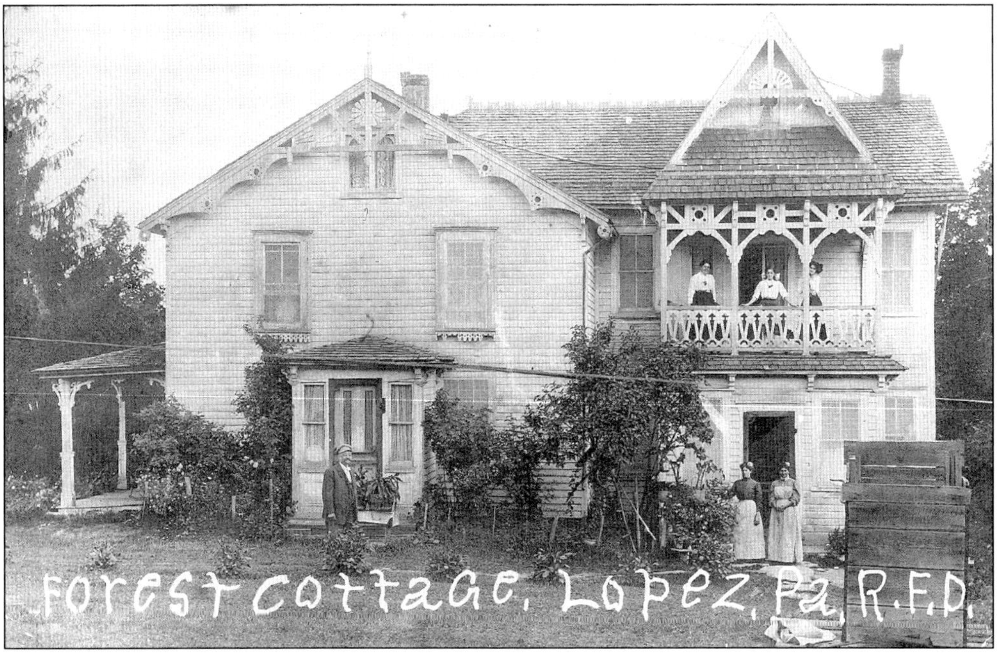

Lopez. The Folk Victorian Forest Cottage had elaborate woodwork and charming details, such as the duck on the ridge crest. The town was named for John Lopez, who was involved in the construction of the Susquehanna and Tioga Turnpike. Residents of the town worked in the lumber and coal businesses, and in the pajama factory of the Joseph G. Smith Company, manufacturers of "the preferred night apparel of thousands of New Yorkers." (Postcard courtesy of Norm Brauer.)

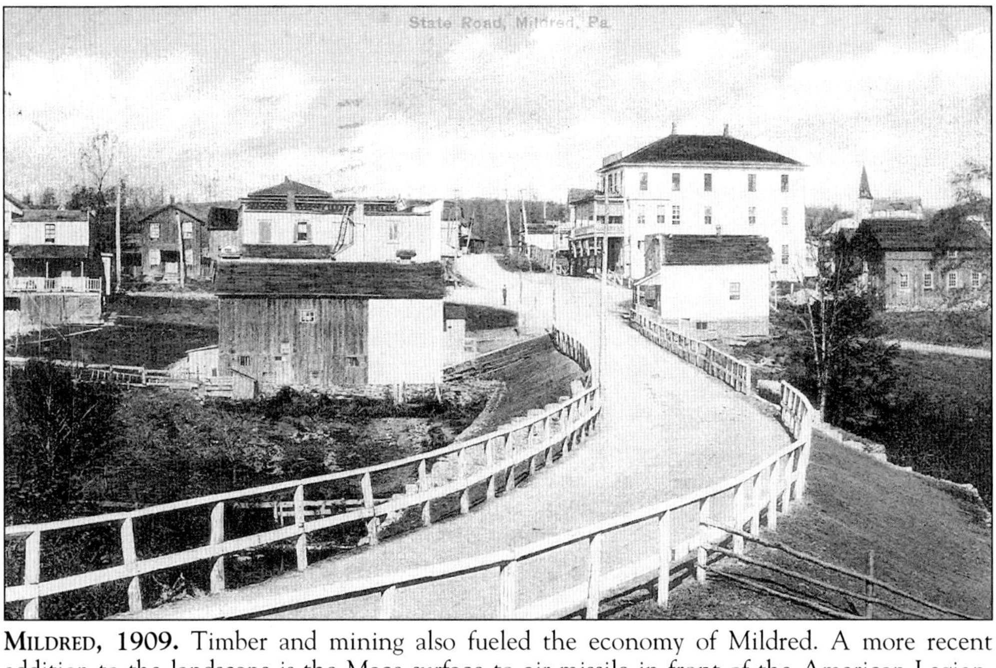

Mildred, 1909. Timber and mining also fueled the economy of Mildred. A more recent addition to the landscape is the Mace surface-to-air missile in front of the American Legion. (Postcard courtesy of Norm Brauer.)

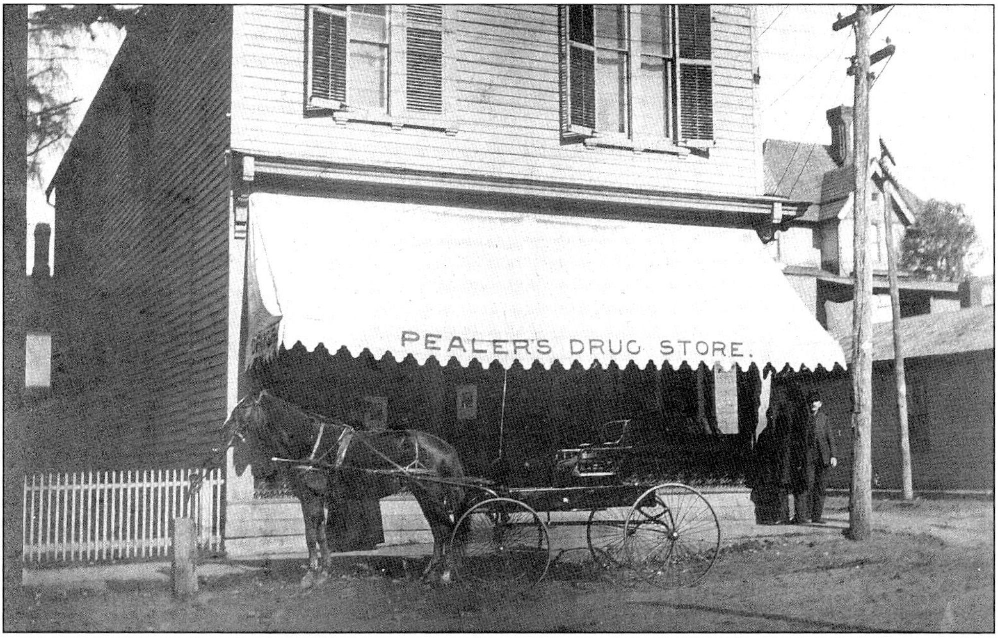

DUSHORE. The town was incorporated in 1859. The name comes from a mispronunciation of the name of an early settler, Dupetit Thourars, one of the Azilum refugees. Pealer's Drug Store was the only pharmacy in Sullivan County. It was run by Charles E. Pealer until his death in the 1920s. Prescriptions were filled and there was a photo-developing and printing service. Businesses other than the one pictured above included Harrington & Company, a milk and ice cream plant; a furniture factory; and a silk company. (Postcard courtesy of Norm Brauer.)

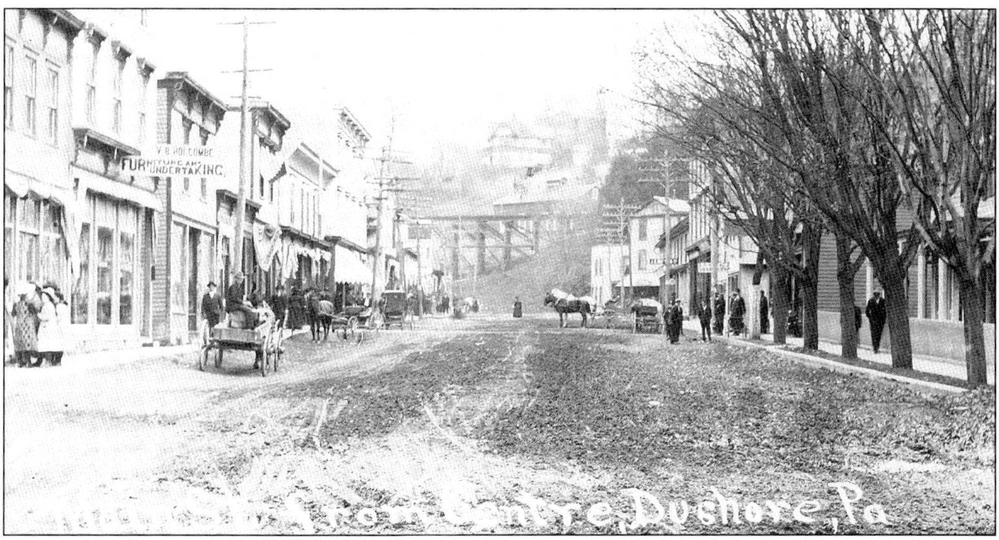

DUSHORE, 1912. On the left side of the street is a sign that reads "V.B. Holcomb, Furniture and Undertaking." These two businesses, which seem so different from each other today, were often done by the same person back in the 19th and early 20th centuries. Mr. Holcomb and his sons carried a large and comprehensive stock of furniture, and in 1928 they were the county agents for Frigidaire electric refrigerators. They practiced the latest approved methods of the mortician's art. (Postcard courtesy of Norm Brauer.)

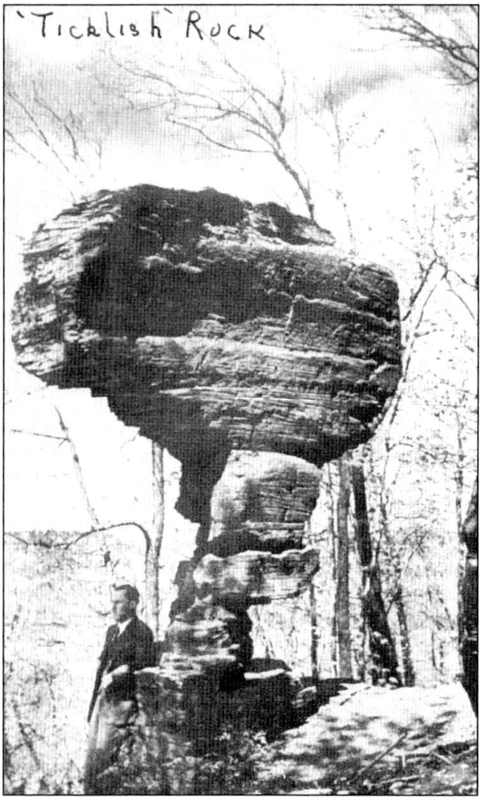

Ticklish Rock. This curious formation is on top of Pocono Knob near the Lycoming County line. It is estimated to weigh 50 or 60 tons, and "by pushing the rock with one's hands it can be made to tremble perceptibly," although why someone would wish to do this with 50 or 60 tons of rock over one's head is a puzzle. It is often written that the effort to climb to this spot is difficult, but photographs of the rock all seem to include a man in a suit. (Postcard courtesy of the Tioga Point Museum.)

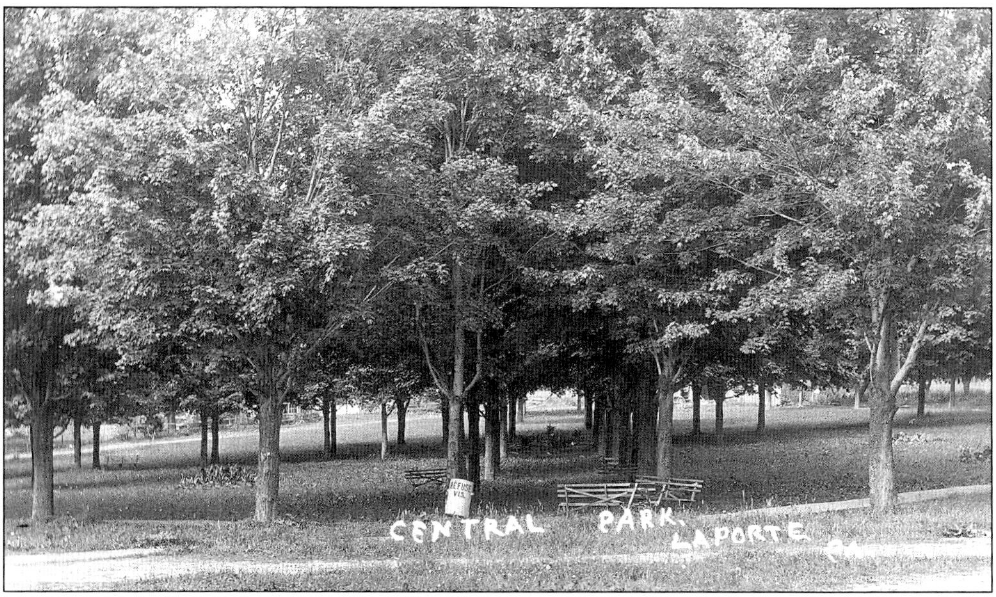

Laporte, 1908. Laporte is the Sullivan County Seat. The county was established in 1847, from land taken from Lycoming County. In 1852 Michael Meylert, who had inherited 30,000 acres at Laporte, erected a new county courthouse. Businesses in the early part of the century included the National Bank of Laporte and the Mokoma Hotel, shown on p. 67. (Postcard courtesy of the Bradford County Historical Society.)

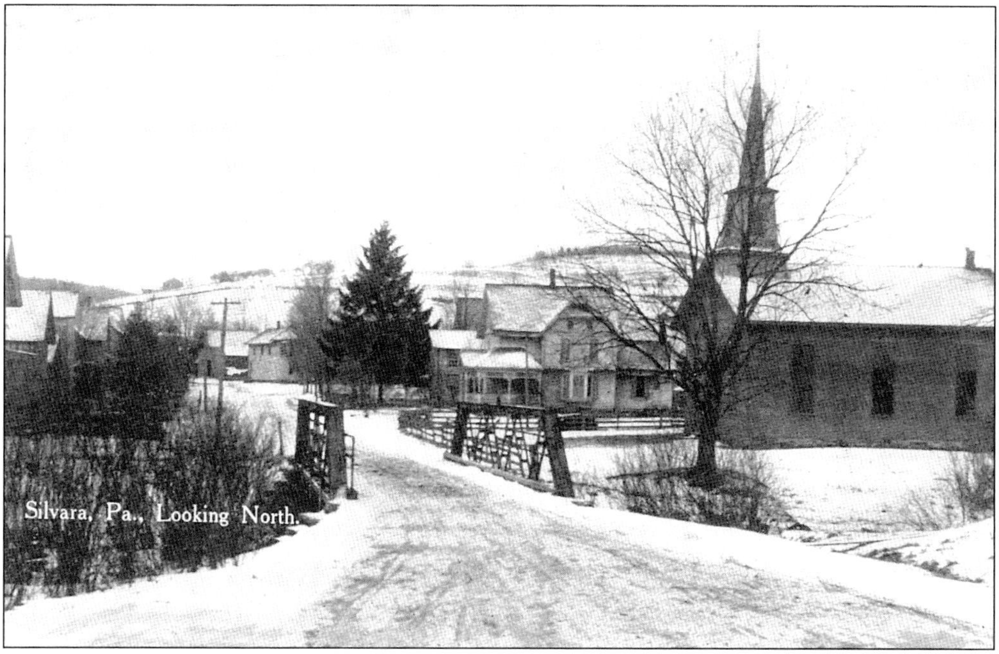

SILVARA, 1910. The town is named for Emanuel Silvara, who came to the United States from Portugal in 1805 by stowing away on a ship. The captain of the ship sold him for three years to pay for his passage. He moved to this area about 1840. (Postcard courtesy of the Bradford County Historical Society.)

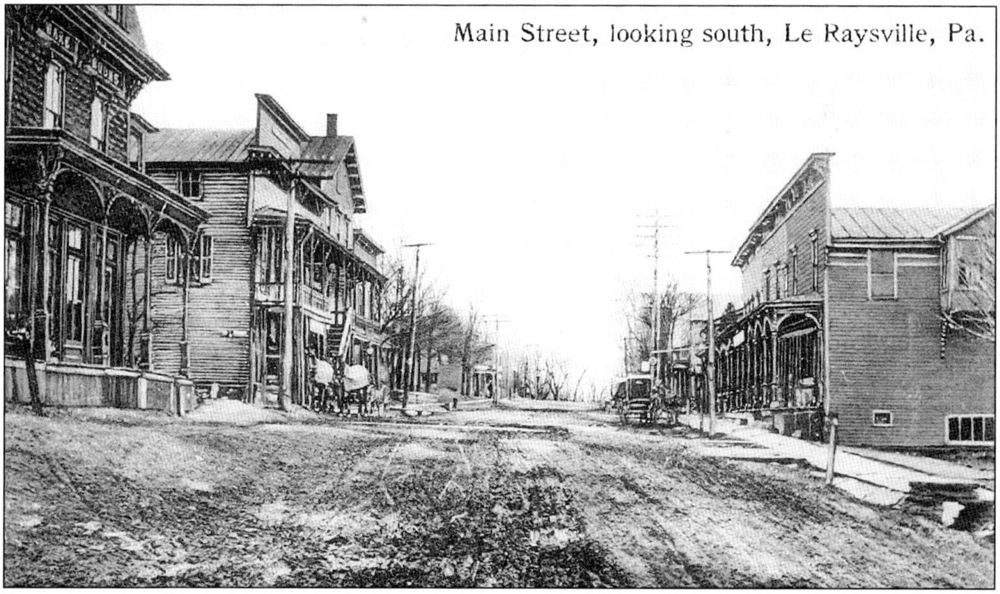

LERAYSVILLE. This town is named after Vincent Le Ray de Chaumont, a Frenchman who owned vast tracts of land in Pennsylvania and New York. An early historian mentions the "LeRaysville Phalanx," an industrial association founded on the principles of Charles Fourier in 1844. These principles called for unconventional living arrangements, and for property ownership and marriage to be radically redesigned. The experiment was short lived. (Postcard courtesy of Norm Brauer.)

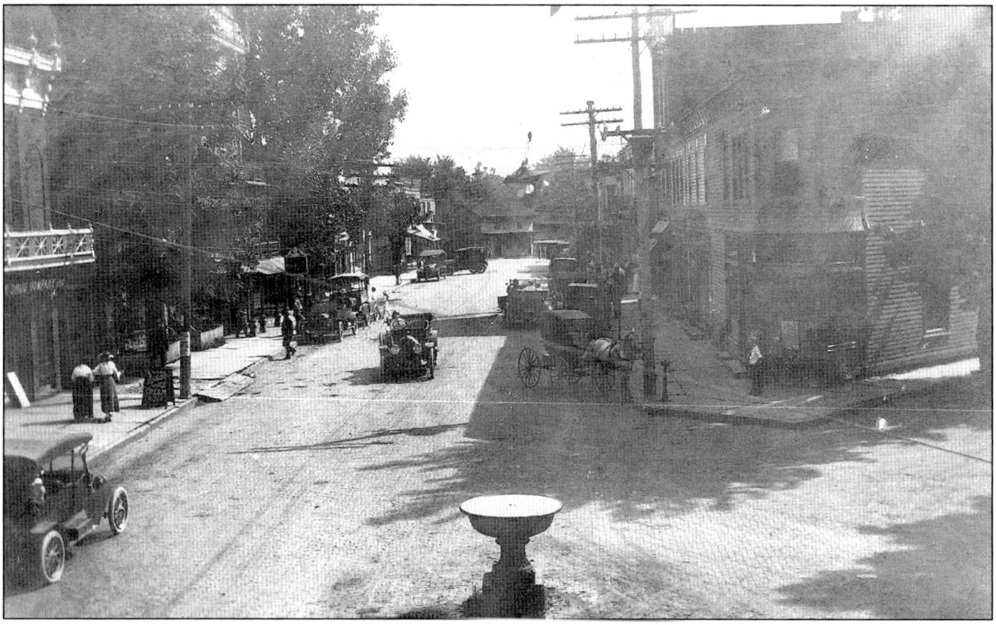

Wyalusing. This scene is from the paved-street era, probably the 1920s. Between 1763 and 1772 David Zeisberger established a Moravian mission not far from here known as Friedenshutten. Wyalusing was the name of a Munsee village that has been translated as "the place of the old man," or, more colorfully, "the dwelling of the hoary veteran." Historical artifacts from the area may be seen at the Wyalusing Valley Museum. (Postcard courtesy of the Bradford County Historical Society.)

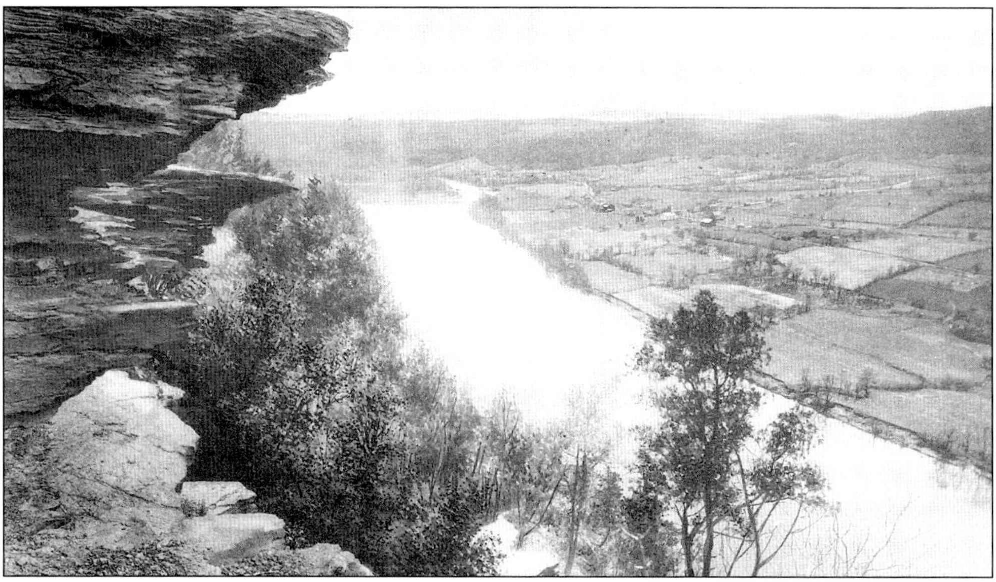

Wyalusing Rocks. Native Americans used this outcropping as a lookout. An officer in Sullivan's campaign wrote that there had been many structures in the valley near here, "but since the commencement of the present war the whole has been consumed and laid waste, partly by the savages and partly by our people." (Postcard collection of the author.)

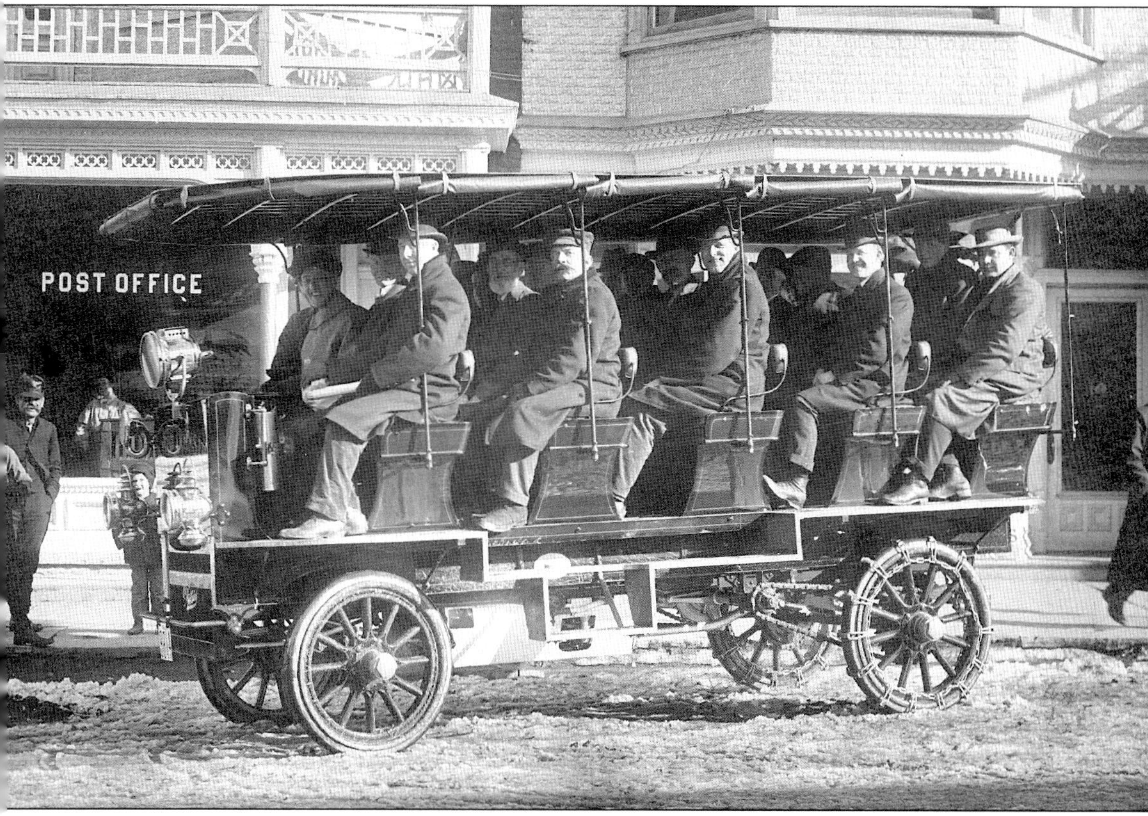

WYALUSING, FEBRUARY 1909. The message on the back of the card reads, "Dear Cousin, This auto is just starting on its first trip out 5 mi. to Camptown. I sit on the second seat back with foot up against the seat in front of me. I only weigh 180# am the biggest of the family. M.D. Durkee." (Postcard courtesy of Norm Brauer.)

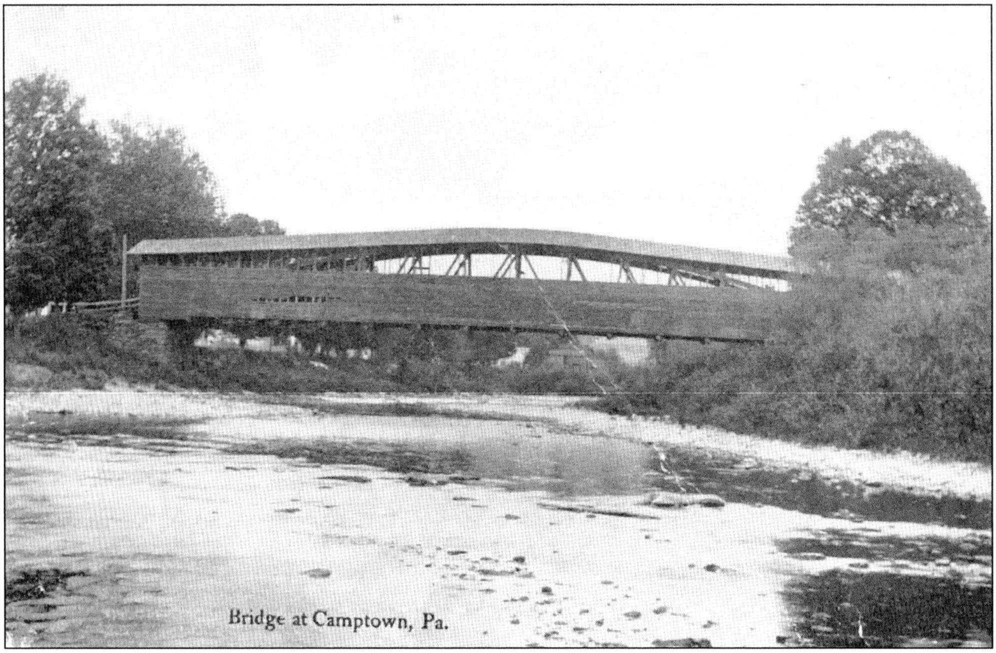

CAMPTOWN. Named for Job Camp, who settled here in 1792, this area is home to the famous races, possibly the ones immortalized by Steven Foster (doo dah). Elisha Lewis and Peter Stevens built the red bridge shown here in 1855, and it carried traffic until the flood of July 8, 1915, took it out. (Postcard courtesy of the Tioga Point Museum.)

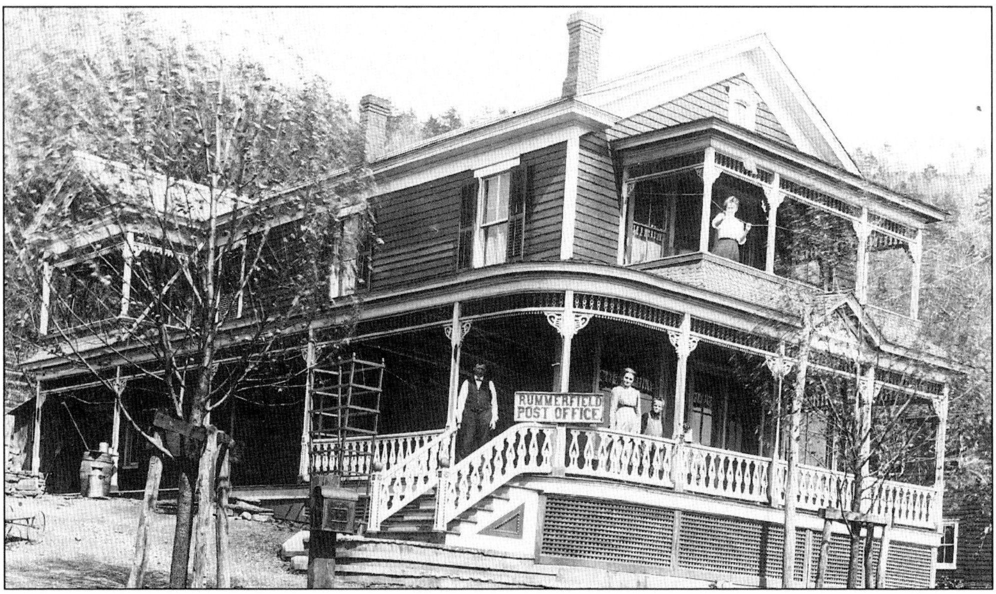

RUMMERFIELD, 1910. The town bustled with commerce during the first decade of the century, with farmers and dairy men from outlying towns bringing their products to be shipped by the railroad and processed at the creamery, and buying supplies to bring back home. In 1940 this town was described as an agricultural hamlet. Back in the days before the Civil War, William Griffis ran a tavern that was a station on the Underground Railroad. (Postcard courtesy of Norm Brauer.)

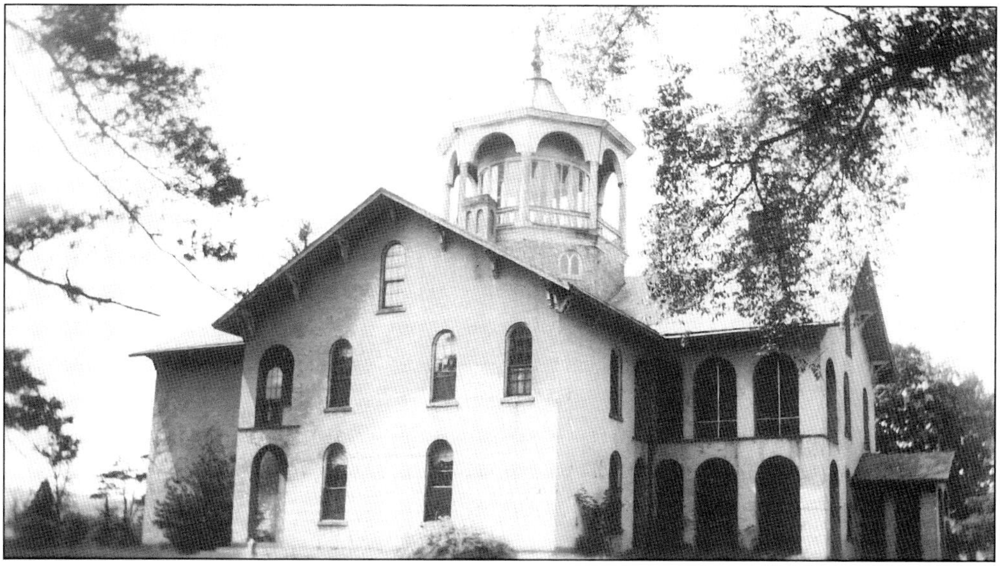

WYSOX. The painted brick Piolett mansion still stands at the intersection of Routes 6 and 187, although it is now missing the glass cupola/skylight. For many years the house was empty and abandoned, with water-damaged books and family papers still strewn about. Recently, however, the building was turned into a store and gas station. (Postcard courtesy of the Tioga Point Museum.)

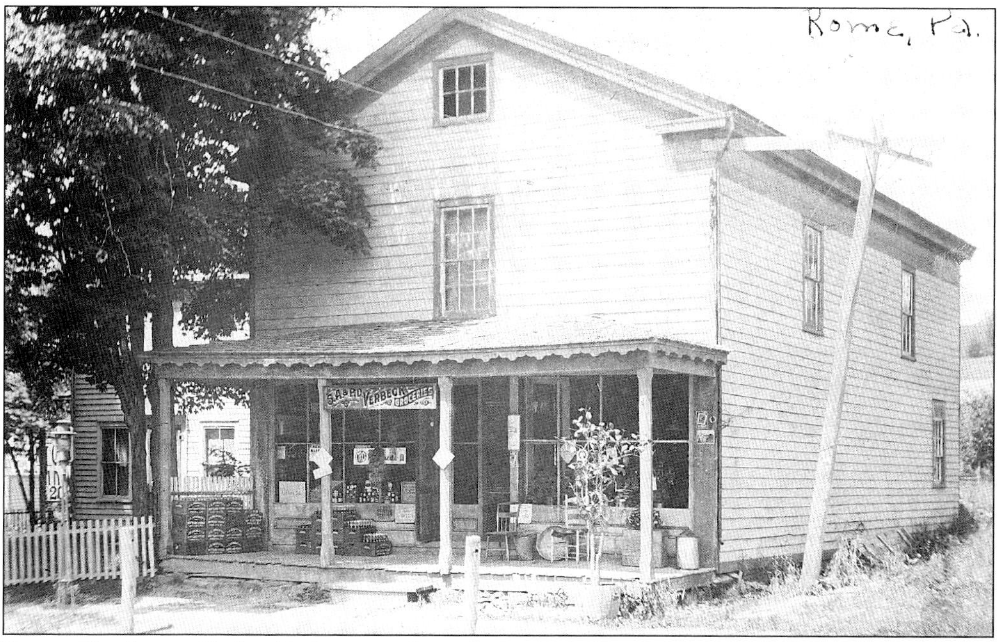

ROME. The fare at Verbeck's Store in the early 1900s was more convenient and less scary than the food available to early settlers. One early historian writes that "the severe toils of the frontier gave a piquancy to the sauce that left no room for dainty palates." One of the foods he mentions is eel, and that particular food is still caught in the river, streams, and ponds of the area. (Photo courtesy of the Tioga Point Museum.)

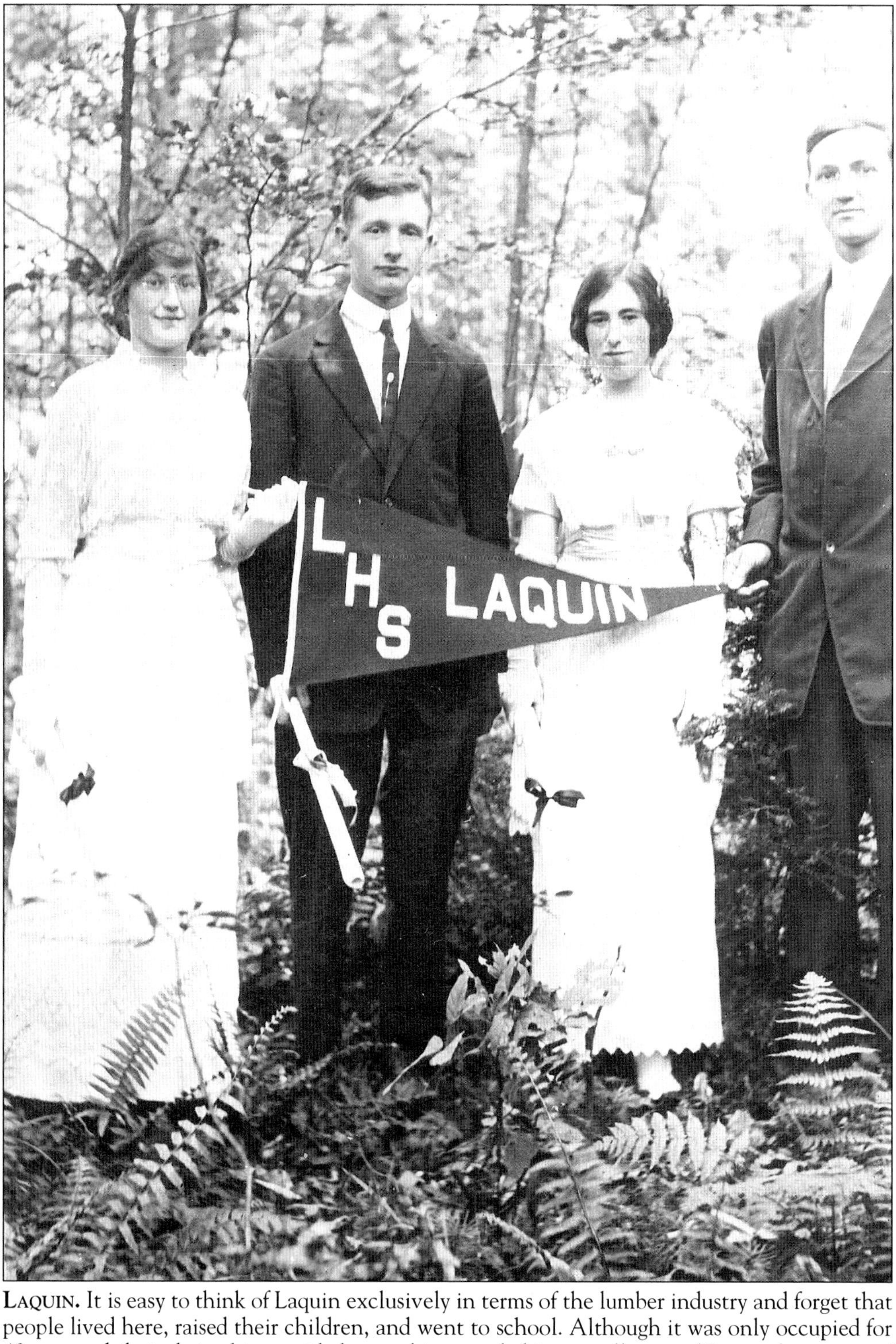

LAQUIN. It is easy to think of Laquin exclusively in terms of the lumber industry and forget that people lived here, raised their children, and went to school. Although it was only occupied for 40 years, while it thrived it provided everything needed in a small town. (Postcard courtesy of the Bradford County Historical Society.)

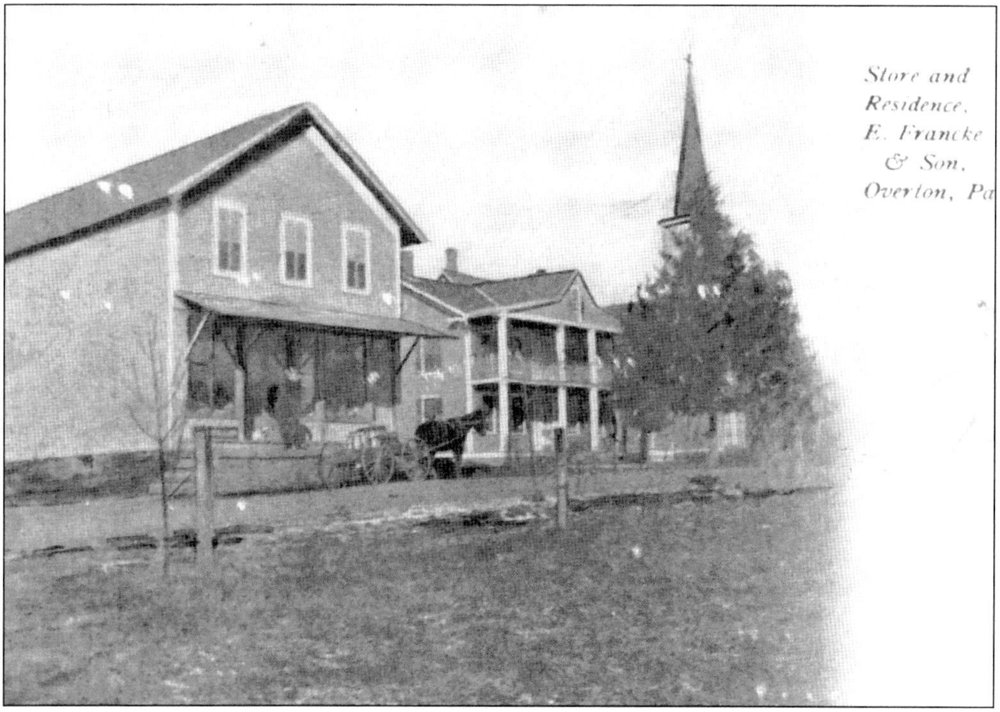

OVERTON, 1909. Only 1/4 mile to the north of the Bradford/Sullivan county line, this village was platted by Henry Sherman in 1856. Overton was the home of the Heverly family; in fact the post office was established as Heverlyville in 1851. (Postcard courtesy of Norm Brauer.)

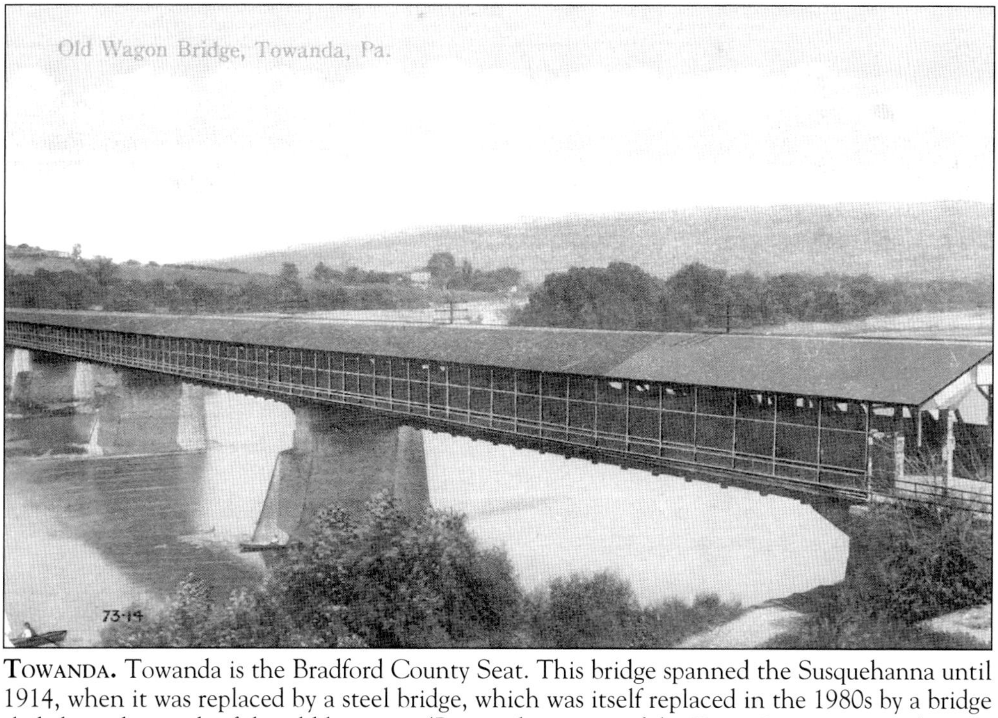

TOWANDA. Towanda is the Bradford County Seat. This bridge spanned the Susquehanna until 1914, when it was replaced by a steel bridge, which was itself replaced in the 1980s by a bridge slightly to the south of the old location. (Postcard courtesy of the Tioga Point Museum.)

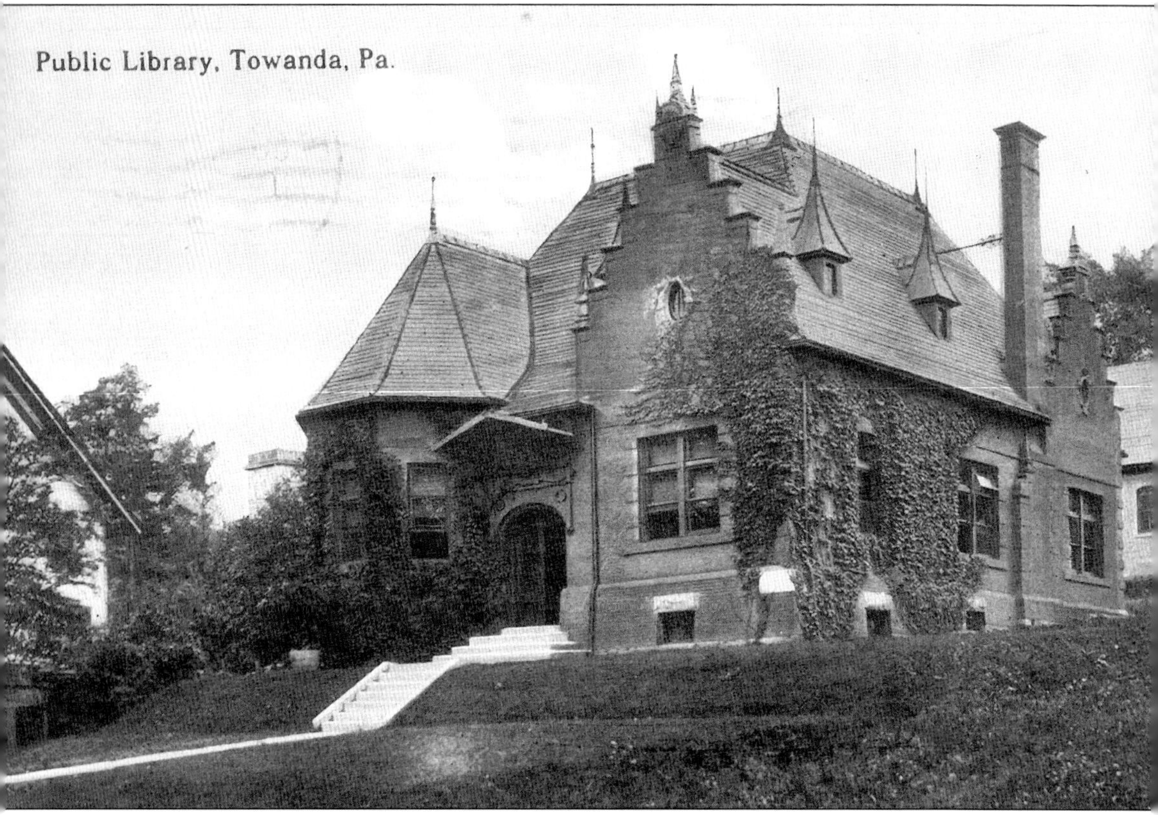

TOWANDA, 1912. The library was begun in 1897 at the corner of Maple and Main with money donated by Frank R. Welles, a Bradford County native living in Paris. The Flemish Renaissance Revival-style building, designed by Henry Chapman of New York City, opened to the public in September 1898. Towanda is justifiably proud of its well-preserved civic, commercial, and domestic architecture. The 100th anniversary of the county courthouse was celebrated in 1998 with a parade down Main Street. (Postcard courtesy of the Tioga Point Museum.)

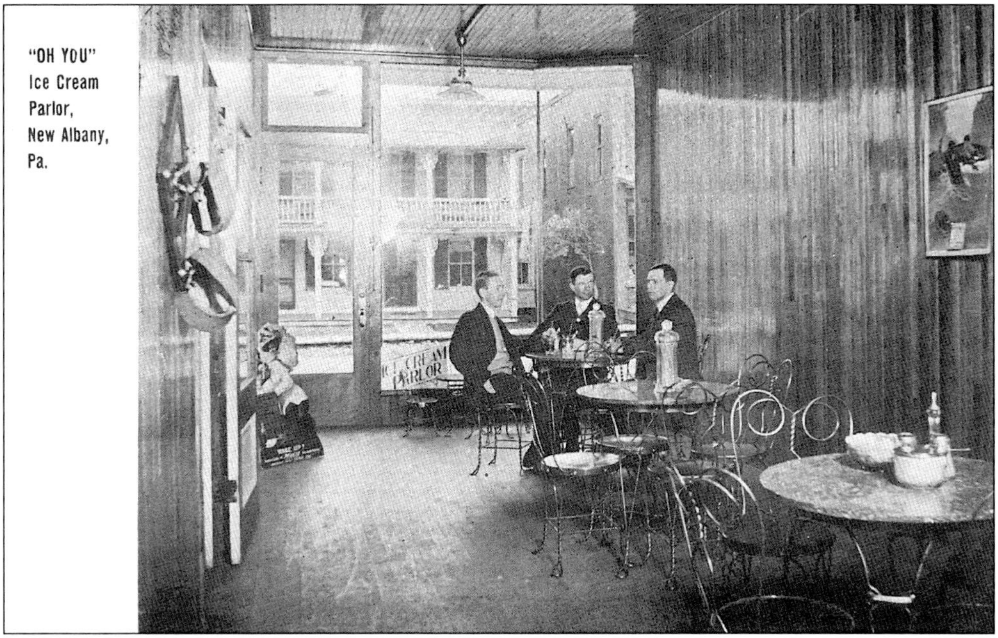

New Albany. This card, published by E.E. Strevy, shows his ice cream parlor. He also ran a variety store on the same site. A 1924 history describes the town as containing a rural graded school, two churches, two gristmills, several stores, a factory, a hotel, a blacksmith shop, and garages. The population was 315 in 1920. (Photo courtesy of Norm Brauer.)

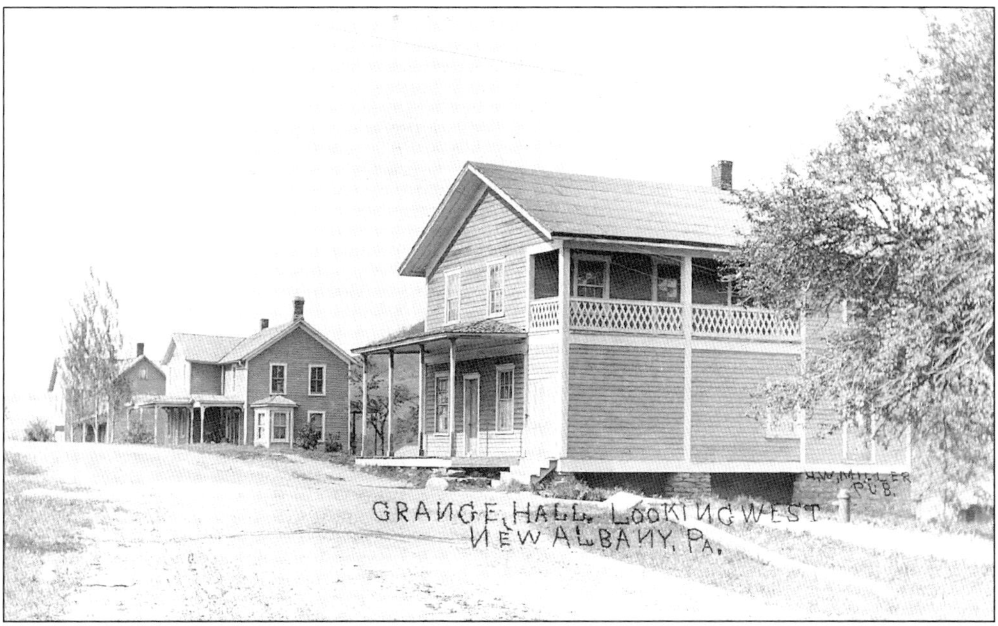

New Albany. The Grange was a strong organization in this farming town, and in the whole region. There were 43 Granges in Bradford County in 1929. (Postcard courtesy of the Bradford County Historical Society.)

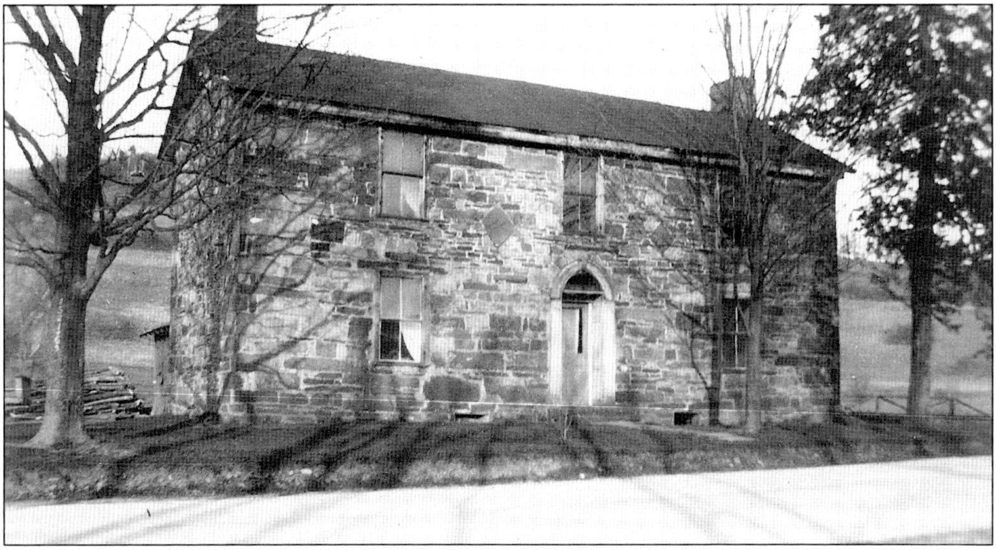

MONROETON. Captain Timothy Alden built this house in 1827. He was a blacksmith and a captain of the militia, and he tended the toll gate on the Berwick Turnpike. The house remained in his family for the rest of the century. On Halloween night one year early this century, the house burned, leaving only the stone walls standing. (Photo courtesy of the Tioga Point Museum.)

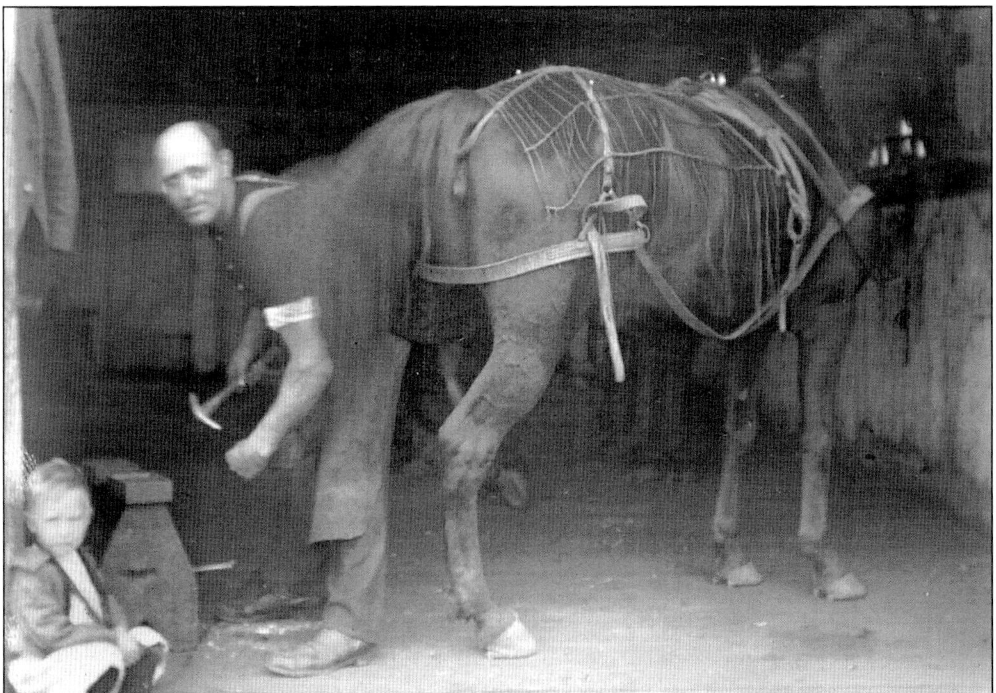

POWELL. This charming card shows the town blacksmith (first name Hugh, according to the signature on reverse) in action, with a child, perhaps his son, waiting in the corner. (Postcard courtesy of Norm Brauer.)

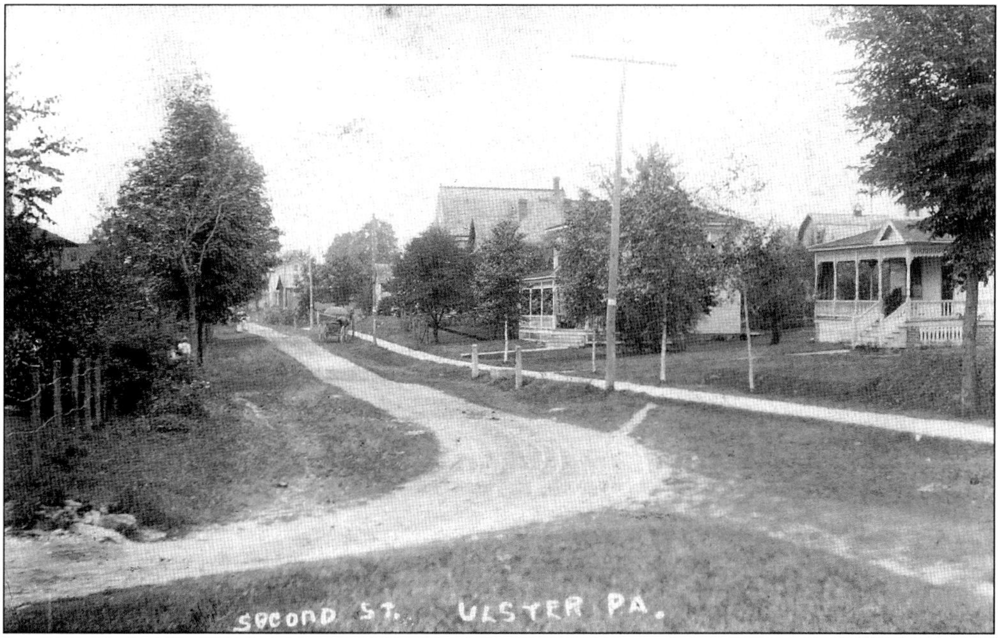

ULSTER, 1909. "A crossroads farming center with neat cottages and large lawns," Ulster has some of the oldest houses in the area. It also has a genuine totem pole, shipped from the Pacific Northwest by train, in the public square. (Postcard courtesy of the Bradford County Historical Society.)

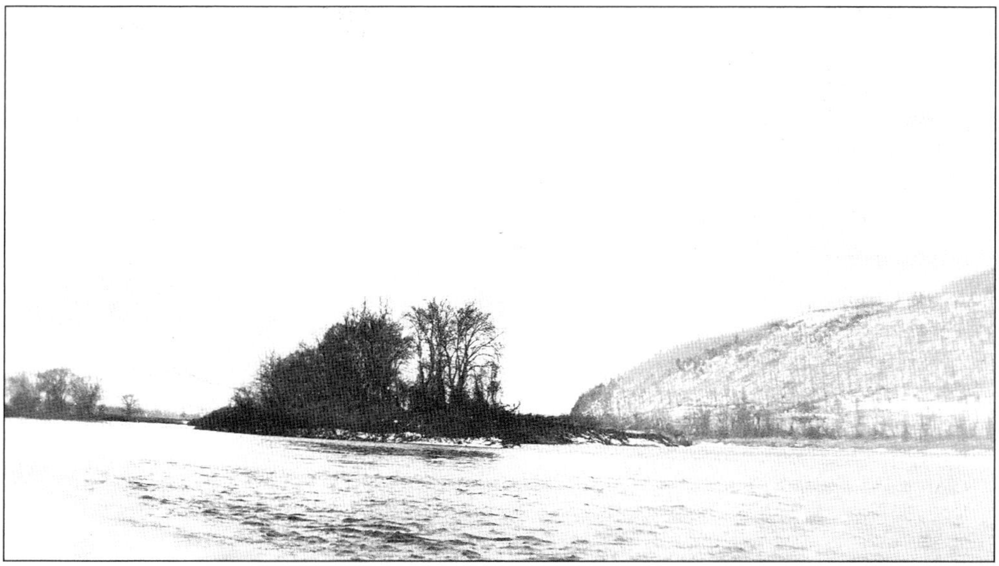

MILAN, 1917. An 18th-century French traveler viewed the area as follows: "The mountains, which form the banks of the Susquehanna, do not lie so close together as in any other part of its course that we have yet seen. The country behind Tioga descends into a plain upwards of three miles in extent . . . The merchants of the place carry on a considerable trade in *etoupés* [hemp, tow, or oakum] which they got from the upper parts of the river and sent to Philadelphia . . ." (Postcard courtesy of the Tioga Point Museum.)

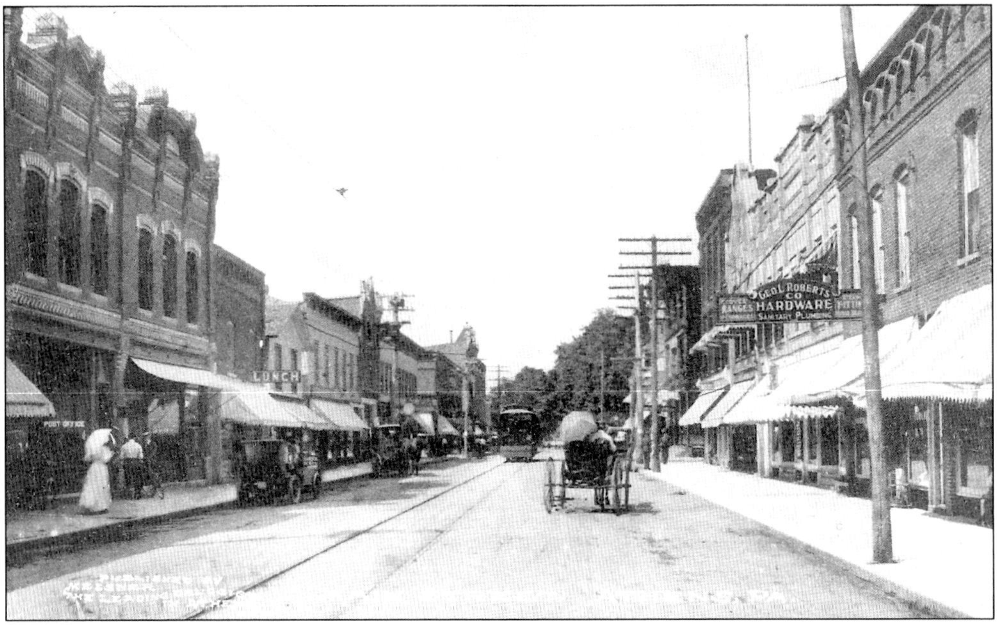

Athens. This view of Main Street shows three different modes of transportation: a horse-drawn buggy, an automobile, and a trolley. One of the large stores in Athens about this time was Karner's Department Store at the corner of South Main and Center Streets. Karner's sold groceries, meat, furniture, hardware, and shoes. It was "three stories wide, three stories high." (Photo courtesy of the Tioga Point Museum.)

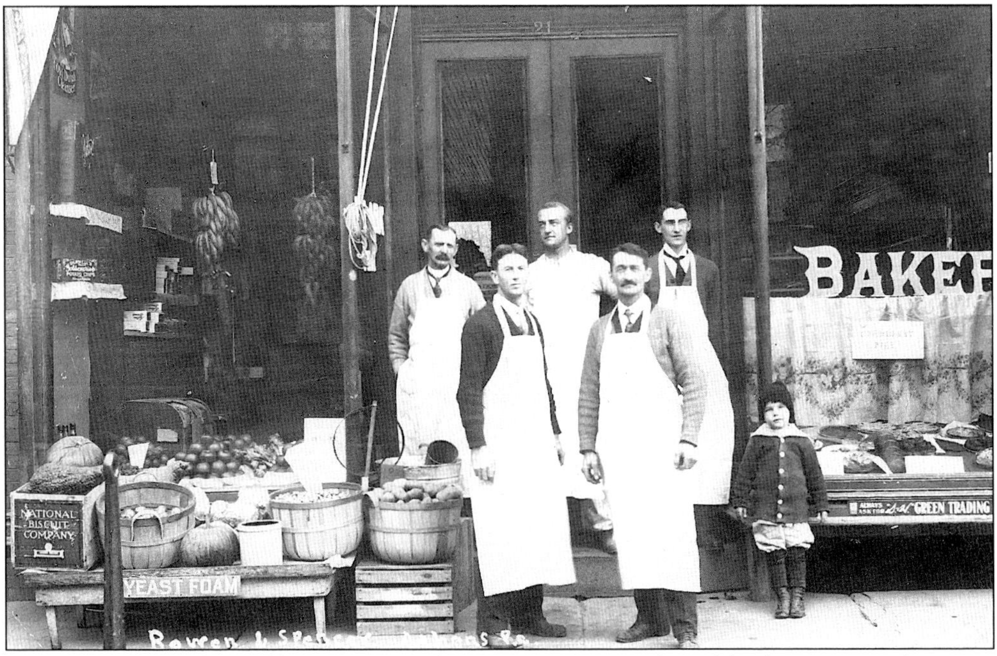

Athens, 1914. The staff at Bowen and Spencer were "working like beavers" at the store, according to one of the bunch, who wrote this card. Some of the brands for sale here are still familiar, for example Nabisco and S. & H. Green Stamps. (Postcard courtesy of the Tioga Point Museum.)

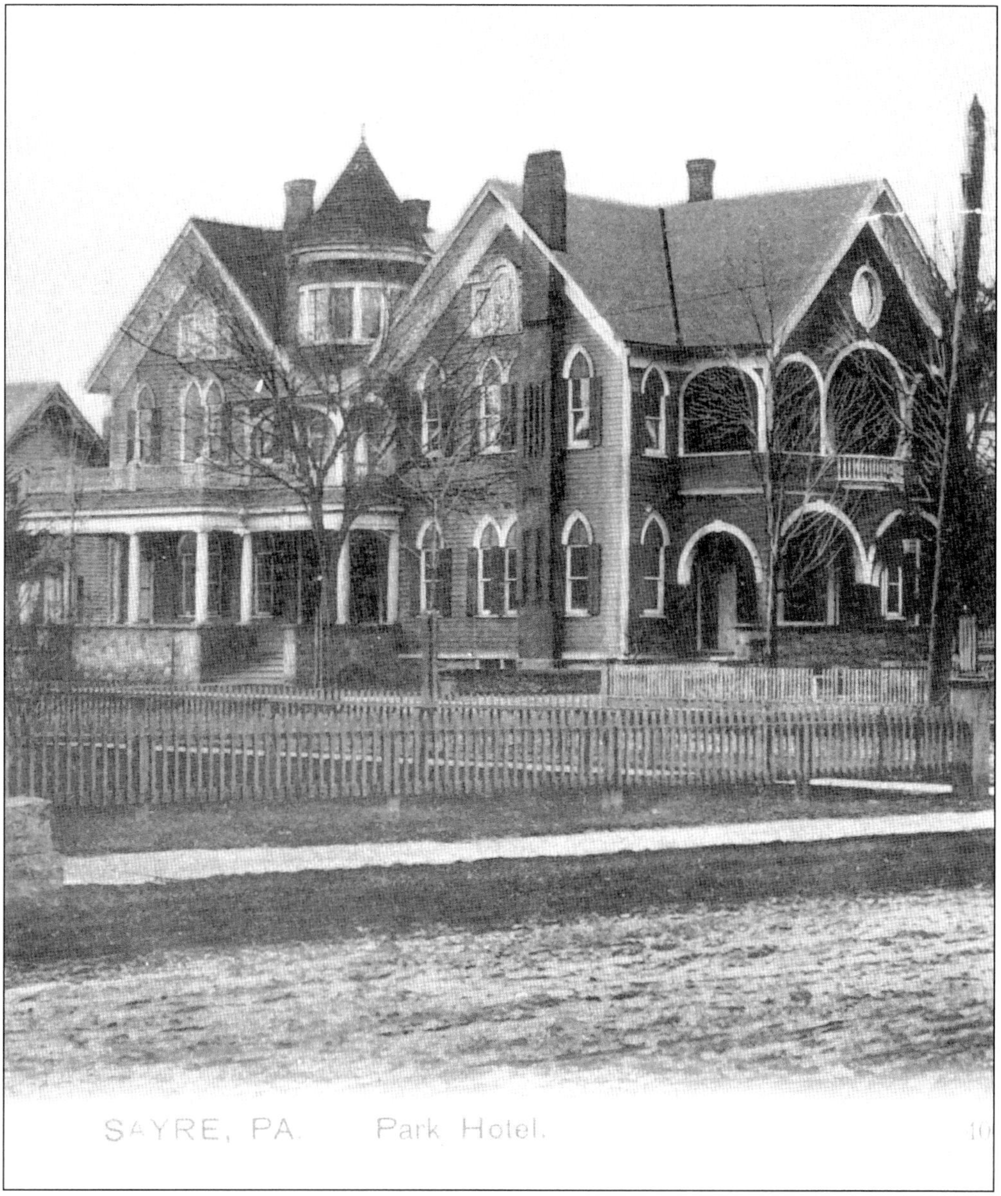

SAYRE. The Park Hotel, now known as the New Park Hotel, stands on Elmer Avenue near Howard Elmer Park. It looks virtually the same as it did when this card was published. Delmar C. Higgins and James L. Sullivan were the proprietors in 1907. Sayre was founded in 1870 and grew up fast around the railroad, although the town was not incorporated until 1891. The youngest town in the valley soon passed the older Borough of Athens and Village of Waverly in population and prosperity. (Postcard courtesy of the Tioga Point Museum.)

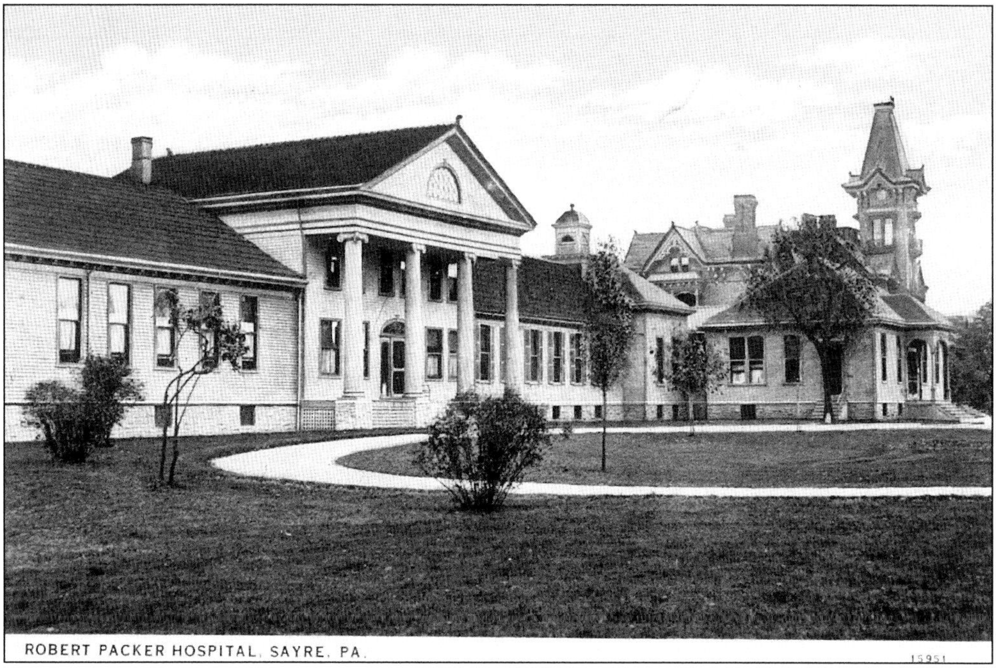

SAYRE. The original Robert Packer Hospital is the mansion on the right-hand side of the card. Formerly the home of Robert Packer, who died shortly after its completion, the hospital was founded in 1885 to serve the many people who worked for the Lehigh Valley Railroad. The Guthrie Clinic was founded in 1910 by Robert Packer chief surgeon Donald Guthrie. (Postcard courtesy of the Tioga Point Museum.)

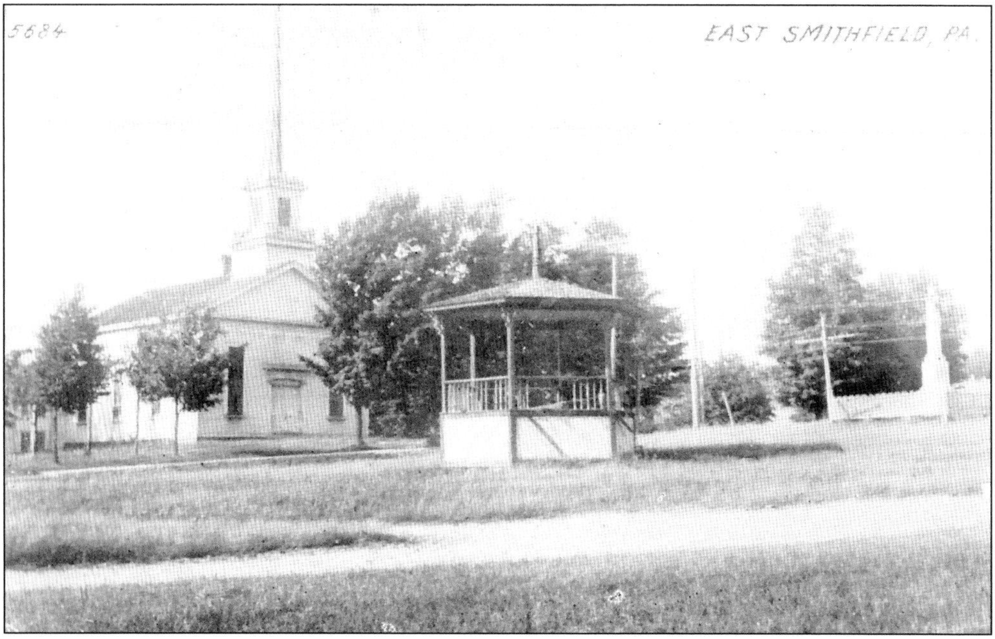

EAST SMITHFIELD. The town square is still an attractive feature of the town. Old buildings surround it just as they did when this card was printed long ago. (Postcard collection of the author.)

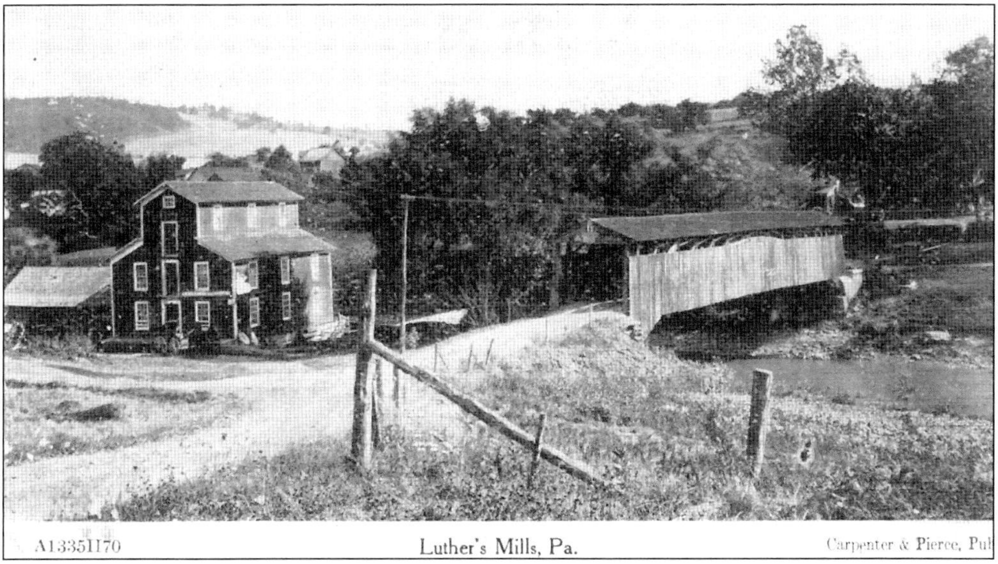

Luther's Mills. Sugar Creek powered the mill that stood here from the early 19th century through 1920. "It is said by persons conversant with the facts that Pennsylvania has more ancient mills with a history than any other state in the union; but Time, the destroying agent, and the new roller process of grinding grain, is fast doing away with the old landmarks, . . . But with it all is yet a mooted question whether the bread of today is any better than the bread of the past." (Postcard courtesy of the Bradford County Historical Society.)

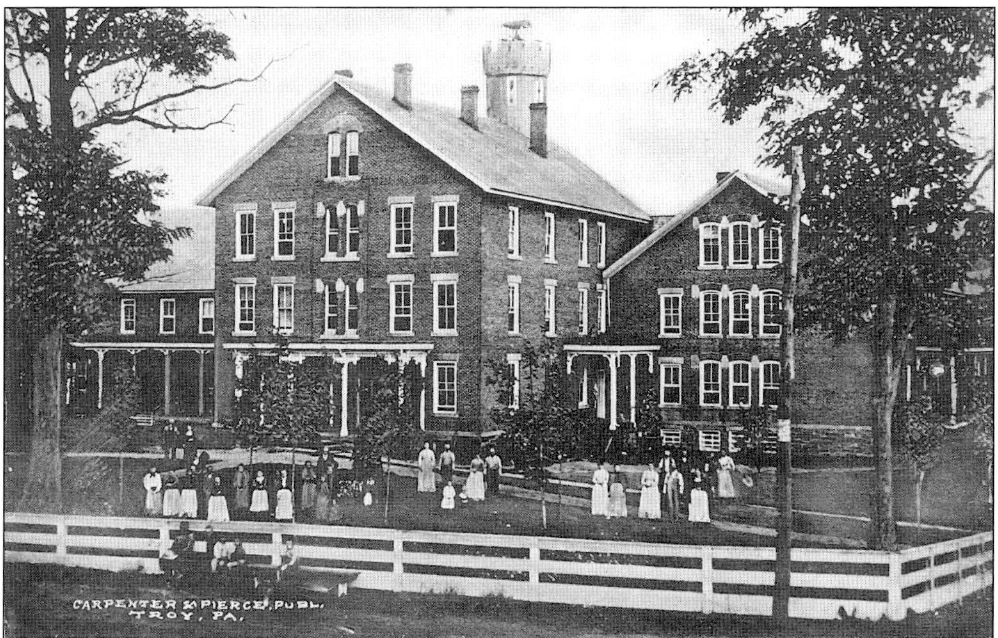

Burlington, 1910. The County Farm, also known as the poor house or alms house, was established in 1879. The building was put up in 1880 and the first inmates received in 1881. They worked a 200-acre farm. (Postcard courtesy of the Bradford County Historical Society.)

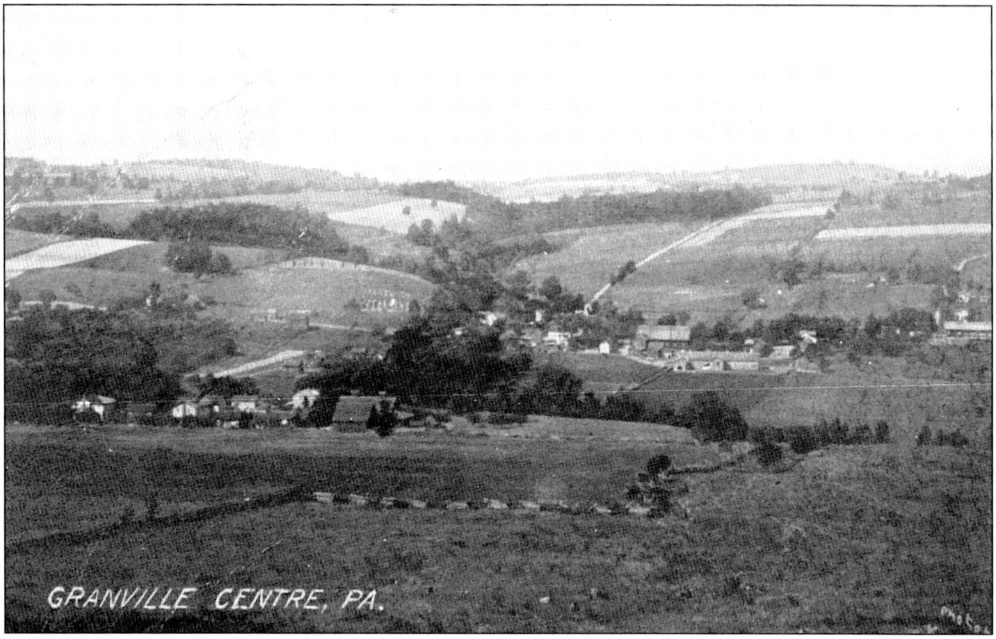

GRANVILLE CENTRE. The rolling countryside around the town is typical scenery of the Endless Mountains. This is dairy country, and at the time this card was printed Glenside Farms creamery operated in Granville Centre. (Postcard courtesy of the Bradford County Historical Society.)

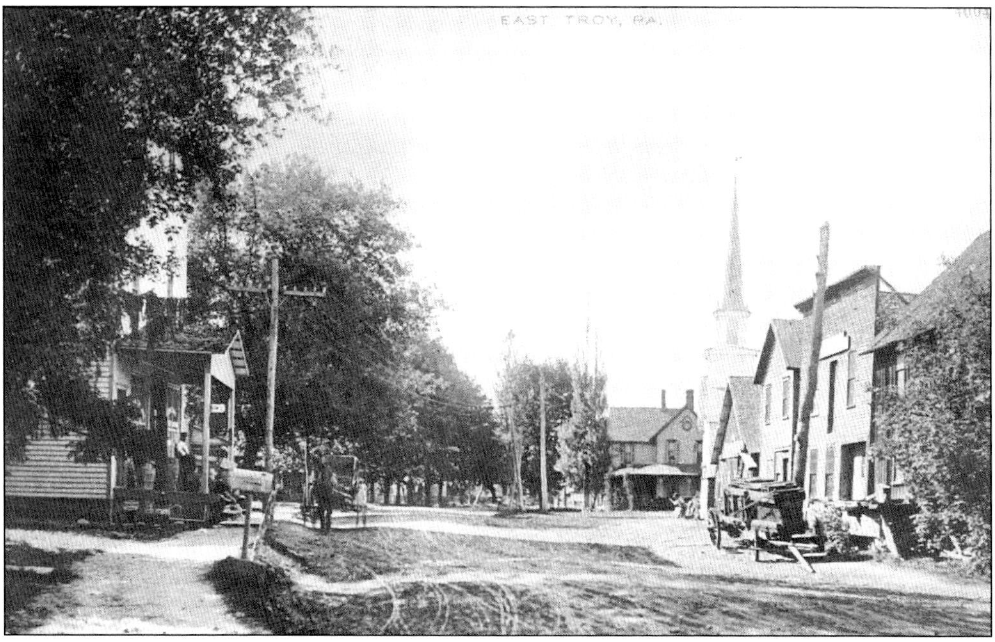

EAST TROY. This was a bustling part of Troy Township when this card was printed, with two churches, a creamery, a feed mill, and several stores. (Postcard courtesy of the Bradford County Historical Society.)

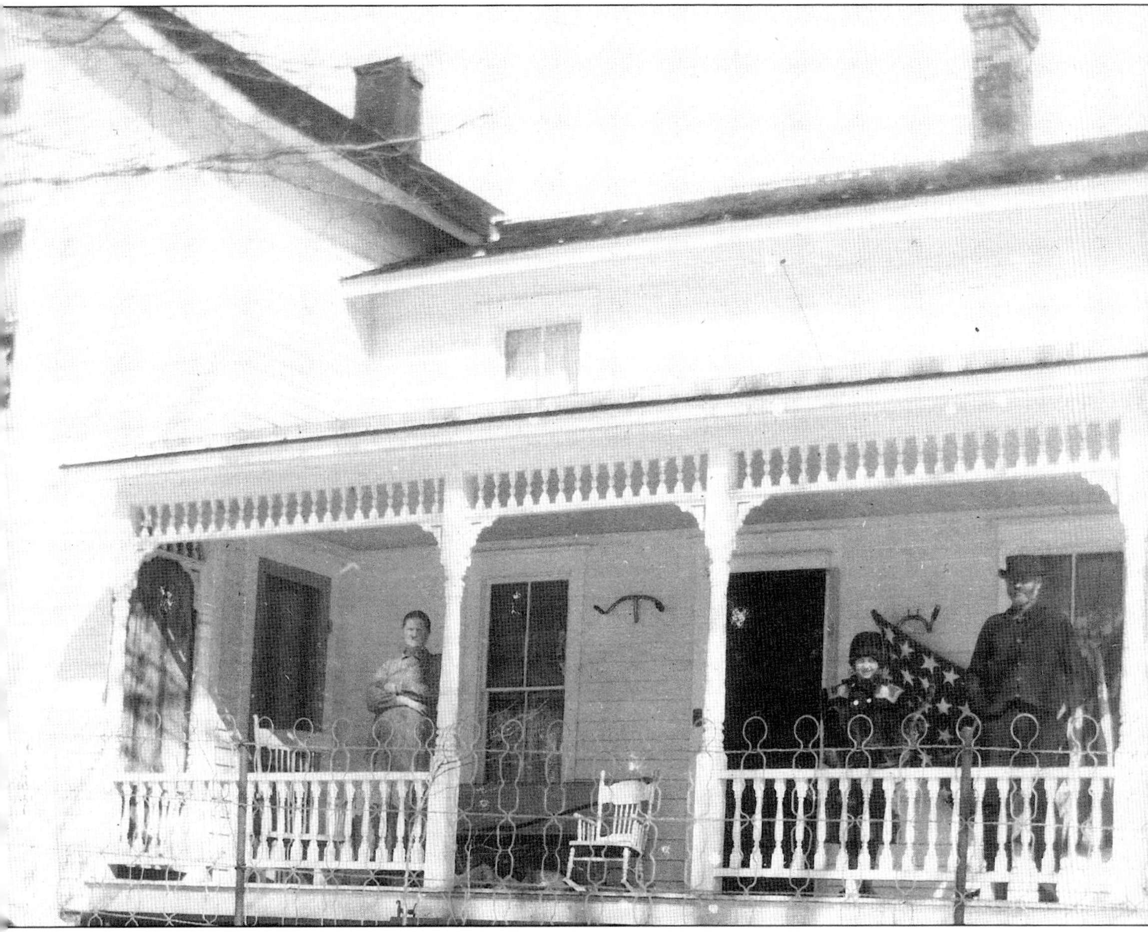

COLUMBIA CROSS ROADS, FEBRUARY 7, 1905. This is the residence of a lady who signed her name Edith C.P. Perhaps she is the one standing on the porch on the left. The roads that cross are the Tioga Point and the Williamstown-Elmira Roads. Columbia Cross Roads profited from the trade generated by Northern Central Railroad and its location on these two busy roads. (Postcard courtesy of the Bradford County Historical Society.)

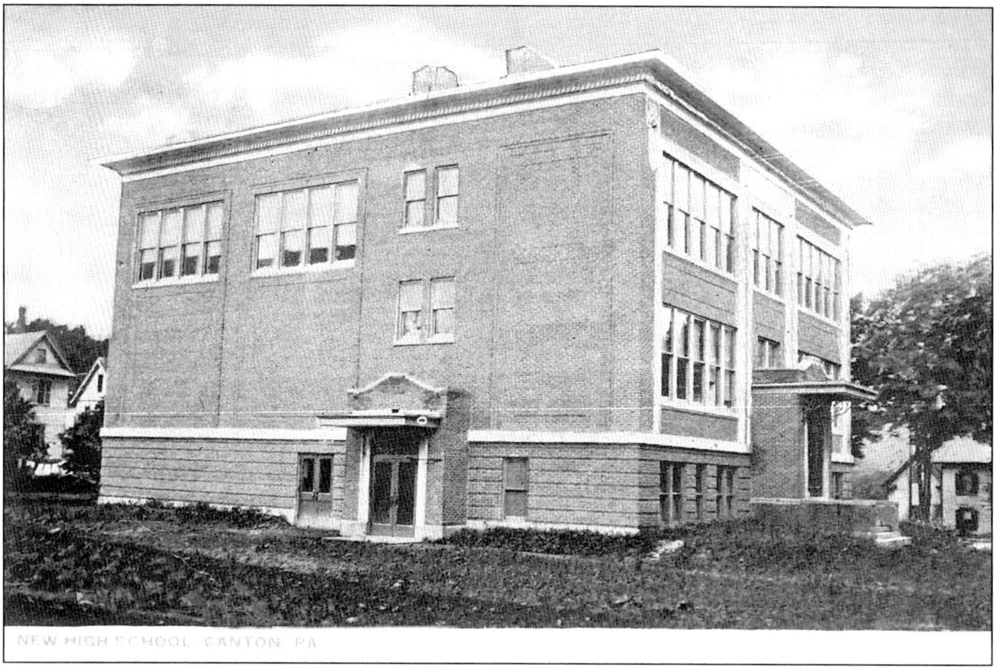

CANTON. This school was constructed in 1916 and contained the modern features of hot-air heating, a telephone, and an aquarium. Canton has an interesting history, including the fact that it was the winter home of Charles Lee's Great London Shows, a circus. (Postcard courtesy of the Tioga Point Museum.)

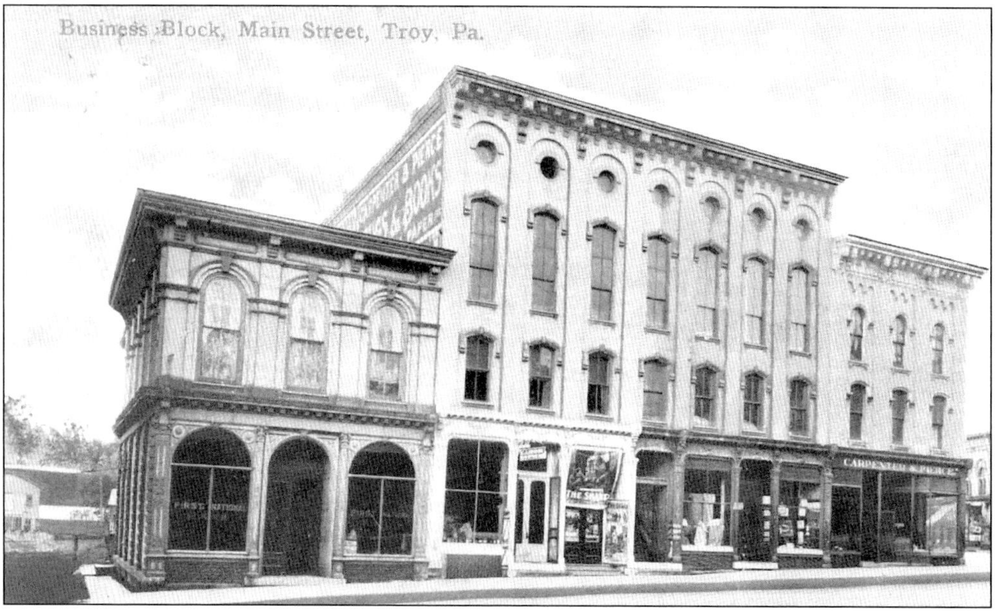

TROY, 1914. The First National Bank of Troy, on the left in this card, respectfully solicited the business of the users of the 1907 Bradford County Directory. It offered 3 percent on deposits left six months and 3 1/2 percent if left one year. Carpenter & Pierce, on the right, sold drugs, books, paints, stationery, wallpaper, etc. (Postcard courtesy of the Bradford County Historical Society.)